Witness to DISPOSSESSION

Witness to DISPOSSESSION

The Vocation of a Postmodern Theologian

TOM BEAUDOIN

Maryknoll, New York 10545

Founded in 1970, Orbis Books endeavors to publish works that enlighten the mind, nourish the spirit, and challenge the conscience. The publishing arm of the Maryknoll Fathers and Brothers, Orbis seeks to explore the global dimensions of the Christian faith and mission, to invite dialogue with diverse cultures and religious traditions, and to serve the cause of reconciliation and peace. The books published reflect the views of their authors and do not represent the official position of the Maryknoll Society. To learn more about Maryknoll and Orbis Books, please visit our website at www.maryknoll.org.

Copyright © 2008 by Tom Beaudoin.

Published by Orbis Books, Maryknoll, NY 10545-0308.

All rights reserved.

No part of this publication may be reproduced or transmitted in any form or by any means, electronic or mechanical, including photocopying, recording, or any information storage or retrieval system, without prior permission in writing from the publisher.

Queries regarding rights and permissions should be addressed to Orbis Books, P.O. Box 308, Maryknoll, NY 10545-0308.

Manufactured in the United States of America.

Library of Congress Cataloging-in-Publication Data

Beaudoin, Tom, 1969–
Witness to dispossession : the vocation of a postmodern theologian / Tom Beaudoin.
p. cm.
Includes bibliographical references.
ISBN 978-1-57075-785-3
1. Philosophical theology. 2. Postmodernism—Religious aspects—Christianity. 3. Vocation—Christianity. I. Title.
BT40.B43 2008
230'.046—dc22

For beloved Tina and Mimi,

We three make "only an altar of earth"
(Exodus 22:24)

Contents

Introduction

I find you, Lord, in all Things and in all
my fellow creatures, pulsing with your life;
as a tiny seed you sleep in what is small
and in the vast you vastly yield yourself.

The wondrous game that power plays with Things
is to move in such submission through the world:
groping in roots and growing thick in trunks
and in treetops like a rising from the dead.[1]

What is it like to remember the opening line, to place ourselves in its tunnel unending? The earliest canonical gospel, the very first sentence, the New Testament's inaugural sounds: Mark 1:1. "The beginning of the good news of Jesus Christ, the Son of God."

The good news begins. What signals this verse as the beginning? Is Mark 1:1 introducing the next verse, quotation, or motif as the beginning of the gospel? Is Mark 1:1 declaring itself as the beginning of the gospel? If so, what is the good news in the very declaration of the beginning of good news?

Is there the gospel of Jesus Christ in the mere gesture that the good news is now underway in the exposure to these words?

Or—is this "prefatory" remark to the oldest of the canonical gospels making an announcement, a heralding, a preparing of the way (verse 2) for the entire gospel of Mark, and even through "the good news," all the gospels as such, so that the entire report of the good news is but a beginning, that Mark 1:1 is framing Mark 1:2 through 16:8, or even through the disputed 16:9 through 16:20? If so, these two thousand years of Christian theology are footnotes to a beginning, elaborations of a commencement—normally taken as a conclusion.

Given the gospel's beginningness, at once showy and shadowy, how can one be sure that this is the beginning of what will prove to be good news? Will the gospel have a middle or an ending that validates its good name?

Reading all of Mark as the beginning of good news projects the search for a validating ending, or even middle (if Mark 1 to 16 is prologue) outside the received text. We must travel outside the text, engaging culture to see what the good news might be, where it might be, beyond its textually announced beginning, and to provide the perspective and experience through which what is good news in this beginning can be appreciated—and what is beginning in this good news.

Mark 1:1 condenses the strangenesses that are the Bible's constant offering. What truth can be made of those strangenesses in psyche and culture is the work of theology.

CATHOLIC THEOLOGY, POWER, AND THE POSTMODERN

This book is a series of essays on theology and culture today that experiment with exposing the concerns of Catholic theology to the ways of postmodern philosophy, namely the philosophy of Michel Foucault (1926–1984). I use this notion of "exposure" advisedly, as my purpose above all is to attempt one small task befalling Catholic theology today: to put to the test what can be believed of the faith in the face of some of the most fundamental challenges available, be they philosophical critique, religious counterclaim, or that personal encounter, felt or imagined, with what must so inadequately be called "alterity." I attempt to sustain theological exposures in this book so as to ascertain where the real challenges lie to thinking with and for, as we so easily say in Catholic theology, "the tradition."

Exposure can also have a theological meaning as an intellectual form of penance. It was Johannes Baptist Metz who argued that Catholicism was faced with the unavoidability of developing a theology that did not try to defend itself against the Holocaust, and did not try to defend itself against the theological control of Judaism that Christianity attempted, and in which it succeeded, again and again. Metz saw that because the Holocaust was a catastrophe for Jews, Christians needed to accept it as a disaster for Christian theology. He counseled relentless exposure to the catastrophe and to its survivors as a condition for ever making theological claims again. This penitential role for theology is summed up in Metz's breathtaking principle for his theologizing: "There is no truth for me which I could defend with my back turned to Auschwitz. . . ."[2] He will keep himself in the presence of the disaster in which his faith tradition and his humanity are implicated.

The consenting to being disarmed by the Jewish other, sister and brother, spells the end not only of supersessionist theologizing, but of a dialectical mode for theology, insofar as an ahistorical mutual critique, correlation, or comparison is allowed to produce theological truths. Penance is not the kind of argument that dialectic is. It is the kind of argument that starts with attention to the incisions made by the other in what were considered settled, essential, or nonnegotiable aspects of a theological whole, and proceeds "*ad intra*" about what is happening in regard to the incisions that are marking up our theological fantasies. As a result of this kind of thinking, we have a dramatically changed situation between Catholic theology and Judaism today, full of new theological proposals that were unimaginable a few decades ago, and are still unacceptable to many American Christians. Metz teaches contemporary theology the absolute importance of exposure as an act of theological penance, as condition for theological survival. Theological penance fosters an affective and intellectual availability to deep challenges to the faith, to think of faith only in face of those challenges, and in so doing, to hand over everything about the previous theological life that fed into the theology that helped create a profoundly intolerable situation for human beings.

This sensitivity to, impatience with, and protest against what is intolerable is what Foucault described as philosophy's task in being attentive to the present. I would like to make a Catholic practical theology, a theology of the present, share in this concern for the intolerable, especially in addressing that which is intolerable for which Christians bear responsibility. Other theologies of the present can learn from Metz's example. However, we should exercise deep caution in drawing anything like direct analogies between the Holocaust and other forms of suffering. There can be other theological exposures that face the intolerable in their own time and place, as Metz did. One such intolerable is the sex abuse scandal in the Catholic Church, particularly in the United States, which has been the geographical space for my own theology.

It is impossible for Catholic theologians to keep writing theology without reference to this profound corruption, one that has affected perhaps over fifty thousand victims and their families in the United States.[3] This scandal has several qualities under-recognized in contemporary theology: it is not only the outcome resulting from an intellectual poverty (poor ecclesiology, for example), a spiritual poverty (lack of mature fidelity to Christ or the church, one could say), a sexual poverty (such as an alleged gay indiscipline with regard to celibacy), or a managerial poverty (like decisions, whether merely wrong, or truly evil, by bishops, to keep abusive priests near minors). In, through, and beyond these many dimensions, the sexual abuse scandal should force Catholicism to the bedrock of its self-understanding. Who can endure unchanged even a single searing testimony from a survivor, melting the most treasured idealizations about this Catholic Church, and throwing back at us the charge that our theology itself may serve these idealizations, or may itself be an idealization?

It may be that Catholic theology has so little to do with the life of bishops, religious, priests, and the laity that it seems excessive to claim that the scandal calls Catholic theology into question at its roots. But if Catholic theology is, at a minimum, learned reflection in service of the flourishing of the Catholic faithful (and in principle of that of all people of good will), that is, if Catholic theology is saturated with concern for just practice in church and culture, claims for theology's irrelevance do not exempt theology from radical critique in face of the sex abuse scandal; theology's very irrelevance to laity, priests, religious, and bishops becomes an index of complicity through silent enabling of the scandal. Whatever theology's influence on those responsible for this Catholic evil, the physical-spiritual violence toward thousands and thousands of young souls in the past several decades calls fundamentally into question the content and purpose of thinking for and with this religious institution. As Stephen Pattison has argued, the "long-overdue 'discovery' of child abuse must be to Western theologians what the challenge of the poor has been to colleagues in South America—an imperative to a fundamental re-visioning of theology."[4] Sexual abuse of minors is the awful lodestar for all future American Catholic theology. A theological penitence that learns from Metz can say that the Catholic Church does not need to be thought of in the same breath as National Socialism in order to merit serious questioning of the role of its scholars in furthering or undermining relations of power that have damaged and even destroyed so many lives.

While there are many faces to this scandal, including most primordially the faces of the individual victims, one important theological face is the visage that power takes in Catholic practice. Exposure to the scandal in its depth requires theological exposure to critiques of power.

James Alison has argued that, as a result of this crisis, Catholics are finally understanding the "mendacity of power," which for Alison includes virulent official denials and betrayals of gay men in Catholic life, leading to the realization of "how vital" the power to tell people false truths about themselves "has been to the structure of our Church."[5] Power is the single most important spiritual, practical theme in the many recent studies of the sex abuse crisis.[6] Though power is not a traditional focal topic for Catholic theology, and Daniel Finn has persuasively argued that this has been to our detriment,[7] Karl Rahner—consistent with his architectonic grasp of Christian theology and its anthropological stakes—understood well the importance of theological attention to power. "Power is not *just any* element in human life. It is," he wrote, "along with sexuality, indeed even more than this, perhaps one of the most fundamental forces in our existence." It impinges even on the deepest spiritual realities: The "exercise" of power, far from being a superficial part of life, or relevant only in the realm of politics, is relevant for theology because power involves "a process either of *salvation* or *perdition*."[8] Something of deep importance for Catholic faith and life, then, approaches in the appreciation of power in Catholic life and thought. Indeed, we must discover what kind of Catholic theology can sustain itself in face of researches regarding power in which Catholicism is directly or indirectly implicated.

Foucault's work considers attention to power essential for analyses of how our construals of truth, subjectivity, and knowledge function together to create a "world" for us. Although this particular constellation of foci for apprehension of social reality joins Foucault to other currents of postmodern thought, the "postmodern" designation should not be considered a stable, uncontested notion. Let us hold on to it loosely for the present volume and presume that its use indicates a critical and reflexive intellectual orientation toward strongly "social constructionist" accounts of reality, and a critical attitude toward the "Enlightenment" as received intellectually by the time of the twentieth century in the West, toward what was presumed to be a modern, liberal, enlightened way of proceeding in Western intellectual life in general and social analysis in particular. This casts the net very wide for what counts as "postmodern," and is sufficient to encourage both a space in which to locate Foucault's distinctive fashioning of analysis of the mutual imbrications of power and knowledge, on the one hand, and to signal the ambiguities in the term itself that can make some thinkers seem postmodern to some commentators and not to others. And at any rate, because Catholic theologians by and large in the United States have barely begun to deeply integrate "postmodern" debates into their theologies, not to mention the integration of the question of power, there is no need here to try to set out with a premature clarity what counts as a "postmodern" Catholic theology. My chief task is theological exposure to Foucault's philosophy, for the sake of a theological penitence regarding power—which will necessarily involve attention to subjectivity, truth, and knowledge.

This book, then, will not be a book about the abuse crisis as such, but a book about theology and power with reference to Foucault and the kinds of questions he inspires, with a particular attention to the implications for the Catholic theological vocation today. Not all the essays deal explicitly with Catholic theology, and not all deal explicitly with Foucault, but the atmospherics of both are present throughout. Thus I should say a bit more about the structure and contents of the book.

THE ESSAYS

This book is a collection of essays that revolve around the theme of the vocation of Catholic theology in the midst of "postmodern" concerns. But the essays not only share a general concern for this problematic; they also each contribute to the constitution of a theological attitude that I take to be of signal importance for Catholic theology today: being a witness to dispossession. Each of the essays, then, has something to say about the activity of theologizing or the identity of the theologian in the midst of contemporary cultural questions understood postmodernly, but each essay also has a word to say about dispossession, about what Catholic theological life must begin to hand over if it is to retain its hope for vibrancy, criticality, courage, that is, its beautiful Catholic strangeness.

That does not mean all the essays were originally written for the purpose of being put together in a collection like this. Four chapters (One, Two, Four, and Seven) have been published in earlier versions elsewhere, leaving six chapters to make their first appearances here. Those whose life began in other publications have been edited to greater and lesser degrees so as to fit in a more friendly way with their adopted siblings for this book, while retaining features of their origins in theological mixed media: as university lectures, academic chapters, journal articles, or general-readership essays.

I have organized the essays by what I consider to be practical-theological themes. While this book does not overtly partake in the energetic recent debates about defining practical theology, but instead tries to advance specific practical theological arguments in service of a "definition to come," my present understanding of practical theology is that it takes as its own charge a focus on the constitution of practice in a critical account of theological knowledge, for the sake of testing how theology can make critical and reflexive sense of practice in faith and culture. The book takes up operating in such a theological atmosphere from complementary angles: Part One of the book deals with teaching, Part Two with engaging culture, Part Three with theological vocation, and Part Four with Christian life. Readers should feel invited to jump in with the theme that most interests them, and work backward or forward from there. In all the essays, I am edging my way toward a postmodern location for Catholic theology. This explains the frequent combination of personal discussion, practical social/ecclesial analysis, and theoretical theological reflection. I am searching for the handle, or a reasonable facsimile, for a postmodern intellectual, spiritual, and social world without evident handles. I hope that these various forms of theological writing will make sense for those for whom postmodernity is not only a series of interlocking intellectual debates about truth, subjectivity, knowledge, and power, but also a profound rocking of the meaning and possibilities of spiritual life in general and Christian spirituality in particular.

Part One focuses on the challenge of teaching theology in face of postmodern attentions to power, and in Chapter One, "Foucault Teaching Theology," I sketch a Foucauldian approach to power and draw out its implications for what theologians do with theological knowledge in the classroom, with particular attention to what theological knowing as a power-bearing discourse means for our relationship to students. This concern carries through into Chapter Two, "Multiple Theological Intelligences?" in the form of a critical encounter between a Foucauldian approach to the construction of academic knowledge and the influential theory of multiple intelligences, with a particular interest in what this encounter means for teaching theology in general, and for the theological significance of music in particular.

In Part Two, the book focuses on theological engagements with culture, which means both a consideration of some cultural problems taken into theology today, and theological production itself as a cultural problem. I consider the limits of American cultural discourse on spirituality and implications for Catholic higher education in Chapter Three, "Is Your Spirituality Violent?" Chapter Four, "Popular Culture Research and Theology," has me returning to what is now an "old" focus for my work, the theological meaning of popular culture. In this chapter, I suggest an approach to locating research in popular culture within the domain of spiritual exercises.

The volume then moves to some problems in the nature of theological work today, under the heading "Vocation" for Part Three. Chapter Five, "Reflections on Doing Practical Theology," continues the theme of spiritual exercises introduced in the previous chapter, and examines how practical theological work might be understood as a way that theologians pay attention to themselves. Chapter Six, "The Ethics of Characterizing Popular Faith," raises the question of what we academics are doing when we analyze the faith of other people, by way of a critical interpretation of recent research on the spirituality of young Americans.

The final section of the book, Part Four, opens up aspects of Christian life implicated in postmodern philosophical and theological questions. Chapter Seven, "I Was Imprisoned by Subjectivity and You Visited Me," overlays Foucault with Dietrich Bonhoeffer in an attempt to construe a postmodern approach to Christian subjectivity that can be of use for Christian life today. In Chapter Eight, "The Struggle to Speak Truthfully," the convergence of Foucauldian research and Christian scripture on the topic of the ancient practice of "frank speech" is introduced, and implications for the way Catholicism governs its own free speech practices are considered. The last chapter is Chapter Nine, "Faith and Apocalypse," which proposes widening the metaphors that govern Catholic pastoral life, from stages of development and maturing adulthood, over to interruption and disorientation, as a way of accommodating a postmodern sensibility and opening Catholics up to the tragic and seemingly contradictory experiences of faith identity today.

Chapter Ten is a Conclusion, "Witness to Dispossession: On the Way to a Pre-Christian Catholic Theology," and represents my attempt at a constructive statement regarding the vocation of the postmodern theologian, as an agent of dispossession. Still, the Conclusion is but another way of commencing the kind of Christian commencement commenced in the gospel of Mark with which I began this Introduction. Its provisionality signals that this entire book is, in my view, a propadeutic to a conversation on the postmodern that will take many more years within U.S. Catholic theology. It is a propadeutic in another sense, as well: this book will be followed by a more constructive second volume, one that examines the possibility of a Catholic theology of practice. As the reader will no doubt notice, I have been interested in the postmodern refiguring of Catholic theology insofar as it bears on theological comprehensions of practice in faith and culture, and reflexively on theological production itself as a cultural practice. I read this volume as a report of what I have learned in this regard over the past several years, for the purpose of next being able to paint a more fulsome Catholic theological portrait of practice in postmodern culture.

As a book limning a theological "vocation," this volume is necessarily personal. As theology written by a Catholic, it is irreparably ecclesial. As the product of the postmodern education of a post-Vatican II theologian, it is almost unavoidably omnibus, interdisciplinary, and very likely an exhibit of the dissipation of the "Catholic whole" that many pre-Vatican II Catholics (including their postliberal acolytes) now mourn. I hope it serves as an aid to a Markan commencement, to a welcome bewilderment regarding what the beginning of the good news really is.

ACKNOWLEDGEMENTS

Robert Ellsberg at Orbis has been a terrifically insightful, wise, supportive, and patient editor. Working with him has provided numerous occasions for affirming my fandom regarding Catholic book publishers.

I wish to thank Gordon Lynch of Birkbeck, University of London, whose friendship and intellectual collegiality in the realm of religion and culture have proven so stimulating these last several years. The ongoing work of the Practical Theology group at the Catholic Theological Society of America and, in particular, the theological expertise and dynamic collegiality of Kathleen Cahalan of Saint John's University School of Theology and Seminary have influenced my academic identity and choice of scholarly interlocutors. The Foucault Consultation at the American Academy of Religion has allowed a welcome space for the consideration of many sides of the relationship between Foucault and theology. I also thank my Santa Clara University students, who have marvelously bent my theological outlook in the direction of reality. In particular, my research assistant for the past two years, Jessica Coblentz, provided invaluable creative and critical assistance in research, editing, and discussion of ideas.

Saint John's University of Collegeville, Minnesota, generously awarded me an honorary doctorate in 2004, and few things in academic life have pleased and inspired me more than this Benedictine embrace. During that trip occurred the initial idea to bring together the present book. I am also honored to have had a Fellowship in the American Psychoanalytic Association during 2006 to 2007, the first fruits of which already appear in this book, and will hopefully flower more fully in future work.

I am also very grateful for the many academic and religious institutions that have invited me to present my work since my last book in 2003, and whose hospitality and space for dialogue contributed to the formation of the ideas that appear in these pages. These include the Frank J. Lewis Institute (formerly) at the University of San Diego; the Hendrix-Lilly Vocations Initiative at Hendrix College; the Koch Chair in Catholic Studies at St. John's University and the College of Saint Benedict; the William H. Shannon Chair at Nazareth College; St. Catherine's College at Oxford University, for the Conference on Media, Religion, and Culture; the Roman Catholic Diocese of Oakland Lay Ecclesial Ministry Conference; the National Federation of

Priests' Councils Annual Convention; the Vancouver School of Theology and Shaughnessy Heights United Church's "Reach Out" Conference; the Regis University Catholic Studies Program; Corpus Christi University Parish at the University of Toledo; the Archdiocese of Detroit Jerry Martin Pastoral Ministry Conference; the Faith Formation Conference of the northern California Catholic arch/dioceses; the Los Angeles Religious Education Congress; the Catholic Book Publishers Association annual meeting; the Diocese of San Jose "Vino and Vespers" program; the San Jose Interfaith Coalition for Race, Religion, Economic, and Social Justice; the Boisi Center for Religion and American Public Life at Boston College; the Interfaith Roundtable Conference at Phillips Andover Academy; and the St. Thomas More Catholic Center at Yale University.

As for my bandmates in Speedwalker—Dave (drums), Pedro (guitar), and Luke (vocals)—I am grateful for their spirited camaraderie in the rock music that continues to deeply shape my sense for reality, in those secular spiritual exercises wherein some of the most important theology is to be found, outside of the academy and the church.

Most of all, there is gratitude beyond gratitude for my family, my wife Martina and my daughter Mimi. Their embrace of my theological life initiates me into the trustful sense that theology may not only be a handing on, but also a handing over.

Witness to
DISPOSSESSION

PART ONE
TEACHING

1

Foucault Teaching Theology

And he said to them, "Truly I tell you, there are some standing here who will not taste death until they see that the kingdom of God has come with power." (Mark 9:1)

Most theologians have classroom teaching as part of their theological life, however unprepared for it they may be. Most theologians also attempt to live a theological life because of the power of the theological teaching they once experienced. How, then, do we as theologians begin to account for the power that runs through us pedagogically?

I contend that no theologian can fail to be disturbed by the disorientation that even a basic account of Michel Foucault's research on knowledge and power introduces: that instead of presuming the existence of ahistorical truths that, however hermeneutically translated, "demand" or "imply" particular practices for the sake of fidelity, he attends to the ways in which truth is practiced, to our changing relations to truth, and to the history of truth. He also seeks to explain the ways in which claims to knowledge of the truth are implicated in practices of power, marking bodies, and affecting and effecting self-understandings.

In hearing Foucault for the theological classroom, I shall first present some of Foucault's primary insights in regard to knowledge and power. Although there are many other basic presentations of Foucault's work on these topics, my supposition is that Catholic theologians, especially in the United States, have not "gotten" these points in Foucault. I will then suggest how the teacher of theology might educate after the Foucauldian, "postmodern" critique. I hope to show the importance for theological educators of developing a pedagogy allied to theological tradition in a responsivity not only to postmodernity, but to the ethical demands of our own teaching and having been taught—with power.

POWER

Foucault's account of power defies simple categorization. As constant expressions of "elementary"[1] force relations in society, "power is everywhere,"[2] but not as a seamless, total, macro, undifferentiated presence. It is instead to be understood as viscous,[3] a "dense web,"[4] an ambiguous, always local, polyvalent, shifting, "enigmatic," and "ubiquitous,"[5] unstable permanence in human relations, or a permanence with no simple "origin" and no singular "location." Foucault's work suspects any metanarrative that would "explain" power because such a metanarrative would require the possibility of getting "outside" of power, which is impossible: "There is no binary and all-encompassing opposition between rulers and ruled at the root of power relations, and serving as a general matrix."[6] Power may be used but is not invented by a person, group, or institution. This is what Foucault means by the paradox that "power relations are both intentional and nonsubjective."[7] Power can be used with certain goals in mind, but that does not mean that one totally controls the effects of the power one has put into use. (As is so common in the classroom, the power that the teacher thinks is being exercised can have a plethora of ambiguous effects, simultaneously supporting and undermining one's intended goals.)

His investigations into the workings of power took him beyond a concept of power as fundamentally repressive (the binary, or dialectical, exercise of force by one privileged and powerful group against another nonprivileged, powerless group), which was the heritage of Marxist theoreticizations of power,[8] and into a conception of power as also productive. For Foucault, power not only prevents and prohibits, but also produces and creates.[9] Power is not to be construed as consistent domination, evenly repressing identities, peoples, or desires.[10] Power has a creative function, being intrinsic to the construction of self-identities, categories of thought, and epistemological limits. Power acts in concert with knowledge so that what can legitimately be known is always already forced and enforceable, so that there is no nonpolitical knowledge, no apolitically organized or socially inconsequential meditation. As Foucault observed in a dense aphorism, "Everything is dangerous."[11] Power has a neutral,[12] functional quality, as something that is, first and foremost, exercised. There is thus a nominalism about Foucault's category of "power."[13] Power is not simply "good" or "bad." All power is ambiguous, and even the most benevolent exercise of it cannot claim innocence. Foucault's subtle and complex account of power suggests that if power is not a zero-sum game, persons, groups, and institutions can simultaneously be victims and oppressors.

To be sure and as perhaps too few Catholic theologians acknowledge, Foucault does not shy away from making judgments about imbalances of power. Foucault suggests that "relations of power" are "the immediate effects of the divisions, inequalities, and disequilibriums which occur" in human relationships, such as "economic processes, knowledge relationships, [and] sexual relations."[14] With Foucauldian provisions in hand, theologians may nuance and complexify attention to now-familiar categories of oppressors and oppressed. Foucault reformulates such oppression in a way that includes the continually renegotiated character of power: "Major dominations are the hegemonic effects that are sustained by [social forces'] confrontations."[15]

Particularly for Foucault's later thought, power is intrinsically related to resistance. Wherever power can be identified as functioning, resistance is possible.[16] Yet Foucault renders any resistance irreversibly ambiguous, undercutting the self-certainty of theories or practices of a however benign, however eschatologically placed, freedom. Every act of resistance is itself an act of power: "Resistance is never in a position of exteriority in relation to power."[17] It is surely for many theologians a reminder of the sinfulness and historicity that condition every theological or pedagogical attempt at, practice of, or concept of liberation.[18] Just as power is multivalent, constantly shifting, and irreducible to a grand explanation, so too is it insusceptible to a final rebellion from one single location. There is instead the possibility of a "plurality of resistances"[19] that are always local. This plurality may express itself in discourses of resistance, which can counteract discourses of power, insofar as "discourse can be both an instrument and an effect of power, but also a hindrance, a stumbling-block, a point of resistance and a starting point for an opposing strategy."[20] And as Jeremy Carrette has shown, Foucauldian resistance may take the form of bodily explorations that resist being told the truth about oneself, what he calls a "spiritual corporality" as counterpart to a Foucauldian "political spirituality."[21]

Foucault's work attempts to show that all knowledge is co-implicated in and an enactment of power. For Foucault, there is no knowledge that does not act on the force of, and produce its own, power. Nor is there any power that is not produced by and productive of particular knowledge. "Between techniques of knowledge and strategies of power," he argues, "there is no exteriority."[22] "Relations of power-knowledge are not static forms of distribution, they are 'matrices of transformations.'"[23] This is evident in Foucault's use of the term *discourse.* By discourse, James Bernauer suggests that Foucault means a "'violence' done to things . . . by a set of rules that determine what can be stated at a particular time and how these statements are related to others."[24] Discourse is never merely a description but always also a production of truth. This does not mean that the search for truth is pointless, rather it is never a search with clean hands: "It's not true that knowledge can function or that we can discover the truth, the reality, the objective reality of things without calling into play a certain form of power, of domination and subjection."[25]

Foucault's most justly famous and confronting investigations of power-knowledge occur in his interrogations of systems and practices of thought and knowledge that are commonly considered liberative, such as psychoanalysis, sexual liberation, and humanism, and disclosing their shadow sides, their subtle imprisonments. A sentence from *Discipline and Punish* may be taken as a summary of Foucault's attitude in this regard: "The 'Enlightenment,' which discovered the *liberties*, also invented the *disciplines*."[26] It is characteristic that Foucault refuses to disassociate the former from the latter.

TWO OF FOUCAULT'S CASE STUDIES

Madness and Civilization

In the book known in English as Madness and Civilization, Foucault argues that the development of asylums for the mad, whose planning and maintenance were driven by concerns for the liberation of the insane from social oppression, undergirded by a concern for the creation of humanizing spaces, was at the same time a dangerous project on subjectivity. Through an ensemble of penal and therapeutic practices, the asylums formed patients and supervisors in a relation to self and others of a different order than the stated plan.

> The asylum no longer punished the madman's guilt; it organized it for the madman as a consciousness of himself, and as a non-reciprocal relation to the keeper; it organized it for the man of reason as an awareness of the Other, a therapeutic intervention in the madman's existence. . . . [B]y this guilt, the madman became an object of punishment always vulnerable to himself and to the Other; and, from the acknowledgement of his status as object, from the awareness of his guilt, the madman was to return to his awareness of himself as a free and responsible subject, and consequently to reason.[27]

The institution's discourses of liberation structure relations to self and others in costly ways. Or rather, the discourses of liberation associated with the claims to truth of psychologies of treating mental illness made possible the asylum and its character as an expected, helpful, and even necessary site in the mental and moral geography of nineteenth-century France. "More genuinely confined than he could have been in a dungeon and chains, a prisoner of nothing but himself, the sufferer was caught in a relation to himself that was of the order of transgression, and in a non-relation to others that was of the order of shame. . . . Delivered from his chains, he is now chained, by silence, to transgression and to shame."[28] Madness "became responsible for what it knew of its truth; it imprisoned itself in an infinitely self-referring observation; it was finally chained to the humiliation of being its own object. Awareness was now linked to the shame of being identical to that other, of being compromised in him, and of already despising oneself before being able to recognize or to know oneself. . . . [M]adness is ceaselessly called upon to judge itself . . . by a sort of invisible tribunal in permanent session."[29]

Interestingly, Foucault's research showed him that even basic images provide the structure for cultural perceptions of madness, in particular the dialectic between mania and melancholia. The smoke and flame of the single fire, an imagined "dynamics of animal spirits," were one organizing image; other explanatory images to organize the perception of madness included metamorphosis, remote causality, physiological motifs of circulation, principles of physics, and operations of electric batteries. What was seen in and as the "mad" person was what was possible to see by the imaginary and relatively ductile cultural-historical structurings of perception.

> What was constituted, in the seventeenth and eighteenth centuries, under the influence of images, was therefore a perceptual structure, and not a conceptual system or even a group of symptoms. The proof of this is that, just as in a perception, qualitative transitions could occur without affecting the integrity of the figure. The essential thing is that the enterprise did not proceed from observation to the construction of explanatory images; that on the contrary, the images assured the initial role of synthesis, that their organizing force made possible a structure of perception, in which at last the symptoms could attain their significant value and be organized as the visible presence of the truth.[30]

The concepts of mania and melancholia, therefore, "were organized around certain qualitative themes that lent them their unity, gave them their significant coherence, made them finally perceptible."[31]

These images are constitutive of and constituted by practices that mediate the self's relation to itself through regnant games of truth which circulate in practice through the images. Thus can Foucault suggest that the "objectivity" of nineteenth-century medicine was "a reification of a magical nature," subtended by an attempted moral constraint of doctor over patient. The practices of psychiatry gained the status of a science, but depend historically on eighteenth-century morality: "a practice forgotten in its origins and its meaning, but always used and always present."[32]

Discipline and Punish

In addition to *Madness and Civilization*, Foucault's discussion of power in *Discipline and Punish* can stand as one indication of his approach to the study of practices of power-knowledge, and serves as a helpful provocation for imagining some dynamics of the theological classroom. In this work, Foucault theorizes the human body as a "political" body, locating the body at the dangerous site of the crossroads of knowledge and power.[33] Punishment can be understood with reference to a "political economy of the body," which is to say that the body has been the object on which political and economic history writes its stories. To serve political and economic ends, bodies are made both useful and docile. But there exists in society not only a "political economy" of the body, but also a "political technology" of the body. In other words, there are specific ways that power is exercised socially on the body. These ways, however are exceedingly difficult to pinpoint with certainty. Power over the body does not issue from one person or one institution; all levels of society reproduce intricate networks of power over bodies; the exploited themselves are often in complicity with this "microphysics of power." It is here that Foucault advances his prime epistemological claim: that "power produces knowledge," that power and knowledge never appear without each other. Indeed, power and knowledge are symbiotic; they aid in continually creating each other. One offspring of the union of power and knowledge in French society, according to Foucault, is the birth of the soul, which—as the seat of guilt, remorse, and morality—serves to make the body even more submissive.[34] The soul, understood in this way, is paradoxically "the prison of the body." Around the soul, an amalgam of historical concepts that have been elevated into essential characteristics of the human have congregated: "psyche, subjectivity, personality, consciousness,"[35] all of which promise privileged access to the truth of one's self.

Foucault describes three "instruments" employed in the disciplinary society.[36] First, "hierarchical observation" is a way of organizing space so that individuals may be constantly observed, including the observation of superiors by their own superiors. Power is made "anonymous" under this sort of observation, because one never knows exactly when one is being observed (thus internalizing a fear of observation as well as the habits of the observer). But who is ultimately responsible for the invasive systems of "hierarchical observation"? As he emphasized earlier in regard to "microphysics of power," it is extraordinarily difficult, indeed impossible, to locate the source of this power. "It is the apparatus as a whole that produces 'power.'"[37] Hierarchical observation becomes so co-identified with a structure that the structure itself seems to "embody" the power being used over others. Foucault's second "instrument" of discipline is "normalizing judgment." He emphasizes that what is considered "normal" is in reality a kind of caprice of hegemonic power, written further into apparatuses of power that take on lives of their own. What is "normal" is enforced through systems of "perpetual penality," with judgment and correction ever possible for nonnormal bodies. Finally, Foucault highlights the instrument of the "examination." The examination is an insidious combination of the first two instruments, observation and normalizing judgment. Examinations have the tendency to objectify the examinees (making them subject to the knowledge of the teacher, and providing the teacher with "objective" knowledge about the student). In addition, and paradoxically, examinations play a key role in creating modern "individuality" by way of "objective" examination criteria. Such individuality actually serves to make students docile by categorizing them for further examination and constant evaluation, practices bathed in the discourses of objective science but serving the unarticulated interests of power.

One of Foucault's best-known categories for interpreting power is the "panoptic."[38] Panopticism in Foucault's works seems to frequently function as a metaphor for the invasive practices visited upon bodies by those in power. The "panoptic" society is one in which its members are under constant surveillance, whose ideals of normality and a productive life are not "natural," but the result of options that have been created for them to serve the interests of power. The "disciplines" of the panoptic society can actually exist alongside or within structures of seeming equality. Relative equality among individuals serves as an opiate of the masses once the cloak of submission has been draped over a society, not allowing the major (yet frequently invisible) systems of oppression themselves to be challenged. Panoptic power is evident also in the knowledge gained by the confessor *and* the penitent in the post-Tridentine confessional, where various refinements of sexual language were enacted, but "the scope of the confession . . . continually increased," expressing itself in "meticulous rules of self-examination wherein," whether to oneself or one's confessor, "everything had to be told" in a "nearly infinite task of telling . . . everything that . . . had some affinity with sex."[39] Transmuting desire into speech (knowledge) was a result of the exercise of productive *and* repressive power.

Thus, knowledge already acts as an initial instance of its own power, having the power to rule in or out "epistemological" options. Foucault's approach strips knowledge of innocence, pointing to the electrocutionary deployability of all knowledge and the "epistemological" expressions power takes in society.

Is such an approach to power-knowledge unrecognizable in the theological education we ourselves have undergone? Might we admit that Foucault has, in his own way, exposed the ambiguity that many of us, heirs of the Enlightenment *episteme*,[40] experience at the heart of all attempts at liberation, the sophisticated self-justifications that seem inseparable from even the best teaching, the ways in which what and how we know are forms of power, power that represses as well as produces—shame, delight, anxiety, self-confidence, and self-definition? Is it difficult to hear the resonance to our own situations of teaching theology, in which to know a certain thing in a certain way is to gain an upper hand, that "knowledge is not made for understanding; it is made for cutting"?[41] Is this experience not one that for all theological educators should hold a special sense of immediacy? Are we not already aware of the "homogenizing tendencies within . . . ideolog[ies] of egalitarian pluralism,"[42] that render, as David Tracy has argued, even our best traditions and attempts at liberative theologies and pedagogies profoundly "ambiguous"?[43] Insofar as these recognitions are meaningful recognitions of our own theological-pedagogical practices, this appreciation of Foucault has a chance of being rendered practicable.

TEACHING THEOLOGY

Exposure to these researches of Foucault opens a specific kind of spiritual discipline in teaching for the theological educator, by which I mean learning to teach so as to honor a "plot of unreadability."[44] "Plot" in its noun forms means a story line, a spot of land, or a planned attack; as a verb it signals the act of mapping out or outlining. A "plot" of unreadability might thus refer to a story whose text remains opaque despite our (pan)ocular straining, a map of our teaching situations whose legend has been partly defaced, a spot of admitted pedagogical inaccessibility and humility or ambiguity, or at the least, a disciplined refrainment from a panoptic attitude toward the "texts" of the pedagogical situation, including one's students, one's teaching media, and oneself, a plan that is no more a hopeless concession to the destructive forces within every pedagogical situation than it is a self-righteous program for living the single correct summation of a heteroglossic, ambiguous religious tradition. The paradox of plotting unreadability: can one plot or "plan" unreadability without already reading its secret meaning, without secretly knowing its code in advance? Plotting unreadability is to plan to read, and re-read, and be read oneself: there would be no knowledge of unreadability were there not attempts to read in the first place. Plotting unreadability, then, demands continued reading without illusions of final readability and without the loss of hope for readability, for to plot is not to guarantee. "You know neither the day nor the hour" (Matthew 24:36).

This plot unreadability can be thematized more concretely into two particular implications: rethinking pedagogical power relations, and as a consequence, reconceptualizing liberation theological pedagogy.

First, in regard to power: this postmodern theological education fosters a pedagogical atmosphere whose "objectives" are not stable but iterative, power-conscious, and critical of potentially normalizing claims. Such a pedagogy must not understand itself as "empowering." Rather, it should dignify and thematize the power relations already at work in any given pedagogical situation, making them objects of pedagogical interest. "Empowerment" is often perceived and practiced as "giving" power to learners, bearing traces of a paternalistic pedagogical approach that does not adequately describe the workings of power.[45] Such education must attend to the workings of power in the particular religious tradition at issue and within the pedagogical setting. "To reveal relations of power is . . . to put them back in the hands of those who exercise them."[46] "It is not to awaken consciousness that we struggle . . . but to sap power, to take power; it is an activity conducted alongside those who struggle for power, and not their illumination from a safe distance."[47]

This is not a demand for the "relinquishing" of power on the part of the teacher, which is impossible anyway. It is rather seeking to keep the dynamic of shared study open for an intention of unendingly reshareable circuits of power in the teaching of theology (without—must it be said?—in any way "reducing" the experience of theological studies to exercises of power "alone"). One implication here is the cultivation of attention to an intentional heterogeneity of power relations in the educational setting. Foucault allows us to see that every theological-pedagogical event is also, but not only, a complex and minute series of exercises of power, in which bodies, selves, and traditions are being "written" and "rewritten."

Second, and as a corollary, perhaps the greatest challenge Foucault poses is reconfronting the problem of education for liberation, a problem whose basic terms Foucauldian thinking may show to have too often been assumed to be all but settled in many progressive theological pedagogies.

Is a liberating teaching of theology possible that will acknowledge power and difference, that will be a theological pedagogy of and for freedom-without-reduction-of-the-other, freedom-without-assimilation, which may mean liberation otherwise than that envisioned by the theologian? Foucault complexifies liberal theological/educational tendencies by suggesting that "there has never existed one type of stable subjugation, given once and for all."[48] Power (which he suggests is "microphysical," resistant to systematization, and multivariate) cannot be simply overthrown following the "law of all or nothing," or by reconfiguring or destroying institutions; nor can it simply be renounced in order to arrive at true knowledge.[49]

Theological pedagogies in the wake of this exposure that seek the aims of liberation theologies must take up a constant self-awareness of their own exercises of power. While theologies of God may manifest an "option for the poor" that is in some way preferential, this does not mean that progressive educators somehow automatically find themselves blanketed by this divine privilege in a way that would remove the ambiguities of power in their own attempts to practice this "option." Nor that the invocation of the injunction, the provocation-impulse to declare this option, is outside of the exercise of power and a servant to intolerable interests.

A thick admixture of repression and production, victimization and domination that are the constituents and effects of power, are ever-present in the theological educator; there is no simple self-emptying, kenotic pedagogical movement on the part of the liberation-theological educator, curriculum, or the general movement of the teaching situation.[50]

It is important to note that this interference of Foucault in the practice of teaching theology does not imply an end of a liberative pedagogy; rather, such practices must seek to understand the real conditions in which power operates. Such practice calls for more than a modern, liberal pluralist "vision of justice . . . spiced up with a heavy salting of deconstructive rhetoric."[51] It is an irruption of the Foucauldian insight into, in Gilles Deleuze's words, "the indignity of speaking for others," which is frequently enough a self-effacing exercise of domineering power.[52] This turn suggests a transgression of the sense of "liberation" that modernity was to have achieved, especially insofar as liberation conceptions rest implicitly or explicitly on an escape from power. Can we approach teaching theology as a set of discourses of knowledge bound up with, supported by, and supporting power relations?[53]

Those who teach theology in the wake of Foucault may affirm that theology may bear distortion when it defines itself as concerned with the limits of knowledge that are the fruit of uninterrogated power-knowledge relations. Has the attempt to teach theology dwelt long enough on Jesus—before Pilate? John's gospel narrates that Jesus remained silent when Pilate attempted to produce a verbalization of truth from Jesus (John 18:38). How can this silence be heard today if not also as warning about the pretension of the theological doctor to produce utterances as power-innocent truths over our students? Jesus' silence, this strange nonteaching, is a tractor beam against which our teaching practices seem to pull, instead of consenting to face his silence, to be a face for his silence. In a practical way, this means radical and unending critique, and not a secret and final access to truth because it has been verbalized, even by an authority like Jesus (who himself refused to do so), but by dignifying the irresolvable tension between the examination of truth as a practice, and the seeking of the impossible possibilities of God.

2

Multiple Theological Intelligences?

AN INQUIRY

A beat poised, a crossgrained rhythm, interplays, imbrications of voice over voice, mutinies of living are rocking the steady state of a theme; these riffs and overlappings a love of deviance, our genesis in noise.[1]

A new mystery sings in your bones. Develop your legitimate strangeness.[2]

INTRODUCTION

In everyday life, we employ an astonishing, complex, and finally non-quantifiable array of resources in working to free ourselves, in attempts both banal and dramatic. Contemporary electronic media multiply these resources for the fashioning of freedom, however ambiguously. In film, music, home video, and comic books, who are their authors, and how are they used in everyday life? What problems do their uses create that become for us unsettled spiritual and intellectual spaces whose ground we find ourselves devoted to clearing? These concerns are of particular interest among progressive theological educators. Perhaps chief among "our" central interests is the inquiry into contemporary resources for freeing pedagogical practices.

The significance of such inquiry for my life has come from two convergent experiences in the academy. First, I realized that my graduate theological education was not structured to make use of the ways of knowing that I had developed as a musician. There were certain codes about theological knowing that most people at the university seemed to take for granted. Those codes protected the notion of theological knowledge as chiefly verbal, conceptual, and linguistic. What I knew, however, after playing bass guitar in rock bands for many years, was that my way of "knowing" musically was in large part nonverbal, nonconceptual, and nonlinguistic. I wondered whether theological education, despite the prevalence of liberationist discourses, was itself not yet liberated in form from a too narrow interpretation of what it means to know theologically.

Moreover, Michel Foucault's work taught me that human ways of organizing or "constructing" reality—physically, emotionally, and intellectually—were to some degree particular and contingent arrangements or "productions" of reality, capable of being drained of their seemingly natural inertia through creative historical and philosophical analyses that commence from what we find intolerable about our present and end in a new relationship being taken up to oneself.[3] It was precisely for the sake of a more "human" freedom that Foucault called into question those structures that had come to be associated with Enlightenment victory: modern prisons, sexual liberation, and psychoanalysis. As James Bernauer has argued, Foucault's work manifested an ethic that protests against every historical construction of the human that announces its inevitability, "bear[ing] witness to the capacity for an ecstatic transcendence of any history that asserts its necessity."[4]

Yet Foucault's work was not restricted to his books. His own understanding was that "the work includes the whole life as well as the text."[5] In seeking to use Foucault as a resource for teaching theology, therefore, it is appropriate to acknowledge that his "work" includes both his academic texts and his biography. Honoring this, I would like to briefly touch on a rarely examined site of his work: his relation to a "nonverbal" domain of knowledge, namely music.

FOUCAULT AND MUSIC

That Foucault, in fact, took much pleasure in music, and that he did indeed "always [have] a soft spot for music,"[6] seems indisputable from evidence scattered across several biographies.[7] His tastes often seemed to run to classical music, although the delight apparently was more in the listening than in any technical appreciation.[8] He clearly did not see rock music as an interesting musical form, although he did find noteworthy its ability to generate lifestyles and attitudes.[9] He also seemed to take pleasure in, and even find inspiration in, other experimental forms of music. The fact that Foucault and the composer Jean Barraqué were lovers between 1952 and 1956 cannot be overlooked here. In addition, Foucault was personally acquainted with the composer Pierre Boulez in the 1950s and again in the 1970s.[10] (Both Barraqué and Boulez were students of Olivier Messiaen.)

Eribon proposes an important resonance between Foucault's philosophy and Barraqué's music, insofar as the latter described music as "tragedy, pathos, death. It is the whole game, the trembling to the point of suicide. If music is not that, if it does not overtake and pass the limits, it is nothing."[11]

Eribon further suggests that the music Foucault experienced while with Barraqué "triggered for Foucault a more general distancing that would permit his escape from the influence of phenomenology and Marxism. This was what he meant when he replied to Paolo Caruso in 1967 that music had played as important a role for him as the reading of Nietzsche."[12] Macey reports even stronger terms, asserting that "the serial and twelve-tone music of Boulez and Barraqué offered him his first escape from the dialectical universe in which he was still living. . . ."[13] Permitting an escape from dialectical thought, and as important as Nietzsche: these are strong claims about and by Foucault. They deserve further thought and research.

In a discussion of Foucault's *Archaeology of Knowledge*, Maurice Blanchot suggests that "many a formula from negative theology" inform Foucault's style of argument with regard to the uniqueness of "the statement."[14] In the following paragraph, Blanchot offhandedly relates this philosophy of the operation of the statement to music, "seemingly comparable to the perverse efforts (as Thomas Mann put it) of serial music."[15] Blanchot nowhere hints of an awareness that Foucault had an interest in serial music, or that such an interest may have proved a significant influence on Foucault's philosophizing and his breaking out of dialectical thinking. Blanchot's association of serial music and negative theology—whether he knew that Foucault had ever listened to such music (or whether Foucault had read much negative theology, for that matter)—provides another provocation. Why this possibly accidental association in Blanchot between the negative-theological impulse "behind" Foucault's philosophy and the workings of serial music?

Further research on these questions may help us not only understand the relationship between Foucault's logical-conceptual cognitive practices and his musical cognitive practices, but may through such understanding provide further paradigms for thinking about how those of us who teach theology might better dignify theological knowledges that until now have been subjugated.

But how are we to think about the possibility of plural domains of theological knowledge? Any discussion of this question takes place in the context of the work of Howard Gardner, a theorist commonly invoked as authoritative.[16] In my work with theological and religious educators, I have found Gardner's work to be the single most frequently referenced corpus for providing a framework for a more broadly human, and more adequately "postmodern," sense of what it means to know. Persuaded by the Foucauldian imperative to interrogate popular structures commonly presumed to be liberating, I would like to investigate closely the conceptual basis for this progressive model of learning.

In the remainder of this chapter, I shall attempt to contribute to the problematization of what counts as theological knowledge. My route to doing so will be through a discussion of the influential work of Howard Gardner on "multiple intelligences." My aim is to lay groundwork for loosening theological knowledge practices from the grip of the dominant construal of the modern theological subject, a subject formed to accept verbal-conceptual knowledge as the privileged epistemic domain of theology. The present work will not entail a critical discussion of Foucault, but will attempt to honor some fundamental Foucauldian "dynamics" by rendering their incarnation within a new domain of thought and practice, by contributing to the creation of a new question regarding what counts as theological knowledge.

Jean-Luc Marion suggests that "theology, of all writing, certainly causes the greatest pleasure."[17] But one need not limit theology to "writing" to find its pleasures. Marion's claim—that "to try one's hand at theology requires no other justification than the extreme pleasure of writing"[18]—is true only if "writing" is writ large, to include music and other domains of knowledge that may be less verbal, though no less at hand.

GARDNER AS RESOURCE

The work of Howard Gardner provides one of the most influential attempts to theorize a plurality of intelligences. The foundational text upon which this progressive pedagogical project is built is Gardner's *Frames of Mind.*[19] Though subsequent works have developed Gardner's ideas, *Frames* is the fullest articulation of his theory and, in my view, remains underanalyzed among progressive theological educators. Thus, I will focus primarily on this text with secondary attention to other of Gardner's books and essays.

Frames of Mind, in marshalling evidence from developmental psychology and brain research, sets an impressive standard for a systematic articulation of the plurality of intelligences. Gardner's project is to describe the different types of intelligence existing as a natural part of human development and flourishing variously within different cultures. He is sensitive to the cost to educators, as well as "nontraditional" learners, of constrictive assumptions about knowing. In pushing back against the "systematic devaluation of certain forms of intelligence,"[20] Gardner is convinced that "only if we expand and reformulate our view of what counts as human intellect will we be able to devise more appropriate means of assessing it and more effective ways of educating it."[21]

Frames makes several substantial positive contributions to a theory of multiple intelligences: (1) it risks naming discrete domains of intelligence; (2) it articulates criteria for an intelligence to be counted as such; (3) it creatively interrelates developmental psychology, brain research, and cultural anthropology; and (4) it attempts to outline the implications of plural intelligences for pedagogical practice. These contributions are offered with a modesty of approach that leaves Gardner's proposal open to further research and critique.

At the same time, Gardner's approach manifests several fundamental unresolved questions and specific deficits in conceptualization. These include (1) an uncritical theorization of the influence of culture on education and formation of intelligence; (2) several problematic criteria in support of what counts as an intelligence; (3) a lack of reflexive consciousness about the power-enmeshed, political-pedagogical uses and effects of delineating a specific set of fundamental human intelligences; and (4) specific problems with the conceptualization of each of the intelligences (of which I shall focus only on musicality). I shall discuss the strengths and weaknesses of the overall theory in turn, seeking to distill a sense of what Gardner's approach provides the present task and what work remains after a consideration of his scheme.

Gardner portrays a richly differentiated account of human knowing, divided into seven specific domains of human intelligence: linguistic, logical-mathematical, musical, bodily-kinesthetic, spatial, interpersonal, and intrapersonal. These domains are construed as individual cognitive competencies that satisfy what he calls general prerequisites and specific criteria for an intelligence to be counted as such. Gardner defines an intelligence as "the ability to solve problems, or to create products, that are valued within one or more cultural settings."[22] He elsewhere elaborates an intelligence as a coherent symbolic domain, with development of a particular intelligence being a matter of mastery of that unique symbolic domain.[23]

There are several prerequisites that must be satisfied for an intelligence to be considered a candidate for inclusion in his theory:[24] First, an intelligence must display its power to resolve or create problems, so as to establish "the groundwork for the acquisition of new knowledge."[25] Second, an intelligence must prove its nontriviality by being "genuinely useful and important, at least in certain cultural settings."[26] Gardner's third prerequisite is that an intelligence display a quality of essentiality, that it not be reducible to some more primary form of knowledge. Fourth, an intelligence must be verifiable empirically. He then adds a sort of metaprerequisite, which is that knowledges considered by the theory must fairly represent the range of knowledges valued by different cultures.

When moving from "prerequisites" to "criteria" for candidate intelligences, Gardner becomes much more specific.[27] His eight criteria include "potential isolation by brain damage," which is meant to limit intelligences to those forms of knowledge whose neural ground is attested to by their distortion as a result of injury to the brain. Second, the study of exceptional intellect in "prodigies" yields clues to the existence of unique domains of intelligence. Third, intelligences must exhibit a unique core of cognitive operations traceable to their neurobiological origins. Fourth, a clear developmental path that culminates in identifiable excellences, or "levels of expertise," is required. Complementary to this developmental history is a fifth criterion, an identifiable history in human biology. That is to say, an intelligence "becomes more plausible to the extent that one can locate its evolutionary antecedents."[28] Corroboration from research in cognitive psychology and intelligence testing (psychometrics) constitute the sixth and seventh criteria. Gardner's final, eighth, criterion is intelligibility to learners (and researchers)—the encodability of an intelligence in symbolic form. His criteria helpfully foreground the terms in which he wants his project to proceed.

Along with these strengths are several problems and a chief conceptual difficulty. Although several of the prerequisites and criteria for intelligences bear the marks of traditional scientific discourse, *Frames of Mind* occasionally hesitates about the scientific status of intelligences. In one passage, Gardner seems to forfeit the scientific confidence he elsewhere employs, writing that the "intelligences are fictions . . . for discussing processes and abilities that . . . are continuous with one another. . . ." In seeming contradiction of his fourth prerequisite of empirical verifiability, he claims that intelligences "exist not as physically verifiable entities but only as potentially useful scientific constructs."[29]

Further, while Gardner's second criterion is a Jamesian utilization of intensifications of everyday behavior (in this case, intelligences) for study and interpretation of more commonplace phenomena, it remains very problematic.[30] Gardner approvingly cites psychologist David Feldman's assertion that "the prodigy may be thought of as an individual who passes through one or more domains with tremendous rapidity, exhibiting a speed that seems to render him [sic] qualitatively different from other individuals."[31] One need not dispute the fact of accelerated individual cognitive progress among certain individuals to observe that theorizing the prodigy in this way seems to function to leave the domain boundaries intact between intelligences that Gardner wants to maintain. It is not clear that "prodigious" behavior, or dynamic and accelerated cognitive abilities, necessarily leads to the maintenance of knowledge domains, or necessarily reveals the "nature" of intellectual competencies "in pristine form."[32] Rather, it seems that truly prodigious actions may in fact transgress knowledge boundaries or create new ones. Moreover, not only may Gardner's construal of the prodigy serve to police the boundaries of knowledge already maintained by his (or another) theory, the focus on prodigies overindividualizes the very concept of "intelligence,"[33] as if prodigious individuals simply rise to the summit of cognitive prowess by force of their own innate prodigiousness. Gardner's interpretation of prodigious intellectuality makes it unlikely that prodigies would ever be epistemologically countercultural, working outside given domains of knowledge.[34] In short, the politically uncritical function of the employment of the prodigy as a criterion disqualifies it as trustworthy. Correlatively, it must be said that in some sense Gardner, and any theorist in similar work, is creating a discourse as much as discovering the essence of seven human intelligences; this political dimension of the productive character of such work on knowledge domains is not entertained by Gardner, who focuses on the "defining" and "discovery" of intelligence by psychology.[35]

Related to this problem is *Frames'* weak sense for the ideological and culturally contested qualities of "knowledge," "culture," or "symbols." While Gardner's interpretation of brain research and its implication for intelligences is rich and suggestive, his interpretation of culture, particularly in *Frames of Mind*, relegates culture to serving as midwife to the natural domains of intelligence striving to find their way in the world. But the question of the different cultural powers that may have a stake in producing and defining "intelligence" itself as a problem remains unaddressed. The undertheorization of the productively powerful role of cultures—in their class, academic, race-ethnic, scientific, and gender dimensions—in birthing, shaping, and governing "intelligence" or "knowledge" represents a significant lacuna. Culture, in his theory, is almost always a benign and secondary force on or support of knowledge.[36] In later work, Gardner and colleagues more complexly theorize the relationship between intelligence and culture, by distinguishing between "*intelligence* as a biopsychological potential; *domain* as the discipline or craft that is practiced in a society; and *field*, the set of institutions and judges that determine which products within a domain are of merit."[37] Despite the turn toward social and institutional formation of intelligence, the absence of a sufficiently critical social theory remains: a lack of theoretical resources for criticism of dominant knowledges and knowledge brokers, and (thus) for the relationship between cultural authorization of knowledge and the very definitions of and inquiries into "biopsychological potential."

Gardner seems in several places to use "symbol" in the sense of an expressive vehicle of human meaning, with symbol systems as shared repositories of cognitive work.[38] "Symbols pave the royal route from raw intelligences to finished cultures,"[39] Gardner claims. As culturally influenced organizers of knowledge, he argues that it is "legitimate to construe rituals, religious codes, mythic and totemic systems as symbolic codes that capture and convey crucial aspects of personal intelligence"[40]—but without any account of the danger within or cultural contestation of the construction and use of symbols.

In addition, Gardner's theory overrelies on grounding the intelligences scientifically. It is not self-evident, however, that for linguistic or musical knowledge to be counted as legitimate domains requires their bonding to a biological limit. This is not to say that brain research is irrelevant to, specifically, formulating what counts as doing theology in the classroom. This is, however, to say that a politically conscious distinction needs to be made between neurobiologically influenced cognitive capacities on the one hand, and domains of knowledge in which theological subjectification might render someone fluent, on the other. Both clearly have to do with the other. But both are not the other. Both need continual denaturalizing, critical investigations as to their conditions and effects. One cannot be made the ventriloquist of the other, else the risk occurs, from one side, of reducing what can and may be known theologically to the rules of knowledge that govern neurobiological discourse; or, from another side, in reinscribing a modern dismissal of the body's materiality as a locus of cognition by failing to search after the body's own processes. Such an approach jettisons the unique and unrepeatable individual cogitating body in favor of a maverick theory of theological knowledges unaccountable to human limits, even while purporting to think them.

Beyond these objections, there remains a major conceptual problem in *Frames*, the tendency to confuse "intellectual capacities" on one hand (as what we might call a psychological and medically potentially determinable set of developmental processes and limits), with "knowledge domains" on the other hand (as what we might refer to as *styles* of knowledge acquisition and the *contents* of such acquisition). For Gardner, what he interchangeably calls "intelligences," "intellectual competences," "forms of knowledge," and "knowledge domains"[41] issue primordially from neural and psychological developmental processes of the individual—cultural differences notwithstanding.

But the problem is not only definitional. For to confuse "intelligence" (as mastery of a discrete realm of knowledge) with "intellectual competence" or "proclivity" (as neurobiologically governed potential for the realization of cognitive capacities) and with "knowledge domain" (as a unique symbolically coded system of knowledge formed by persons, institutions, and cultures) is also a political-pedagogical problem—about who creates or controls what counts as "knowledge." Such a conceptual confusion also elides the role of philosophical contributions with respect to the constitution and politics of knowledge.[42] This conceptual problem is crystallized in Gardner's summary of his work at Harvard Project Zero, which attempts "to arrive at the 'natural kinds' of symbol systems: the families of symbol systems which hang together (or fall apart), and the ways they might be *represented* in the human nervous system."[43] Such a binding of the symbolic character of knowledge (if such character exists) to the nervous system, as if one could be "read off" the other, represents a leap.

Those of us who teach may not only formulate, as Gardner indicates, a stance about "the *identity*, or *nature of the intellectual capacities* that human beings can develop."[44] A fully critical account needs also to formulate a politics of cognitive capacity, which would be the practice of remaining open to and critically articulating the cost of denominating the "nature" of "intellectual capacities," particularly as we strive to establish their givenness as natural competence. After all, the desire to open up many domains of theological knowledge in which the student may be formed may tempt any teacher or pedagogical institution to bind individual differences too readily and firmly to the history, psyche, childhood, anatomy, or neurobiology of our students.[45]

To render the conceptual confusion of Gardner's book more clearly as a task for theological educators: we must resist satisfying ourselves with equating what knowledge "is" with where it "comes from." We must also ask what knowledge does, how different domains function.[46] What are their effects, who gets to define them, how have they been made possible, what are their situations or roles in various pedagogical contexts?[47]

In short, a distinction must be posited between what might be termed "cognitive potential" and "cognitive practice." Cognitive potentials are the inherent cognitive strengths of each individual that may or may not ever be exercised, whether these be inherited or otherwise present in a person (as Gardner evidences) neurobiologically. Cognitive practices, by contrast, are the actual exercises of knowledge within interrelated personal, cultural, and institutional realms (and that always affect the individual's cognitive life, but are surely not reducible to it).[48] (These latter are the practices that populate many of Foucault's texts, from medical knowledge in his earlier work to self-knowledge in his later work.)

The distinction I am proposing between cognitive potential and cognitive practice does not imply a separation between the two. Indeed, Foucault's work would suggest that much, if not all, of the discourses around cognitive potential (such as Gardner's) are always already implicated in cognitive practices. At the same time, cognitive practices rely on cognitive potentials—as elusive to articulate as they remain to the present day—as a condition of their possibility. This distinction serves at least two functions. First, it delineates the primary task of the theological educator: attention to cognitive practices (not, as some appropriations of Gardner's work suggest, to cognitive potentials). Second, this distinction intends to situate both cognitive practices *and* cognitive potentials within a politics of knowledge.

In sum, what does Gardner's theory provide for a more liberating teaching of theology? It offers a pathbreaking example of a creative collation of psychological and medical evidence for a specifiable plurality of knowledge domains, attentive to forms of knowledge commonly used in practical ways, sensitive to individual and cultural differences in competence and ability within these domains, and rendering any contemporary attempt to continue to educate for one primary or sole intelligence deeply problematic.

What remains is the need for a critical, pedagogically informed and directed, practice-oriented account of the multiplicity of extant and potential knowledge domains. This account could critically invite all disciplinary contributions while avoiding the temptation to overclaim for the relation of knowledges to neurobiological "origins." Specifically for the discipline of theology, what is needed is a rendering of this task that furthers the aims of theological work. In other words, becoming a theological "subject" through the teaching and learning of theology needs to be rendered more adequately as fluency in several irreducible domains of knowledge. This move is demanded as an attempt to liberate theological judgment or practices of knowing from the dominant construal of the modern theological subject, formed to accept only one domain—whether we call that domain verbal, conceptual, or logical-mathematical knowledge—as *the* privileged epistemological domain of theology.

MUSICAL KNOWLEDGE: A TENTATIVE PROPOSAL

As an initial step toward constructing a new question about the potential diversity of theological knowledges, and building on Gardner's delineation of musical knowledge as an irreducible domain of knowledge, I posit the following theses:[49]

First, musicality is a domain of knowledge irreducible to other domains. In the present terms, musicality is both "cognitive potential" and "cognitive practice." By this I mean that it is both a psychobiological potential, in Gardner's terms, and that it is an area of cultural contestation of meaning, a unique symbolically coded system of knowledge formed by persons, institutions, and cultures.[50] Here I can only indicate some promising lines of thought on the topic.

From within the experience of playing music, a few examples may be invoked. Jeremy Begbie examines the practice of musical improvisation to observe that that type of musical experience is a "thinking in notes and rhythms; not thinking 'before' them, or on to them, or through them, but thinking *in* physical sound—notes, melodies, harmonies, meters."[51] Begbie argues that jazz improvisation affords its own style of knowing through a relationship that one takes up to other musicians, to the music itself, and to one's instrument. Improvisation schools one in the skills of collective artistic creation by linking musicality to dialogue with one's fellow musicians, to give and take, to attentive listening to others, to a sense for the importance of graceful timing in relation to others and to the shared artistic work.

Jazz pianist David Sudnow gives such arguments phenomenological depth. In his remarkable book *Ways of the Hand*, Sudnow attends in intricate detail to his history of learning to play improvisational jazz at the piano. He relates the changes that took place in his hands during their "schooling" in formal study with a jazz teacher and in informal experiences of playing in clubs, practicing on his own, and simply watching mature players. The book demonstrates the ways in which hands are able to *know* in a style and content that are unique to the body. The process from beginning lessons to mature jazz playing was one of letting his hands take over their own knowledge of the terrain of the keyboard, not simply carrying out the orders of his conceptual intentions articulated outside his body, but a thinking *through* his hands.

To begin with, his hands had to learn the myriad jazz scales. Then, he tried simply applying those scales in ways his teacher had modeled. The breakthrough came when he was able to distinguish between how his mentors talked about their playing, and how they actually used their bodies while they were playing (in breathing, shoulder rolls, position of the lower back), in order to effect jazz. The latter began to free him to understand that the hand's knowing in jazz was not a matter of repeating his mentor's thinking about jazz, nor planning one's playing route conceptually in advance of fingers striking keys, but about thinking through his hands by singing through them. This required conceptual knowledge of jazz musical patterns, but it also required an immersion into his body in order to let the hands practice their own handful knowledge of the musical terrain. He came to call his jazz a "joint *knowing* of voice and fingers."[52] He calls this embodied perception in jazz music, which can be trained, an "incorporated" sense for place and distance, a thoroughly contextualized, felt knowing. It happens that ". . . finding the named, recognizable, visually grasped place-out-there, through looking's theoretic work, becomes unnecessary, and the body's own appreciative structures serve as a means of finding a place to go."[53] Thought as singing through the body would certainly enrich theological thinking were it allowed into the theological classroom, if our thinking were encouraged to be more "at hand," and not to falsely attempt to "partitionalize [the] body. . . ."[54] Teaching theology has not yet come to terms with Heidegger's notion that "Every motion of the hand in every one of its works carries itself through the element of thinking, every bearing of the hand bears itself in that element."[55]

From within theological interpretations of music, a few examples are appropriate. Karl Barth found the music of Mozart to be epistemologically *sui generis*. Mozart functioned for him as theological persuasion against the evil of creation, in favor of its goodness in and through creation's finitude and duality. For Barth, this was a proof, interestingly enough, "better than any scientific deduction."[56] Barth heard in Mozart "a final word about life insofar as this can be spoken by [humans]," and added that "perhaps it is no accident that a musician spoke this word."[57]

From a Catholic perspective, Richard Viladesau has carefully elaborated a case for "aesthetic theology," defined as "reflection on and communication of theological insight in a way irreducible to abstract conceptual thought."[58] He has argued for the facility of music in constructing "kinetic," as opposed to pictorial, images. He concludes that music's kinetic images "may not usually represent concepts directly (although in some cases they may do so, functioning as a learned symbolic language). But they are in any case associated with bodily states, emotions, and high feelings (affects), and these in turn embody . . . implied understandings and visions."[59]

Despite their differences, these different interpretations from Begbie, Sudnow, Barth, and Viladesau share one key insight about the nonverbal character of musical knowledge, namely, "A solution to a [musical] problem can be constructed *before* it is articulated."[60]

This position neither implies nor requires that musical knowledge be immune from discursive enmeshment—from the effects of power-knowledge formations operative in and across all knowledge domains. There can be no question of uncritically naturalizing musical knowing. Indeed, such discursive enmeshment can be seen in the works cited above. What Begbie's theology selects and interprets as musical knowledge serves to endorse—not undermine or radically correct—prevailing notions of Christian orthodoxy. And *that* music itself may be caught up in and interpreted through contesting ideologies seems missing in Viladesau's claim that "What distinguishes beautiful music from noise . . . is precisely its patterns, which create a unity out of disparate elements."[61] On the contrary (and as Viladesau elsewhere admits), music's own "images" can become culturally associated with particular symbolic content. What counts as musical knowledge, then, will be heavily mediated by complex vectors of discourse, power-knowledge forces that make musical knowledge no different from other domains of knowledge with respect to its functioning *as* knowledge, its valence in the contestation of truth.

The thesis of the preceding paragraphs, on musicality as an irreducible domain of knowledge, bears resonance to what Theodore Jennings calls "ritual knowledge." He writes that

> Ritual knowledge is gained through a bodily action which alters the world or the place of the ritual participant in the world. . . . Ritual knowledge is gained in and through the body. . . . It is not so much that the mind 'embodies' itself in ritual action, but rather that the body "minds" itself or attends through itself in ritual action. When engaged in ritual action. . . . I do not first think through the appropriate action and then "perform" it. Rather it is more like this: My hand "discovers" the fitting gesture (or my feet the fitting step) which I may then "cerebrally" *re*-cognize as appropriate or right.[62]

Such connection between musicality and ritual knowledge may open new lines of relationship between systematic and liturgical theologians, for example, and the respective teaching of their theologies. Having limned the initial important thesis on musical knowing, I describe the following theses more succinctly.

Second, musicality is an irreducible domain of theological knowledge insofar as it functions as a *source of* theology. This thesis follows from the first. It has particularly strong warrant if theology is construed as a revised correlational practice, as David Tracy has argued, and as Kathryn Tanner has helpfully problematized.[63] One side of this correlation, interpreting particular "operations" or "uses" of the cultural materials that constitute the "situation," surely includes uses of musical materials, from popular media culture to classical materials, including those consumed over television or those produced in a local garage band.

Third, musicality is an irreducible domain of theological knowledge insofar as it functions as a *mode for* theology. It is largely accepted by Catholic theology that a plurality of methods, as persuasively articulated by Tracy, need to be put to work for interpreting the "classic" texts of theology.[64] What is often overlooked is that not only are plural methods required, but also a plurality of *modes* as well. To dwell too intently on the need for a critical pluralism of *methods* has had the effect of reifying one particular mode of theology, the linguistic-logical-conceptual, which all methods eventually must then serve. To limit theology in this way may not only be an unjust exercise of power by its gatekeepers over against others in the academy. Such limiting may also bear negative class and gender biases, as Margaret Miles has suggested, by making the written text the ideal source and mode for theological work.[65] To dignify theology's fragmentation and fissure into a multi-modular discipline constructively problematizes what counts as doing theology, refashioning assumptions about what we may interpret as theological work in the past, present and future. Further, it opens us to take seriously the subjugated theological knowledges (again, of past, present, and future) and the plurality of theological modes not accounted for within conceptual theology.

What follows from this position is that each knowledge domain may be free to develop its own methodologies and epistemological models (and, importantly for pedagogy, its own practices of critical "thinking" or critical knowing)—open to correction in mutually critical conversations with other domains, to be sure, but not to be conformed or reduced to other domains.[66]

Fourth, musical knowledge can provide knowledge that reworks other theological knowledge domains. It is not enough to say that musicality provides "language" for other domains, even though that is how I must necessarily express this claim in a written work. While musicality can and does provide language (such as metaphors) for linguistic knowledge,[67] it also can declare its own sensemaking logic (such as improvisation) for logical-mathematical knowledge, as well as offer unique orchestrations of the body (such as the relation between hand and head) for bodily knowledge.[68]

In sum, I propose the following: that in the subjectification that takes place in pedagogical sites of theology, musicality is a domain deserving of fluency. Indeed, it would seem to be required by a postmodern theological pedagogy that confronts the reality that "every educational system is a political means of maintaining or of modifying the appropriation of discourse, with the knowledge and the powers it carries with it."[69]

In concluding this brief discussion of musicality, it is important to note the reformulation of what it means to be a theological "subject" if theological work is construed as fluency in various knowledge domains, plurisourced and multimodal. This is a very different image of the theological subject than that of the master of conceptual knowledge. At the limit, this reformulation allows theology "to put into question the signifying subject" by "try[ing] out a practice . . . that ends in the veritable destruction of this subject, in its dissociation, in its upheaval into something radically 'other.'"[70] Less dramatically, we could say that it is one way to "develop a form of subjectivity that could be the source of effective resistance to a widespread type of power."[71]

What follows from this is that it is an inappropriate exercise of power on the part of any one domain to exclude its sources and modes—its practices of truth—from the other domains. The more the domains are allowed to be intercritical, or critically complementary, the richer and more liberative theological subjectification is likely to be.[72] And the more likely theological educators are to honor Psalm 49:4, which raises the possibility of relating verbal and musical knowledge theologically: "I will solve my riddle to the music of the harp."

TOWARD PLURAL DOMAINS FOR THEOLOGY

Finally, we may consider here some preliminary implications for teaching theology. What Gardner observes of the modern Western school system in general seems an adequate description of many classrooms of theology, investing a "premium on logical-mathematical ability and on certain aspects of linguistic intelligence."[73] Gardner and Walters suggest that "in [U.S.] society we are nearly 'brain-washed' to restrict the notion of intelligence to the capacities used in solving logical and linguistic problems."[74] Certainly classrooms of theology typically relegate nonverbal or nonlinguistic knowledge to prefatory or satellite status, deploying music, for example, as "worship," "liturgy," or some other marginalizing disciplinization. My own tradition, Catholic academic theology, is no exception, as Richard Viladesau summarizes, having been since "the post-Tridentine period largely dominated by a philosophical and conceptual approach."[75] Insofar as this is the case, students of theology, like most Western students, are subjectified as "*Homo rationalis*, as a coherent, rational, and noncontradictory (i.e. unified) individual; a source of conscious action whose mental capacities can be augmented with technology."[76]

Regardless of the intelligence or knowledge domain implicitly or explicitly regnant in a theological-pedagogical context, the uncritical privileging of any single domain is likely to be a dominative power/knowledge practice. Moreover, the privileging of one single domain of knowledge is a restriction on the freedom of theology to do its work, and on the theological subjectification allowed and enforced by a classroom pursuing pedagogical practices of freedom. Respect for a diversity of domains is "predicated on the assumption that the innate attributes of the individual student," or in the present terms, their cognitive potentials, "are fundamentally constitutive of her/his identity. These must be explicated and incorporated into the educational process out of fundamental respect for the human dignity of the student."[77]

The theological educator must, then, guard against the "systematic devaluation of certain forms of intelligence,"[78] allowing for what Foucault called the "insurrection of subjugated knowledges."[79] A dominative pedagogical power has forced theologically inflected voicings of protest knowledge to operate only on the fringes of theological teaching and learning.

The predominant, modern domains of theological knowledge need not remain untouched by other knowledge domains. Gardner suggests, for instance, that bodily knowing can inform logical knowing. He quotes the research of psychologist Frederic Bartlett to the effect that "most of what we ordinarily call thinking—routine as well as innovative—partakes of the same principles that have been uncovered in overtly physical manifestations of skill."[80] By this Bartlett means such skills as a sense of timing, moments of repose, and a clear sense of direction. This is an important clue about the possibilities for fruitful interrelationships between domains of theological knowledge.

It is imperative that we consider a reconstrual of the teaching of theology, not for the sake of the maintenance of boundaries of knowledge domains, but for the freedom of critical pursuit of all things "theological."[81] Theology may then yet be a practice of freedom, whether positing a diversity of knowledge domains leads to freedom through a powerful "tear in a dialectical universe,"[82] or a more mundane, careful and subtle redistribution of our intellectual resources for taking up new relations to ourselves and others.

PART TWO

ENGAGING CULTURE

3

Is Your Spirituality Violent?

THE EMERGENCE OF VIOLENCE AS A THEME IN MY THEOLOGICAL LIFE AND WORK

My recent book, *Consuming Faith*,[1] described corporate branding as a challenge for Christian theology, as well as the problems Christian theology poses for corporate branding. Or so I thought. As I have settled not only into the problems involved in this theological work, but also into my theological life of which this work is a part, I have come to see that there are other dimensions of the problem that attract, implicate, and perplex me. I have come to see the powerlessness of Catholic theology in face of the dangers of American spirituality. In this chapter, I trace some of those dangers, and bring the question of a spirituality that allows violence home to my own context—Catholic, and specifically, Jesuit higher education.

Yet, as recent studies of the formation of theologians have shown, biographical factors play a significant role in specifying what counts in shaping the attention of the theologian.[2] Thus, before proceeding to sketch a composition of the theological place of violent spirituality, I relate some elements of my awakening to violent power.

A Social Awakening to Violent Power

A few years ago, several women spoke at Boston College, where I was then teaching. They were from a factory in Honduras, manufacturing clothes for a major American entrepreneur. I knew of the brand because some of my students wore the clothes. These workers were on a tour of college campuses sponsored by the National Labor Committee, describing working conditions in their factory. They sewed sweatshirts that sold for at least \$50 in the United States, and for which they got paid about \$0.25 per shirt. They had asked for a tiny raise and were denied. There were restrictions on bathroom use, no unions were allowed, no overtime was paid, and there were no days off.

I saw their faces, heard their voices, and felt disgust start to burn inside. Soon after, I took a train to New York City to join a protest led by the National Labor Committee at the brand's newest store. A few dozen of us chanting slogans and holding signs for a few hours, in the bright klieg lights, were enough to get attention. Within a week, all of these negative conditions were reversed. The list of immediate reforms was stunning, heightening the scandal of their absence beforehand. To quote from the National Labor Committee follow-up report,

- The most abusive supervisors have been fired—workers are now treated with respect: Chief of production [. . .] and her right-hand assistant have both been fired. Workers report that their treatment in the factory is much improved.
- Overtime is now voluntary and paid correctly[. . .]
- Locks taken off the bathrooms: Workers are no longer required to get a "toilet pass." Guards are no longer posted at the bathroom doors. The bathrooms are clean and supplied with toilet paper.
- Clean drinking water: Purification filter systems have been installed, and the workers now have clean, safe drinking water to drink.
- The factory is now kept air-conditioned.
- Social Security health care is on the way: [The factory's] owner has pledged to the workers that he will soon inscribe all the workers in the national Social Security health care system, which provides free health care and medicines for workers and their children.
- The workers believe that the mandatory pregnancy tests will also be terminated.
- [. . .] On December 8 [2003], workers organized and won recognition for their union[.] [3]

This was a stunning example of the authority of one powerful company to ease the conditions of violence imposed on others.

Around this time, I walked into one of the coffee shops in my neighborhood, part of a national chain. I found one of the managers, and offered a proposal: I would travel to the sites, in Latin America or elsewhere, where the coffee sold at this particular shop was harvested. I would interview the coffee farmers, get their stories, take their pictures, and interview their families. And I would feature the results of my journalism on the walls of this coffee shop. After all, the only pictures we saw in the coffee shop were romantic scenes of Latin American sunsets over green fields or romanticized portraits of happy coffee farmers. I offered to pay for this expedition myself (though I was hoping my university would help fund it). The manager listened to my story; his surprised face turning eventually to bemused skepticism. There is no way, I was then told, that they would allow such a thing to happen in their store. It was too risky and too controversial. But thanks for asking about it, he said, and did I know that they now offered one fair trade coffee on their menu?

Through such experiences, one thing was becoming clear to me, as it has become clear to so many liberation and political theologians: the dangerous power of the face, of the suffering face, the excluded face, the face of a victim or survivor. A *story* of suffering may become a morality tale or be co-opted by theory. A *face* calls in a different way.

The Jewish philosopher Emmanuel Levinas famously argued that to be human is to be responsible for the suffering of the other, for the person whose well-being our very existence may be threatening. This obligation to others is encountered and symbolized in a unique way in the face-to-face relation. The faces of others present persons genuinely different from us, exposed to us. The vulnerability of the human face presents us with the claim: do not kill me. In a sense, Levinas says, the bare face of another says "do not deface me"; allow me, it says, my otherness without violation, shame, or indifference.[4]

Wherever we are kept from seeing the face of the other, I was slowly seeing, whether of the other who stitches our clothing, or dies from our taxpayer-supported bombs, we make it easier for ourselves to act as if we, too, are not responsible for that other. It is an option the privileged have available to them.

An Individual Awakening to Violent Power

When I was 23 years old, I was sitting in my Kansas City apartment with my girlfriend late at night. Outside, I heard my roommate and his girlfriend arriving in his car, and I got up to open the door. I saw them through the window walking up to the door, arms full of presents and other things from a party. I opened the front door, and as they stepped up to it, several men—four or five—suddenly rushed out from behind some bushes and drew guns, forcing all of us back inside. Most of the men ran through the apartment, cutting phone lines, stealing money, keys, and other things, including a guitar I had borrowed from my next door neighbor. One of the men, waving a metallic blue gun at us, commanded the four of us face down on the floor. He tore the necklaces and bracelets off the two women, yelling to keep our faces buried in the floor. He stood behind us, and when my roommate stupidly started to mouth off, I turned my head slightly and saw the gun right behind his head and mine. Time slowed down interminably. I thought how stupid it was to die when I was so young. I knew that there had been a gang responsible for dozens of robberies and many rapes in our part of the city that summer, and I wondered if these were the men. The overintensity of the situation prevented me from being able to anticipate, or even force myself to wonder, at what it would be like to be shot in the head, or for my girlfriend or friends to be shot or raped next to me. Each second was full enough of a strangely peaceful terror, and I was also conscious of thinking of important people and experiences in my life. Then, suddenly, the men were running out the door, and the leader said to us, "If I see your face through the window, I will put a bullet through your skull." He ran out, and we were motionless for five minutes. Then there was quiet crying. Slowly, I was aware of a paralyzing and astonishingly helpless sense of violation whose residue has never fully left me. At least one of the men was later arrested, and the police told us it was indeed the same gang responsible for the other acts of violence. The experience disabused me of any naïve trust in humanity remaining from my childhood, haunting me in almost every late-night noise, unlocked door, violent movie scene, and aggressive male posturing I encounter.

Remembering this apocalypse does not qualify me to understand all other forms of violence, as if from above or deep within. I see these autobiographical episodes as clues to the ways that life's disorientations can begin to add up to a new personal theological outlook. The memories spur a continued destabilizing of my theology, making me wonder what awful human capacity I have encountered, and how theology might help encounter, think through, and even, perhaps, help to heal it.

Settling into the lasting effect of this trauma and other similar experiences have helped me to see that there was a deep ethical point in my last book of which I was unaware: the problem of relations of violence in which we are involved. How are we involved, I want to know, in the traumas of others? And as a theologian, I want to know whether and how our spiritual commitments involve us in violence. And so I have gone back to the question of branding that I raised in *Consuming Faith* from this perspective of a theological concern for violence. Wasn't what I was concerned with in that book the violent effects of branding on those employed by the branding companies?

This chapter will eventually turn toward a consideration of my own "placement," Catholic higher education, as trending toward violent practice. Although, and because, few people think of Catholic higher education as a system participating in violence, a comprehension of the violence allowed by Catholic higher education must first take place within a composition of the place of American spirituality. This means having a felt sense not for spirituality as theorized in the official discourses of the church's theology or the state's religious studies, but for spirituality as practiced, a process of analysis I would define as *what we can learn of American spirituality not from what it professes, but from the kinds of things that it fails to contest.* Such a project, in its fullness, would extend far beyond one essay, but I would like to dwell briefly on the public emergence of torture as an "acceptable" American practice in recent years, as part of the "war on terror." Let me be clear that in allowing ourselves a patient awareness of torture's reality, Christians undergo a necessary training for awareness of even subtler forms of violence in our midst enabled by our spirituality. This is the pedagogical and political link I presume between our torturing society and our dangerous slide into an ever more capitalistic system of Catholic higher education in the United States. No one would suggest that torture is the same violence as socialization into consumer capitalist higher education, but I propose that both evince something of American spirituality's weakness in face of contemporary social power, whether economic, military, or educational. From the stance of such an awareness, it becomes more possible to see Catholic higher education, especially in its more elite and striving forms—forms that set the pace for all the nonelite Catholic colleges and universities—as a way violence is held and governed by Catholic spirituality. An unsavory outcome, to be sure, but a truly practical theology cannot take as its starting point the avoidance of unhappy deflations of what were held as articles of faith.

Michel Foucault helped in giving language for a relation between branding and violence, a construal of branding as a violent power. This was, as I have said, a relation I had already begun to make in *Consuming Faith* but which I did not yet see clearly enough in its starkness, which means I also did not take seriously enough theology's stake in an intervention against branding as violence, which means I did not see clearly enough what a theology of nonviolence in a branded world might look like. I did not see clearly enough, in other words, that spirituality can support violence when it is indifferent to the violent power of branding.

BRANDING AS A VIOLENT POWER: FOUCAULT

Foucault was not even really talking about "branding" in the sense in which we typically mean it in postmodern capitalism. Yet he analyzes an important thread of the history of Western culture that helped produce the power relations that govern corporate branding. This thread has to do with the institutional affixing of identities to individuals—what can be rendered in English as "branding"—on both a larger scale and a more fundamental level. Specifically, it has to do with the way in which prisons fixed and enforced the culturally marginal and dangerous identity of the criminal, the offender, the delinquent, and the recidivist. The complex of penal institutions, "after purging the convicts by means of their sentence, continues to follow them by a whole series of 'brandings' (*marquages*)," such as continued surveillance and the permanence of police records, "and which thus pursues as a 'delinquent' someone who has acquitted himself of his punishment as an offender."[5]

By rendering a person outcaste, dangerous, or abnormal, by rendering him or her permanently fixed not only to their past but also to an identity embedded in the social adjudicator of "security," branding is a sort of protoviolence. It is a condition for discrimination, enchainment to a harmful network of relationships. Branding and social exclusion are bound up in the same power of modern forms of social control.[6] This is not the kind of exclusion that keeps some people purely segregated from the rest of society. Foucault seems to use the term *branding* to talk about fixing an identity, through the capacity for ongoing social control of the nonnormal, in a way that is useful for those who benefit from the docility and usefulness of branded peoples. After naming modern delinquency as a sort of "visible, branded [*marquée*] existence," Foucault suggests that "delinquency, controlled illegality, is an agent for the illegality of the dominant groups."[7] In other words, Foucault suggests that branding is a practice of social control under modern forms of penal power. Dominant groups benefit when people become branded as useful delinquents. Foucault gives the examples of prostitution, arms and drug trafficking, and illegal alcohol sales.[8]

There are thus, he implies, the branded and the unbranded, the marked and the unmarked. This is a distinction familiar to queer theory, which has shown how "normal" identities go unmarked in society (and religion), and abnormal, unnatural, hybrid, or otherwise troubling ("queer") identities are (re)marked (upon), noticed, tracked, in a word, branded. And by branding the abnormal or socially marginal who remain useful for dominant groups, power is given a foothold by which to attempt to manage social relationships.[9]

This brief encounter with Foucault productively complicates how I and others have set up a theological analysis of branding in particular and our economy in general. First, it places branding within contemporary power relationships, and thus within social relations of force and, potentially, relations of violence. Second, it problematizes who is branded in our society, suggesting that branding has a political, managerial function of maintaining certain ways of life for some at the expense of the health, social status, and ultimately, flourishing, of others.

It also proposes several specific problems for theological analysis: How do we learn to desire to be branded by corporations? What forms of violence are we part of when we consent to branding practices? Even if we take pride in not being mastered by the corporations whose brands we individually (through purchases) and socially (through laws) "support," do we allow our relation to ourselves and God to be interrupted by the way in which our branding practices brand others? For in a globalized economy, it is never only about us. Every economic decision is a potential branding in Foucault's sense: the maintenance of a politically docile marginal identity which privilege finds useful.

The deep formation in violent branding practices goes hand in hand with the imperial psychology our culture has allowed.[10] But it bears pausing on the question of "spirituality" and its state in American life in order to appreciate more fully how the privileges of empire, or at least imperial psychology, structure our lives today.

CONTEMPORARY SPIRITUALITY AND VIOLENT POWER

Many theologians and religious thinkers show us that violence is the negative index of human transcendence, the strange and mysterious power we have to construct, tolerate, enforce, and even then have the privilege of forgetting about the denial of the strange mystery proper to created being.[11] A power paradoxically radical and banal, violence is the forced denial of the freedom of creation to flourish. Violence is not power as such, but the effect of pleasure in dominative and irreversible power over others. As so many adults who have frankly reviewed their own upbringing have realized, and as many historians and philosophers who have surveyed the United States' own history have shown, violence need not register as conscious to be effective, need not be intentional to be real. The psychological violence to which many children are subject, the institutional racism that has been the shadowy spouse of American history, the fear of the religious other that has almost constitutionally been the product and nemesis of Catholic history, these are all different "forms" of violence, yet all reminders that violence can operate at a social depth extraordinarily resistant to both tolerant politeness and critical thinking. Joyce Schuld has shown something like this when she argues that Foucault and Augustine converge in their understanding that there are profound constrictions on us that circulate through us, with and without our conscious permission, showing us how corrupted relationships permeate our social-historical and everyday existence.[12] Grace Jantzen shows, even more radically, how violence itself may well be foundational to the Western intellectual tradition, insofar as philosophy has constructed itself with a remarkable thoroughness on fantasized control of women's bodies.[13] Whatever else these theological and religious researches show, they demand our attention to our own implication in the circulation of violent practices, regardless of our goodwill and enlightened intentions.

Does spirituality, as typically understood today, license such violence? Indeed, it seems difficult today to see "spirituality" as even remotely related to violence.

One of the most common ways for Americans to describe themselves today is as "spiritual" persons (as distinct from "religious"). Someone's "spirituality" may be their way of talking about faith in a deity, in nature, in a particular value, or in themselves. The fact of diverse spiritualities today testifies to the seriousness (sometimes through irreverence) with which people take their quests to discover the significance of their lives, to honor and interpret their deepest passions. Our contemporary passion for spirituality wants to distinguish itself from religion. This seems evident when spirituality is defined as experiential (as opposed to juridical), interior (versus external or doctrinal), individual (as opposed to institutional), freeing and trustworthy (neither restrictive nor suspect), pure (not sinful), and a connector between religions and faiths (as opposed to a wall between them). Today's understanding of spirituality enables people of various religious traditions—and none at all—to respect each other's "journey." It gives a common faith language to the recovering addict and the gym junkie, the gang member and the politician, the passionate faith practitioner and the indifferent secularist. Notably absent from popular understandings of spirituality are questions about responsibility for power, much less license for violence. The very question "Is your spirituality violent?" seems to be seldom if ever asked in contemporary America.[14]

Jeremy Carrette and Richard King, in *Selling Spirituality*, provide an analysis that helps explain the strange silence of spirituality in regard to violent relationships.[15] Carrette and King survey the rise of the discourse on spirituality in Europe and North America, and look at the way in which Christianity and the so-called "Eastern religions" get repackaged in the current interest in spirituality. Religious traditions whose spiritual practices are bound up historically with social responsibility, with cultural criticism, and even radical political activism, find their practices detached, depoliticized, and made nonthreatening for Western spiritual practitioners. Meditation, yoga, dietary habits, prayers, and other spiritual exercises lose their social "dangerousness" when they become dropped into the shopping cart of our overindividualized, overpsychologized sense of spiritual entitlement. Theirs is a challenging diatribe in the tradition of the Frankfurt School, putting before people of conscience what is at stake in the appeal to spirituality in Western everyday life.

Insofar as they are right, we can see how spiritualities are tempted to forget their affiliations with violence. Once spirituality as a form of experience does not understand itself as caught up in, and in some measure responsible for, relations of power, and therefore of violence, we are all in a more deeply dangerous situation, especially the vulnerable among us and around the globe who do not have the luxury of a nonpolitical, noneconomic spirituality. In the light of Carrette and King's work, I now see that the route I have been trying to map is a geography of the spiritual license to abusive practices. Let Christians not think that members of other faiths are the only ones capable of faith-based violence. Our country may still be, in a very qualified sense, a "Christian nation," but one whose construction of spirituality allows victims, and of them, far too many.[16] It is hard to ignore the interrelation of the major movements of our culture, the twin passions for both consumption and spirituality. Might these dual appetites be comprehended by a third term?

IMPERIAL PSYCHOLOGY: OUTSOURCING AND TORTURE

I propose to irradiate their connections by the way these twin passions serve an imperial psychology. This imperial psychology, a state of soul, keeps the form of experience that we call "spirituality" from letting through deep questions about and personal responsibility for the suffering caused by our cultural practices, such as economic or military practices—what we buy, and who and how we fight. Thus our spirituality is kept from experiencing the outrage that would lead to greater and more varied resistance to violence by Christians and other people of conscience. Imperial psychology configures a spirituality that imagines that one is not finally dependent on others.

Imperial psychology assumes that the suffering of Americans is of greater spiritual significance than that of anyone else. It has the privilege of choosing to not care about people who might teach us about ourselves, who might interrupt the security of our American and Christian identity. Thus, imperial psychology lacks interest in Iraqi body counts, European attitudes toward the United States, or in seeing itself as one member—among others—of a global community. This state of soul thinks that American security and freedom are the highest forms possible to anyone—especially because we have worked so hard for them. From this position, no quarter can be given to any possible ambiguity in our own motives or any vulnerability that we might share with those who threaten our "way of life."

This imperial psychology that lets on to a violent spirituality is horrifically evident even in our own day in the way the United States has permitted and practiced torture, including the nightmarish practice of "extraordinary rendition," the secret transport of people arrested by the United States to be interrogated in countries with questionable human rights records. Questions also remain about secret American prisons in foreign countries. But is it not too easy to allow such practices to be branded as part of the "war on terrorism"? If we are not to allow the brand its defacing power, theology can and must undergo the hearing of experiences of the tortured.

As has been reported in the American press, Maher Arar, who was born in Syria and is a Canadian citizen, was apprehended by U.S. authorities in New York City at Kennedy International Airport, on September 26, 2002. Here is how Bob Herbert in the *New York Times* reports the story. At the airport, Arar

> was locked in chains and shackles and accused of being "a member of a known terrorist organization." There was no evidence to support the accusation, and no evidence has ever come to light. Nevertheless [. . .], Mr. Arar was shipped off to Syria, where he was kept in an underground rat-infested, grave-like cell, and tortured. (When I visited him in Ottawa last year, he told me how he had screamed and wept and begged both God and his captors for mercy.) After 10 months, he was released. No charges against him were ever filed. . . .
>
> The reality, he said, is that his life has been all but completely destroyed. He is fearful. He has become psychologically and emotionally distant from his wife and two young children. He has nightmares. He can't find a job. He spins dizzily from one bout with depression to another. And some former friends who are Muslim will no longer associate with him because "they're afraid to be the next target."
>
> "I mean, you can tell, no one wants to hear about me," he said. "After 9/11, everyone [is] branded with the terrorism label—they're doomed."[17]

There is also the account of Khaled el-Masri, a German citizen who was picked up while vacationing in Macedonia and taken to Afghanistan to be abused and intimidated at a secret CIA prison. No evidence was found for abducting him, much less torturing and holding him from December 31, 2003, through May 28, 2004. According to his testimony, he was kept for twenty-three days in a hotel in Macedonia in isolation, threatened with guns, and interrogated; he then went on a hunger strike in protest. His testimony continues:

> On January 23, 2004, I was handcuffed, blindfolded, and placed in a car. The car eventually stopped and I heard airplanes. I was taken from the car and led to a building where I was severely beaten. Someone sliced the clothes off my body, and when I would not remove my underwear, I was beaten again until someone forcibly removed it from me. I was thrown on the floor, my hands were pulled behind me, and someone's boot was placed on my back. Then I felt something firm being forced inside my anus.
>
> I was dragged across the floor and my blindfold was removed. I saw seven or eight men dressed in black and wearing black ski masks. One of the men placed me in a diaper and a tracksuit. I was put in a belt with chains that attached to my wrists and ankles, earmuffs were placed over my ears, eye pads over my eyes, and then I was blindfolded and hooded. After being marched to a plane, I was thrown to the floor facedown, and my legs and arms were spread-eagled and secured to the sides of the plane. I felt two injections, and I was rendered nearly unconscious. At some point, I felt the plane land and take off again. When it landed again, I was unchained and taken off the plane. It felt very warm outside, and so I knew I had not been returned to Germany. I later learned that I was in Afghanistan.
>
> Once off the plane, I was shoved into the back of a vehicle. After a short drive, I was dragged out of the car, pushed roughly into a building, and left in a small, dirty, cold concrete cell. That first night I was interrogated by six or eight men dressed in the same black clothing and ski masks, as well as a masked American doctor and a translator. They stripped me of my clothes, photographed me, and took blood and urine samples. I was returned to my cell, where I would remain in solitary confinement, with no reading or writing materials, and without once being permitted outside to breathe fresh air, for more than four months.
>
> During this time, I was interrogated three or four times, always by the same man, with others who were dressed in black clothing and ski masks, and always at night. The man who interrogated me asked about whether I had taken a trip to Jalalabad using a false passport; whether I had attended Palestinian training camps; and whether I knew the September 11 conspirators or other alleged extremists. As in Macedonia, I truthfully denied his accusations. Two men who participated in my interrogations identified themselves as Americans. My requests to meet with a representative of the German government or a lawyer, or to be brought before a court, were repeatedly ignored.[18]

Can there be any surprise in learning that it took five years for a declassified report to show that Arar was never any threat to American security?[19]

Christian theology in the United States must also hear the testimony of those who, in "our" name, took part in carrying out torture, such as Anthony Lagouranis, an Army interrogator in Iraq in 2004 to 2005.

> When the chief warrant officer at our interrogation site in Mosul first told me to use dogs during interrogations, it seemed well within what was allowed by our written rules and consistent with what was being done at Abu Ghraib and other detention centers. The dogs were muzzled and held by a handler. The prisoners didn't know that, though, because they were blindfolded; if they gave me an answer I didn't like, I could cue the handler so the dog would bark and lunge toward them. Sometimes they were so terrified they'd wet their jumpsuits. About halfway through my tour, I stopped using dogs and other "enhancements" like hypothermia that qualify as torture even under the most nonchalant readings of international law. I couldn't handle being so routinely brutal.[20]

There is a damning metaphor for the U.S. practice of torture that unintentionally links it to the way American companies are allowed to conduct themselves: "outsourcing." To "outsource" in business is to contract out part of the work that goes into a product, usually for the purpose of saving costs. Almost all abuses of human dignity in the manufacture of clothing by American companies abroad are linked to "outsourcing" as an economic rationale. Similarly, to "outsource" in regard to "homeland security" is to send suspects abroad to be squeezed for information in ways that would be unconscionable were they to (publicly be known to) take place on American soil. The use of the term *outsource* to describe both practices provides an unsettlingly illuminative connection between branding and torture: to outsource is to attempt to hide the face—the face of those at the receiving end of the power to outsource. Punishing those who are unfortunate enough to fall beneath our boots, or should I say to fall beneath that middle-class youth fashion, moon boots? Or our tennis shoes, sandals, or jeans, most all outsourced to those who must work under conditions about which the best we can feebly say is, "Well, at least they have jobs and aren't really working in sweatshops"?

Outsourcing, torture, invisible foreign labor: A hellish circle among whose enabling powers is the license provided by the hand-washing "spirituality" of American faith. It is indeed an "extraordinary rendition"—of the tune we like to hear played, that "we" are Christians, that America is a majority Christian nation, one with "values." Can we any longer be surprised that our spiritually hungry society is at the same time a "torturing society"[21]?

For myself, American spirituality's shadow role in this awful tale could also be glimpsed in one almost-invisible vignette from the halls of Abu Ghraib.

In 2004 to 2005, the world learned that under U.S. Army Specialist Charles Graner, detainees were subject to a regimen of physical and psychological abuse and torture, including forced masturbation, being made to lie naked in a pile with other prisoners while their captors jumped on and beat them, suffering strikes from a metal baton to a detainee's wounded leg, being handcuffed to a door for eight hours, sleeping naked in cold and wet cells, being urinated on by soldiers, having to eat from a toilet, enduring threats of sexual violence against them and their wives, and being forced to eat pork and disavow Islam.

Strikingly, this physical and psychological damage was then put into a spiritual frame. According to detainee Ameen Said al-Sheikh, "Graner told me to thank Jesus for keeping me alive." With that statement, this torture suddenly and irreversibly enters the theological realm, casting the abuse as part of a Christian sensibility.[22]

Without overfocusing on Specialist Graner, we can say that it is entirely plausible that an American could make such a statement. The statement and its context accurately sum up the way many American Christians feel about the treatment of detainees. This statement, however, is a direct challenge to American spirituality. Why? Because Americans pride themselves on a faith that is essentially private. Indeed, when we use the term *spirituality* rather than *religion*, as I have suggested, we are usually describing faith as an individual experience, as something separate from obligation to a tradition or community, something more pure and freeing than the walls of an embarrassingly particular, and probably broken, "religion." Yet a private spirituality cannot provide any help in thinking about why this alleged theological claim is wrong. To do so, it must become public, it must risk proposing an alternative vision of Christianity, and it must engage in reasoned argument about faith. To keep spirituality private, in the face of this concrete abuse of persons in the name of Christianity, is tantamount to endorsing the alleged torture. If you can claim that your Jesus is private, Graner can claim that his is, as well, and the prisoners are the ones who pay the price for our private spiritual pleasures.

Yet every Christian, and person of conscience, who is repulsed at this use of "thanking Jesus" shows by their very outrage that spirituality and attendant theological claims are necessarily public. The alleged abuse is a *public* enactment of a theological claim (that Jesus accepts violence toward these detainees). The resistance to that theological claim drags spirituality out of its private captivity and into the publicness of righteous anger, an anger that can and must have good *public* reasons to denounce that image of Jesus.

But where is the modern Confessing Church to question how our contemporary spirituality licenses violence? And in my own Catholic Church, have we begun to comprehend the irrelevance of Catholic theology to questions of violence, power, and spirituality in our larger society? One need not romanticize the days of the public "theological giants" like Tillich, Murray, and Niebuhr to ask such questions, nor be ungrateful for the achievements of an entire generation of American Catholic theologians in making theology a respectable and critical discipline—in the academy.

Any search for the form of theological work today that will be most responsible to both the intellectual and political, not to mention mystical and ecclesial, responsibilities of the theologian, and in the U.S. Catholic Church in particular, can initiate a resistance to the appeal to spirituality to control or ignore the other by starting on our own most prized territory: Catholic education, especially Catholic higher education. The avoidance of our own betrayals of young people provides a way of dealing with a kind of violence that for many of us is too close to acknowledge.

VIOLENCE ON THE AMERICAN CATHOLIC LANDSCAPE

It is not, then, as if Catholic practices take place in a cultural vacuum. They must be located today in the violent relation to self and others into which we are initiated in our "torturing society." Do we see violence in need of theological attention on the Catholic landscape today? I propose an arena of Catholic life for consideration: higher education. Specifically, the violence now inherent in the tuition-debt structure of a good (and influential and well-respected) portion of Catholic higher education.

In his recent book *Lessons of the Masters*, George Steiner asks, "How is it possible to *pay* for the transmission of wisdom, of knowledge, of ethical doctrine or logical insights? What monetary equivalence or rate of exchange can be calculated as between human sagacity and the bestowal of truth on the one hand, and an honorarium in cash on the other?"[23] Most of the twenty-eight Jesuit colleges and universities in the United States, such as the one in which I teach, have decided: well over $40,000 a year. This figure includes tuition, room and board, insurance, and school supplies. It is becoming routine for Catholic colleges and universities in the United States to top $25,000 to $30,000 a year when all expenses are calculated. Indeed, many of the top Catholic college and universities are less than a decade away from a four-year degree costing $200,000.

If you have not been in college for a while or do not have relatives in school, the numbers may shock you. As of 2006, at least half a dozen Jesuit colleges and universities charge more than $30,000 for tuition and fees. The average tuition rate for all Jesuit colleges and universities is well over $25,000 a year.[24] According to a College Board report, four-year private college and university tuition and fees alone in the United States average $22,218.[25] Remember that to these tuitions must usually be added approximately $10,000 a year for room, board, books, and other necessary supplies and expenses, and it is easy to see how $40,000 is quickly becoming the new normal cost for a year in a good-quality private college.

Can it be any accident that the extraordinary tuition rates being charged at Catholic universities are correlated to an increased attention to the branding of Catholic higher education? We more or less freely now talk about the uniqueness of the Catholic brand, the Benedictine brand, even Notre Dame itself as a brand, as easily as we imagine and treat Harvard or Yale as brands.

Anxiety about how much ground has already been lost to the corporate takeover of Catholic education has led to many conversations inside Catholic institutions, and the beginning of public explorations of the issues. For example, an entire issue of a Jesuit publication was devoted to debating whether branding was appropriate for Jesuit education—and those in favor featured voices that represent strong, established, and influential constituencies in Catholic higher education—not least among them, the business schools.[26] People are actually paid to be concerned with Jesuit universities' "logos," and to manage Catholic higher education branding for parents, students, and the media. At a Jesuit university where I was teaching, faculty were sent a new sticker with the university "logo," which was, they were informed, recently "refreshed" (the language of university symbolics now being borrowed from the ephemeral world of the Web). Faculty were asked to display the new logo publicly, and therefore assist in the branding of the university.

Those who defend the use of branding most often say that Catholic education has the right to use what the larger society uses, and put it to better uses. In this reading, "branding" is essentially politically and theologically neutral, and depending on the intentions of the institution, can be used for either good or ill. But as both Foucault and the experience of contemporary capitalism shows, branding is a form of social control built on exploitation, trafficking in violence. It encourages not an economy of grace, but of force: whether the psychological coercion of advertising or the physical coercion of the sweatshop.[27] This does not mean that our religious institutions do not try to brand us in particular ways. But insofar as those practices share in the forms of power that structure corporate branding, they are at least proto-violent. And no incipiently violent form of relationship should be undertaken by Christians without very serious consideration.

Few would dispute that students receive an excellent education at Catholic colleges and universities. Fewer still would argue that services, supplies, or salaries should be cut in order to bring down costs. (Paying the expanding ranks of lay faculty like me help fuel the tuition increases.) And no student is ungrateful for the many grants that help take a bite out of these costs. Such grants, however, often fall far short of what most students need to be free of negative financial pressures on their educational and vocational decisions in college. The crucial point is that, now that the cost of Catholic higher education is essentially indistinguishable from that of other private upper-tier schools (Santa Clara, for example, costs almost as much as Stanford; Boston College almost as much as Harvard), and now that the endowments of many leading Catholic schools reach into the scores or hundreds of millions of dollars, it is worth asking whether Catholic colleges and universities should make themselves distinctive in the landscape of higher education, not only by how and what they teach, but also by how they deal with tuition.

While the high cost of Catholic education purchases a certain cultural "distinction" in a society where economically elite institutions are associated with excellence, influence, and power, the prospect of a $200,000 education moves Catholic education into a dangerous zone of handmaid to the structural violences apparent in American capitalism in an age of growing inequality fostered by the current American class structure, raising the question of becoming an inordinate burden on the middle and lower classes, not to mention introducing an array of problems that are counter to its own best hopes.

Many of my undergraduate students from disadvantaged or even middle-class backgrounds, for example, forgo the social and intellectual benefits of campus "cocurricular" activities like social, political, or academic clubs, or artistic performances, because they must work to pay their own way. Many others, willing or not, go into substantial debt from age eighteen to twenty-two to get the education they want, a loan debt that for each college graduate now averages around $20,000, according to Anya Kamenetz's research.[28] The anticipation of that debt very quickly and deeply restricts students' freedom to follow God's call of vocation. Anticipating years of loan repayments, they are lashed to "bottom line" life decisions for decades. Let us not miss the fact that Catholic schools outsource the loan arrangements to non-Catholic loan agencies who have never been bothered by the theological debates about usury, nor the contemporary concern for Catholic education as discernment for God-given vocation.

For students whose parents can afford to pay several thousand dollars a month, the money frequently becomes a constricting force on educational decisions. Parents who are forking over so much cash increasingly pressure students in overt and covert ways to buy a "redeemable" degree. Neil Howe and William Strauss, in an influential study of this generation and their parents, describe some zealous Baby Boomer parents who overmanage students' educational decisions, from choice of major to selection of courses. These are the "helicopter" parents, hovering above students' daily life, in regular contact through cell phone and e-mail, securing their entrée in students' lives by the power to write tuition checks.[29]

Deficits of in-house research tell the story in negative: Just as Catholic schools are not known for careful internal research about how staff and faculty manage to pay their bills, nor for what the tenure process actually does to the lives and goals of young faculty, studies of students whose lives are managed by the money issues are virtually nonexistent. I mean students at these schools who work full-time; who drain their parents' savings or put parents in lifelong debt; students who carry such debt themselves for what should otherwise be their most energetic, creative, and barnstorming years of their twenties to forties; who change majors under pressure from parents or imagined future employers; who graduate early to avoid paying more tuition, thereby missing irreplaceable rituals and relationships in the last year of college; who drop out of Catholic institutions for financial reasons, or, most damningly, who take on the capitalist logic of the system by redefining their own desires from the first year of college, or maybe even before they set foot on campus, because they know that they need to play the system so as to get a degree that will cash out for them later, that will have made the $100,000 to $150,000 or more "worth it."

If I mention in class that at one point in my life I lived in public housing and was on the government's free lunch program, I inevitably get students following up by discreet e-mail asking me for advice about how they will survive their Catholic education financially. Some are surprised that we might even say a few words about the students' or professors' social class within the classroom; it brings the realities far too tightly in focus—for the privileged, the underclass, and those in the dicey and anxious middle. Such are the informal sets of data too many of us already have, and even more than that: we have a felt sense for the ways in which a promising student's deep needs were not met—and could have been, were it not for anything more than a lack of courage and creativity on the part of each of us responsible for this mission. And there is no institutional way of remembering these students, of openly discussing, much less memorializing, these failures of mission.

When middle-class parents must scrape bottom to send one child to school; when parents with several children experience despair in face of the hundreds of thousands of dollars a Catholic education would cost, and must choose which children will go to their first-choice schools and which will settle for the hometown college, or less; when the pressures of making a college major "worth the cost" make wealthy and wealth-aspiring students narrow their future goals to medical school, law school, or "free market" business school training; when students routinely calculate how much each course, class, or minute of instruction is costing them; when, in other words, those who undergo a Catholic education become unduly positioned by capitalist ways of proceeding, then Catholic schools are in deep danger of becoming merely a way station for America's stratified life, a socioeconomic violence both structural and personal, with little hope of effectively naming and understanding this violence, much less interrupting it.

Perhaps, then, the deepest and most dangerous cost of tuition elitism in Catholic education is the twin damage to American society and Catholic educational ideals. By rising up to name-brand prices, Catholic schools unwittingly help perpetuate the economic violence of the operative class system in American higher education.

No doubt people will ask: Is it not too extreme to call this a violent system? I would only ask you to place yourself in imagination over the life span of students so affected, and to imagine what else could become of their lives were such debts not so foundational for so many. I would ask you, especially if you graduated from college some time ago, or if you yourself came from a privileged family, and even though it feels so unsporting and even disloyal to do so, to consider the violences of this system: to remember that we are talking about four years of a young adult life when desires are shaped, values are incorporated, debts (psychological and financial) are incurred, when an entire orientation to a set of adult possibilities, indeed to a vocation, becomes available, to varying degrees, in a way never possible in the same way again in life. I call the demolition of dreams, the subtle inculturation into forgetfulness of one's deep desires, the indoctrination into a scale of values that sidetrack the most creative, courageous, hopeful, and distinctive elements of a college student's personality and potential—I call all this violence, at once psychological, spiritual, and financial—directed at an age group we would rather control than set free. You can start a second or third career at age thirty, forty, or fifty, but you can never again pay such reckless attention to your desires, in the context of needing to please neither parents nor employers, as you can at age twenty-two. No one gets a second chance at that opportunity to feel what it might mean to try oneself on for size.

And because I teach in Jesuit universities, let me note that in the case of Jesuit higher education in particular, this damage to American society is also a threat to the unique identity of Jesuit education. While education priced for the aristocracy is a mark of distinction in our society, it is not the sort of mark that makes a school more faithful to the Ignatian charism. After all, a Jesuit college or university's way of "doing business" models powerfully what it really means, in the formulation of Superior General Peter-Hans Kolvenbach, to educate the whole person for solidarity with the world.[30]

Have Jesuit colleges and universities forgotten the original free-tuition vision of Jesuit education? As a way of living a vow to poverty, of affirming the God-given potential in students of all social classes, and thus of making concrete a belief in God's freely bestowed gift of grace, Jesuit schools early on strove to work entirely from endowments. As John O'Malley has written, from their "religious motives," early Jesuits started "the first systematic and widespread effort to provide free education for large numbers of students in a given town or city."[31] The spirituality of the society helped ensure that a Jesuit education should in principle, and in practice, be open to anyone. The advent of the $200,000 Catholic education ought to shake us to a reconsideration of that initial vision of free tuition and Fr. Kolvenbach's contemporary challenge to students.

Free Tuition in Catholic Higher Education

My proposal in this regard is simple: It is time for Catholic higher education to free itself of the burdens of playing according to the rules of American socioeconomic stratification; it is time for Catholic colleges and universities to reclaim the uniqueness of Catholic commitments to justice and dignity; it is time, too, for a shared Catholic penance for another violence I discussed in the introduction to this volume, Catholic sexual abuse of children and teenagers.[32] It is time for a definitive commitment to reparations in the form of a blanket graciousness to all young people who desire to study in Catholic colleges and universities.

In short, I propose that it is time for Catholic colleges and universities to become 100 percent tuition free. Free tuition for all students at Catholic colleges and universities could be a guiding image of our day for Catholic education, a symbol of the vibrancy and daring fidelity to forming the whole person for intellectual excellence and faith that does justice. This commitment should make of Catholic schooling a call to radical hope, a socioeconomic sign of peace.

Can we afford it? There are indications that money is out there for projects that call Catholic education into a new and hopeful vision. Whether one looks to Voice of the Faithful or many of the other Catholic community organizations that have gained steam in recent decades, there are donors to be tapped. And Catholic charitable organizations, or organizations that have given to Catholic educational institutions, might well be interested in being associated with the ground floor of such an endeavor. Moreover, recent political history has shown that hundreds of thousands of Americans can and will donate very large sums of money if they are moved by inspiring ideas and shown the urgency of the cause—and if it is easy for them to donate. And there are many employees in Catholic institutions, including myself, who would happily go out and "beg alms" in support of such a vision.

But this is not just a newer iteration of an old-fashioned fundraising strategy. I am willing to beg alms because I share in the sinfulness of my church and so should share in its penance. But so too should the bishops, who should be on the front lines begging alms. Allow the vision for even a moment: bishops next to professors next to students and staff, next to people of good will all making a global appeal for free tuition in American Catholic colleges and universities, as both penance and promise of God's reign.

Of course, the money would not come all at once, but success could breed success. By staggering the goals, potential donors could easily observe the progress of the free tuition initiative. So, for example, a Catholic college or university might aim to reduce tuition by 10 percent in five years, by 25 percent in ten years, by 50 percent in twenty years, and eventually by 100 percent. As at each stage the goal is met, donors would see that the goal is realistic and the project serious. A Web site that would communicate the progress of the initiative to the world, and allow people of good will to send in donations toward the final goal, would keep potential and actual students, their parents, and the rest of the world informed about progress.

There would also be some secondary benefits of free tuition. Applications to a good school with a free tuition initiative would undoubtedly increase, perhaps even skyrocket. This would elevate admissions competition, allowing Catholic schools to be even more selective about their student body while retaining a commitment to invite students from disadvantaged backgrounds.

The increased applications and decreased admission rate would affect the school's rankings positively. The school would become more elite in status—but for the right reasons. And the challenge of going to 100 percent free tuition would garner constant media attention. Meeting the goals every few years would occasion worldwide coverage, and undoubtedly pressure other Catholic places of higher education to explain why they themselves could not do this. The secular media might, surprisingly, be the best evangelizers for education as a socioeconomic sign of peace.

Committing to free tuition may seem absurd because unrealistic. Where would the money come from? How could this ever possibly work?

Understandable as they are, such questions are conditioned by a modern instrumental and bureaucratic imagination, a way of thinking about Catholic education that accepts what similar educational institutions, like elite secular schools, take to be "realistic." Here the *theological* importance of committing *in principle* to free tuition becomes clearer.

Metz and other Christian theologians have rightly emphasized the apocalyptic Christian imagination in the Gospels, daring to hope for the impossible, allowing itself the wonderment of exposure to the radical vision of the reign of God. This vision is a *classless* vision, one that today demands excellence in education for all persons, and prevents Catholic educational institutions from being satisfied with reproducing the American class system. The apocalyptic imagination does not accept what seems "realistic" to modern society, but seeks God's grace in the divine power to do a new thing now, as a symbol of finally making all things new.

The more "realistic" we continue to be, from this perspective, the more students of all classes, especially the poor, will suffer. Even though it is not "realistic," free tuition can be affirmed *in principle* by Catholic colleges and universities. Free tuition, as expression of the reign of God, is blessed apocalypse, both promise and hope.

Whatever the pace of success might be, then, even if a free tuition initiative were to fail, it is the right thing to do. It makes Catholic schools, and by extension the Catholic Church, both more faithful to its own ideals and more credible to the outside world. This would be the sole area of Catholic life in which most of American culture would be rooting for us, wanting to see a Catholic institution succeed.

But first one Catholic college or university must step forward, and in so doing make a daring stand for the distinctiveness of what we do, in terms that will likely surprise and fascinate the larger society, a public act of faith that would be—unlike many today—neither sectarian nor shallow. This stand would represent a bold educational identity, deeply Catholic and American.

BEYOND FACELESSNESS

Without the space for serious theological reflection, we are faced with a spirituality that licenses violence, with branding as a way of managing violence against the faceless other—that is, the other kept faceless by force. Spirituality and branding do so by outsourcing the hard and unpopular work—the torturing of our suspects, the stitching and sewing of our clothes, the loaning of money to students, the paying off of those loans for decades.

What are the powers of violence that our spiritual commitments fail to comprehend? How can those who want to call themselves Christians avoid the demand for the spiritual practice of fostering an anticapitalist, nonviolent relation to God and our sisters and brothers, especially our sisters and brothers whose faces we will and can never see? For too long, the facelessness of the economic and religious other—student, worker, gay priest, terrorist suspect—has kept God faceless. But now Jesus returns to open for us the gospel of Matthew, chapter 25, and says to postmodern, consumer capitalist, American Christians: whatever you did to the most faceless of my sisters and brothers, you did to me. An idoloclastic strain in the Christian tradition may now be married to the ethical demand of our time: Jesus calls us by remaining faceless, by being present in and through our relation to the faceless. Jesus is the faceless man, who is kept anonymous by the way our spirituality fails to challenge our economic and religious practices. Jesus is the faceless man, whose flourishing is pinned, governed by our practices.[33]

Yet early Christianity also described Jesus as a *parrhesiast*, one who spoke confidently, freely, frankly. As a ritual reactivation of the dangerous memory of this *parrhesia*, we can ask, and ask again: How often do student voices about tuition inform university policies? How often do we "consumers" hear from those who make our computers and cut our flowers? Who speaks for those arrested in the "war on terror"? Does Christian spirituality search out the face and the voice, not of the random other, but of the other of the body of Christ and of the globalized economic body—the other on whom we depend and to whom we are related through politics, church, or economy?

What would a nonviolent Christian spirituality look like, both in the Catholic world and on the American scene? We might have to begin by freeing ourselves from the desire for spirituality itself.

4

Popular Culture Research and Theology

Is there any way of going on that is not a turning back?
—Teresa of Avila[1]

There has been a tremendous interest in relating theology and religion to "popular culture" in the last few decades, with a surge of publications in the last ten years alone.[2] While the reasons for this deserve their own research, the developments presented by these studies afford an opportunity to stand back and look at some of the larger questions raised by this turn to the popular and media culture in religious and theological studies.

I have had the opportunity to review many manuscripts in this burgeoning field. While I have learned something from each new exploration, I would like to recall one specific moment that provoked a question that drives the queries of this chapter. I was studying one of the many recent edited collections of essays about religion and popular culture. In this manuscript, movies, television, and music were made to interact with analyses drawn from sociology of religion, psychology of religion, and Christian theology, usually grounded conceptually through borrowings from cultural studies. Such collections have become one influential shape for theological and religious research in popular culture today.[3] Their form and content provoked fundamental questions in my reading that I shall submit as questions for the field; namely, what is the value of our work? Whence do we draw a critical appreciation of such value? The emerging field has not been able to sufficiently raise or answer these questions.

In the collection before me—as in the field more generally—it was not self-evident why certain researches were grouped together and made to represent a field called "religion and popular culture."[4] One minimally unifying element was that these particular essays dealt in some way with popular culture. Using Simon Frith's broad definition of popular culture—as the production of cultural objects "of," "by," or "for" "the people"—these essays, and most all approaches in the field today, qualified.[5] Another minimally unifying feature could be found in the use of religious or theological frameworks to situate popular culture, showing its overtly or covertly religious or theological character, or making it the site of critique—either from or toward religious or theological positions. Frequently, such research also celebrates popular culture's religious or theological character.

In asking about the value of our "diversity" for a relatively young field, I do not mean to suggest that there needs to be one point of all such work, nor that such a "point" or "purpose" ought to be final, transparent, or available to a normative assessment. I raise the question not for the purpose of forcing a "field" called "religion and popular culture" out of a productive heterogeneity of scholarly advances. My interest, in other words, is not to attempt yet another theological disqualification of academic heterogeneity in method, commitment, or theme. It is, rather, to find a way both of understanding the significance of this heterogeneity, on the one hand, and thematizing this critical appreciation into a task for the future of the field, on the other.

What might theology have to contribute to the question of how a reader might receive a collection—or a field—that manifests a strong plurality, if not polycentricity, of topics, methods, and ethical, religious or theological commitments? Perhaps due to the "blessed rage for order" so characteristic of the contemporary theological mind,[6] Gordon Lynch and Kelton Cobb have recently advanced research that attempts to name the ambiguities about the theological significance of popular culture, and its research, and to find a way of making clearer spiritual distinctions about the value of popular culture.[7] Both seek to go beyond mere religious studies commentary, on one hand, or a poorly theorized spiritual celebration or condemnation, on the other hand. Lynch portrays what is at stake in the field as a matter of judgment, and in particular, of "normativity." That is, how is one interpretation of popular culture authoritatively to be judged better or worse than another? Cobb discerns what popular culture has to say about classic theological topics in ways that may lead postmoderns toward or away from devotion to God. The question becomes how one can spiritually "sort out what is going on in the depths of popular culture."[8] I shall render the chief problem before us slightly differently: What is at stake for readers and writers of religious or theological engagement with popular culture? What I share with Lynch and Cobb is a curiosity whether an indifference to judgment adequately fulfills the ethical task of the one who attempts to think and teach theology or religion in the academy.

POPULAR CULTURE AND THEOLOGICAL PRODUCTION

I would like to frame this problem as a question about the production of meaningful claims in the theological or religious scholarly engagement with popular culture. In so doing, I mean to locate such questions about our work in popular culture in broader queries regarding the ethics and politics of academic theological production. In other words, how do we come to think that something significant occurs when we read or write of relating popular culture to theology or religion? To state this as a problem of ethical formation, how do you and I learn to read each other's pop culture analyses? Or to state it as a more personal and rarely raised problem: How do we learn to read our own analyses of pop culture?

Approaching a way of thinking about these questions requires a brief consideration of two commonalities of work in the field: its self-involving character and the economies of analysis generating such work.

Self-Involvement in the Field

In this field, scholars of religion or theologians are typically personally invested in their research topic in a particular way. They seem to have some experience, usually not without pleasure, of the popular culture they are analyzing, or on rarer occasions, pleasure and personal investment in the religious renunciation of pop culture's relationship to religion. In other words, despite many of the topics dealt with in this "field" being bound up with consumer capitalist culture, the academic engagement with them seems the occasion for, and the fruit of, the subjectivity of the scholar being thrown open. Indeed, one defense sometimes given for writing about pop culture and religion is that the topic allows for the pleasures of the scholar to be explored: "To enter into reflection on the meanings and influences of popular culture [. . .] because 'it's fun' is an effective starting point that requires no apology."[9]

Sometimes the personal relationship of the scholar to the topic is evident, sometimes only indirect; sometimes unabashedly foregrounded, and sometimes all but occluded by recourse to a sophisticated theoretical scaffolding (as if to signal, yes, this is fun, but it is also quite serious, and even if I didn't like movies, rap music, comic books, or *Sex and the City*, please understand that I am treating universal human themes, delimited qualities of a particular community, the construction or reception of meaning, or a critical issue of concern to contemporary religio-theological discourse). In many ways studies of popular culture emerge from and refer back to the level of self-reference. The participation of the subjectivity of the scholar in the analysis of culture is conceptually striated, worked up, organized, made clear or obscure, but made nonetheless. Religious and theological studies of popular culture seem to draw the sort of scholar who is involved emotionally and intellectually, existentially, with popular culture. "We" tend to be scholars who are aware that our sense of ourselves has been governed by popular productions, who are "subject" in some way to, in and through popular culture, usually in a pleasurable or meaningful way, however qualified, although sometimes in a negative way, in the pleasure of critique.

Such intuition-observations have become clues about how to begin learning to read works in this field, allowing me to acknowledge that such an existential involvement was also true of my own writing about popular culture. My published theologizing began a decade ago with a rhapsodic essay on theological themes related to the musical *Rent*, continuing through essays on media, suffering, and the Iraq war, music video, the "What Would Jesus Do?" phenomenon, and corporate branding. I have been more or less aware from the beginning that in doing this sort of theology, I have been attempting to justify, appreciate, question, or expunge certain formative influences on who I have become in my dealings with pop culture, the theological life I have or have not been able to lead through my relationship with pop cultures, and also, who I see my students, friends, co-religionists, and North American others becoming in their relation to popular culture.

Such placements of the popular culture scholar are both signaled and withdrawn by many instances of autobiographical glimpses into scholars' vital investments in popular culture. These are rarely considered of significance, however, for the basic argument itself. For example, when Margaret Miles writes about the freedom that movies offered from her restrictive and confusing religious upbringing,[10] or Randall Holm writes about being "strangely drawn" to the singer Jon Anderson through the "undeniable spiritual import" he experienced in the rock music of Yes,[11] or Robin Sylvan alludes to a "long strange trip" taken spiritually through profound musical experiences in Africa and California,[12] such comments play the rhetorical role of "prefatory" personal introduction to the more serious scholarly work to be done, although they presuppose and invite an analogous sympathetic identification from the reader, and more or less acknowledge that the relation of author to reader is that of fan to fan.[13] It is at least as likely that the formative experiences hinted at by such modest disclosures play a silent structuring role in the work itself. As Bruce Forbes allows, "Many of us come to the analysis of popular culture with a particular special interest, related to our own private enthusiasms (comic books, the Beatles, soap operas, or whatever). . . ."[14] It also seems significant that so many such "peeks" allowed in scholarly work reference experiences with media culture during deeply impressionable stages in life, from childhood through young adulthood.

It seems, then, that scholars of religion or theology think about pop culture because we have felt the significance of being involved in it, or more, because in doing so we are also writing about ourselves, or further, because in and through this exercise we are aiming, with irremediably crooked arrows, to hit a target not yet in view—or already too much in view: ourselves. It makes sense to read our intellectual engagements with popular culture in religion and theology not only as scholarly productions, in the accepted academic sense, but also as a form of work on, or "therapy" (properly understood) for, those who write and read them or in other words, what I would like to call "spiritual exercises"—spiritual exercises at varying degrees of awareness of themselves as such, whether conscious, inchoate, or potential, or most likely, a humid admixture.

Economies of Analysis

While Frith's three categories (and the schematizations of others[15]) provide a way of giving the field some coordinates by which to locate what it means by popular culture, the question of the economies of the production of meaningful works in our field can be productively examined, and can be related to the constitutive role of self-involvement previously outlined. Indeed, the cultural formation of the scholar in their personal and academic life, which "peeks through" our field with perhaps more frequency and legitimacy than many other areas of the academic study of religion and theology today, suggests a development of Frith's tripartite definition. As noted earlier, he defines popular culture as those cultural "products" constructed "by," "for," and "of" the people. However, the present consideration of the unacknowledged and pleasurable involvement of the scholar in their work in this field calls for attention to a fourth and perhaps counterintuitive aspect, the popular culture of popular culture studies itself: that is, the question of how and why we are incited to write about popular culture and religion. In other words, the culture of the popular that facilitates the constitution of our field can be understood as that which scholars are permitted and encouraged to think about their own basic categories by their own religious and secular understandings of religious experience.

Why draw attention to the popular culture of this field itself? Kathryn Tanner has made a thoughtful and creative argument that academic theological production is its own form of "popular culture," analogous to everyday popular culture in its provision of cultural materials for authorized use (from materials like books and conferences to ideas like *physis* and *psyche*) that are reused by scholars to gain political advantage in the field by rhetorical strategies that fabricate weaknesses in others' texts as the site on which to take things in a different direction, to "trope" prevailing readings so as to be appropriately within and without acceptable boundaries—to be considered fresh research.[16] This is analogous, Tanner shows, to how people in everyday life make do with the products and notions they are given, turning them to their own purposes based on the political and personal needs at hand. From such a perspective, it becomes possible to see how research in "religion and popular culture" is not (only) the furtherance of a well-defined field of study, but a way of operating in and constituting objects for that field itself.

It is not Tanner's project, however, to more specifically define a way of thinking about what might be at stake for those who operate in these "popular" fields. I wish to complement Tanner's locating of the academic study of theology in postmodern cultural theories with Michel Foucault's journey through his development of theories of social practice.

In particular, I refer to the research of Foucault on the fashioning of historically particular understandings of the popular, and the creation of the experience of the existence of a popular culture, through the governance of peoples by way of cultural practices that conduct in a certain "population."

This focus has been highlighted by several of Foucault's recently published Collège de France lecture courses from the 1970s.[17] This period of Foucault's work is the time of "discipline" in his research, as famously schematized in *Discipline and Punish*.[18] It is this period that is of particular preparatory importance for his later turn to an understanding of philosophical research into culture as a spiritual exercise. In short, a comprehension of the history of the Western disciplining of subjectivity was the clearing away and clarifying about religion as social control that helped prepare for his so-called "ethical stage," the exploration of a more "positive" sense of discipline: spiritual disciplines and experiments with *askesis* in his late work. But before I get to the more "positive" meaning of exercise, I would like to indicate something of the exercises of social control from one of his works of this period.

We can take *Abnormal* as exemplary of this period of his work. In seeking to find out how Western culture came to be a site of continual incitements to declare one's sexuality and other "deep truths," allowing one to be fitted into modern regimes that govern everyday life, he returned to the Middle Ages to ask this: How did Catholicism create a population that thought that in order to be Christian one had to confess, and to confess in a certain way? In other words, how did a culture of confessing people come to be created and rendered normal in Western culture? In short, he answers, through the technology of the confessional. That is, through the creation of the experience of being part of a human society with unruly desires, and an ecclesial society with the cathartic redemptions of confession, so long as one can learn the practices that allow the passage through speech of one to the other.

Foucault comes to discuss the confessional as a way of explaining what happened to penance in the Western Catholic tradition: how penance became bound up with practices of confession, and those practices were then situated in the official ecclesial language of "sacrament," and as a result, penance became a way that the power of the church was exercised over the faithful. In other words, the ancient Christian practice of penance becomes, with the Council of Trent, the site for an extension of "ecclesiastical power" over the faithful, over their souls, desires, and bodies. Such an extension and concentration of power needs not only juridical declarations, such as Trent propounded, requiring yearly reception of the Eucharist and, in preparation for that, yearly confession. It required more than a juridical interlocking of these two sacraments. It also required a material space in which to symbolize this power and to practically allow it its reach. The confessional became such a space. As Foucault argues, the confessional was "the material crystallization of all the rules that characterize both the qualification and the power of the confessor. . . . There were no confessionals before the sixteenth century."[19]

Confession becomes a technology that operates in society under the jurisdiction of the church. As the church manages confession through the sacramental system and ties it to the Eucharist, then that ecclesiastical power tightens by an elaboration of erotic investigation. Charles Borromeo is an exemplar of this power, in its ability to open a relationship between people and themselves, on one hand, and their confessor, on the other. To teach people to manage themselves according to this detailed and rigorous investigation of desires, temptations, excitements, curiosities. In a word, the "flesh." This is what Foucault names the "Catholic technology" that is one of the major contributions of Christianity to Western culture. This governance of the Christian conscience becomes a way of teaching clergy and faithful a certain way of relating to themselves: through exercises of self-examination, they learn to suspect interior movements, feelings, and desires. The existential value of the sacrament becomes its ability to affect surveillance over the body, or more specifically, that aspect of the body that threatens: the flesh.

What we learn from this movement in Foucault's thought, for present purposes, is that an ethics of popular culture and religion research can emerge from genealogizing the problem of the study of religion and popular culture itself, which would mean an examination of the cultural constitution of the disciplining of the popular and of popular religion, which—as Foucault's trajectory shows—raises also the question of the *askesis* not only of popular religion in culture but of the thinker of the questions him- or herself, insofar as to be concerned with the popular is, given Western history, to risk being accomplice to social control.[20] Foucault speaks directly to our academic "discipline":

> For a long time ordinary individuality—the everyday individuality of everybody—remained below the threshold of description. To be looked at, observed, described in detail, followed from day to day by an uninterrupted writing was a privilege. The chronicle of a man, the account of his life, his historiography, written as he lived out his life formed part of the rituals of his power. The disciplinary methods reversed this relation, lowered the threshold of describable individuality and made of this description a means of control and a method of domination. It is no longer a monument for future memory, but a document for possible use.[21]

In other words, what we are doing in this field when we attempt to render clear the religious or theological plane of popular culture should be considered an ethical problem analogous to inviting people into a box to speak of their unruly desires. How does one imagine one's place as an ethical subject in a field such as ours?

For assistance, I turn to conceptions of spiritual exercises as I have learned them through Foucault and Pierre Hadot. From them, we can begin to comprehend that intellectual work on cultural problems can be a way of changing one's relationship to oneself in accord with a desire to live a certain sort of life, that making religious or theological sense of popular culture can be a spiritual exercise.

SPIRITUAL EXERCISES INTRODUCED

Foucault

In the last several years of his life, Foucault began to suggest that his researches were a way of working on his relationship to himself, of changing his relationship to himself and others.[22] Although such a clarification was perhaps never fully spelled out, the last years of his works are marked by this reframing of intellectual work as a spiritual exercise. [23] The question of how one evades entrapment by a presystematized relation to self was already built into Foucault's philosophy of practices of subjectivity, knowledge, and power.[24] Foucault worked on his own attempt at greater freedom through careful intellectual work; practicing philosophy, he saw, could affect one's very mode of perceiving the world, one's existential orientation.

One of the clearest expressions of this new appreciation for his philosophy as a spiritual exercise occurs in his book *The Use of Pleasure*, published the year of his death, 1984. In this work, Foucault named his motivation for his research the "only kind of curiosity . . . that is worth acting upon with a degree of obstinacy: not the curiosity that seeks to assimilate what it is proper for one to know, but that which enables one to get free of oneself." He contrasts a mere "knowledgeableness" with the importance of "the knower's straying afield of himself."[25]

> There are times in life when the question of knowing if one can think differently than one thinks, and perceive differently than one sees, is absolutely necessary if one is to go on looking and reflecting at all. . . . What is philosophy today—philosophical activity, I mean—if it is not the critical work that thought brings to bear on itself? In what does it consist, if not in the endeavor to know how and to what extent it might be possible to think differently, instead of legitimating what is already known?
>
> The "essay"—which should be understood as the assay or test by which, in the game of truth, one undergoes changes, and not as the simplistic appropriation of others for the purpose of communication—is the living substance of philosophy, at least if we assume that philosophy is still what it was in times past, i.e., an "ascesis," . . . an exercise of oneself in the activity of thought.[26]

The path to dealing with, and exchanging, one's self is indirect; a game of doubles. James Miller argued that Foucault tried on many occasions "to unriddle a part of himself by writing about someone else entirely."[27] Miller argues that Foucault's different interpretations of Kant, Saint Anthony, and Diogenes were windows on Foucault's own struggles to comprehend and change himself.[28] For Miller, Foucault struggled profoundly with a preoccupation with death that expressed itself in dangerous gay sexual practices.

"All of Foucault's books," argues Miller, "comprise a kind of involuntary memoir, an implicit confession," all witnessing to his struggle to deal with "the truth about himself."[29] "I take *all* of Foucault's work to be an effort to issue a license for exploring [the] *daimonic* possibility—and also as a vehicle for expressing, 'fictively,' his own Nietzschean understanding of [his] harrowing vision of a gnosis beyond good and evil, glimpsed at the limits of experience."[30]

But one need not agree with Miller's judgment about Foucault's *psyche*[31] in order to acknowledge Miller's insight about the exercise-styled forms of Foucault's spiritual and intellectual explorations. David Halperin disagrees strongly with Miller's deep psychological claims about Foucault, while agreeing that Foucault's life and work can be understood as *askesis*.[32]

Halperin has read exercises in the context of Foucault's life as a gay philosopher. "Foucault ultimately came to understand both philosophy and homosexuality as technologies of self-transformation."[33] Gay sexual experience was parallel to and intertwined with other strategies and practices of truth in Foucault's books. Agreeing in a sense with Miller that the erotic is a central reference point with respect to which he changed his relation to himself, but finding Miller almost violently voyeuristic and "knowing" about gay sexuality, Halperin shows how Foucault's philosophical writings and understanding/living of a gay sexual identity was a spiritual exercise insofar as it allowed him to get free of himself, to gain a critical distance from forces of social control that would organize, even "humanely," his relation to himself and others.

Halperin comprehends Foucault's commitment to the study of culture, especially to "historical inquiry . . . as a kind of spiritual exercise."[34] To enact new possible relations to ourselves by understanding the historical contingency of who we have been is the spiritual work of Foucault's historico-philosophical scholarship. Halperin suggests that for Foucault something about the self escapes the self and this "alterity" of the self to how it has been constituted is that to which Foucault's politics and intellectual work appeal. Foucault's political work and scholarship show us experiments "we [can] perform on ourselves so as to discover our otherness to ourselves in the experience of our own futurity."[35] Gay sexual practices and the recent history of American gay life, for Halperin and Foucault, have helped "cultivate in ourselves the ability to surpass ourselves, to enter into our own futurity."[36]

Recently, philosopher Todd May has summarized helpfully that and how Foucault should be read as a "philosopher engaged in spiritual exercises," working on his relationship to himself through his intellectual exertion in thinking through the complexities of the European history of subjectivity.[37] This happened through three forms of inquiry: showing the historical contingency of the knowledge of ourselves; showing that "who we are is not so much the product of disinterested inquiry into our nature but instead of the result of social practices that have their own power arrangements"; and through offering other possibilities in history of relating to oneself and others as subjects.[38] It was this sensitivity to the imperative to change our relationship to ourselves that allowed Foucault to write of the "fascism in us all," in "our speech and our acts, our hearts and our pleasures," "in our heads and in our everyday behavior, [a] fascism that causes us to love power, to desire the very thing that dominates and exploits us."[39] Foucault's comment about the imperative of Deleuze and Guattari's work is also a reference to the spiritual exercise performed by his own philosophy: "Do not become enamored of power."[40] The philosophical-historical study of "the popular" and of cultural practices necessitated a form of ethical attention to oneself, with exercises that come through and beyond one's intellectual work.

A Defense of Foucauldian Exercises for the Future of Theological Studies of Popular Culture

Many who have had some initial exposure to Foucault, especially through the power-knowledge texts that have become so influential in the study of religion, may be surprised at both this focus in his work and its being termed a spiritual exercise. Foucault seems to have adopted for his own work the notion of spiritual exercise from, among other places, the historian of ancient philosophy Pierre Hadot,[41] who argued that ancient philosophy understood itself not as a mere rationalistic, speculative, or theoretical sparring, nor as a mere "intellectual" or "academic" discipline, a potential "major" or even "profession," much less "career," in the various senses that we think of the study of philosophy. Indeed, limiting philosophy to "study" is our modern error—or at least impoverishment. Ancient philosophy, he argues, was a lived experience, a "way of life."[42] Philosophical schools were not for the purpose of making a philosophical argument, but for training in the living of a philosophical life. Schools did this by forming philosophers to become a certain sort of person in the world through their unique spiritual exercises, practices that would help them to think and live according to wisdom.

In these works, there is an important link to the Christian theological tradition. Hadot shows how many early Christian theologians conceived of their work as a philosophy precisely in relation to the ancient sense, by which they meant both a way of thinking and a form of work on themselves, ways of changing one's modes of being in the world in quest of the divine life, which is the supreme life of reason: the *Logos*. Self-control and meditation thus make their appearance in Christian philosophy as spiritual exercises leading to life with God, manifest in a variety of ancient philosophical—now become Christian—practices of theology: exegesis, denomination of revelatory texts, arguments about the proper order of their study, examination of conscience, transcription of misdeeds, cultivation of a peaceful mind, a mindfulness of death, and in all, an attention to oneself. Hadot's exemplars of this trajectory of theology as therapy, that is, as Christian philosophy, are representatives of mystical, monastic, and patristic theological traditions. He discusses theology as attention to oneself in Justin Martyr, Clement of Alexandria, Origen, Augustine of Hippo, Basil of Caesarea, Gregory Nazianzen,

Gregory of Nyssa, Evagrius of Pontus, Athanasius of Alexandria, and Dorotheus of Gaza.[43]

At the same time, the future for which I am arguing in popular culture studies makes the new research on spiritual exercises an occasion and space for unseating the advantage frequently given to the Christian theological character of spiritual exercises.[44] This advantage has been so taken for granted that it has not been seen as an advantage in theological culture. Spiritual exercises have been, in theology and spirituality, more or less generally taken to be Christian provenance, property, or propensity. But if I can restrict myself to my own Catholic tradition for the moment: what if Christian exercises are full of holes that have already let in an ancient philosophical air that Christians have been inhaling and renaming in the same breath? Foucault's work can be read as arguing that it may not be so much a matter of continuity of themes and topics between ancient philosophical exercises and Christian exercises as the form of the exercises themselves that migrated from "pagan" to "Christian" practice, perhaps like a Rubik's Cube that is at once quite limited in the ways it can shift in relation to itself, but at the same time within that narrow morphology can allow itself thousands of possible recombinations of colors.[45] What cubes traversed (what we often too confidently think of as) "the divide" between the "pagan" and "Christian"? Examination of conscience; rehearsal of aphorism; meditation on text; slow maturing progression through authorized writ; recollection of the master; memorization of useful and essential verses; remembering and rehearsing death; remembering and rehearsing birth; envisioning life from on high; serious conversation; teaching to influence the soul: through one's classes and through one's writing . . . and even (with Plotinus, says Hadot) through one's writing as a reflection of the dynamics of the classroom itself.

In our present moment, acceding to the depth of the "technologies of self" that Christianity took over should occasion a radical sobriety on the part of Christian theology. It means that some of the most valued, respected and trusted forms of "Christian" experience are strongly "pagan," however much the contents may have shifted during transit. When Christians engage in exercises, they give themselves over to pre-Christian experiments in relationship, claiming their own version of Iamblichus' ancient neoplatonic conviction: we shall be saved by rituals of incomprehension.

But this also means that theology, if it can bear this *askesis* in and of its thinking, can help point the way toward a clarification of the ethical dimension of engagement with culture. After all, all of these exercises were "moral" in the senses Foucault outlined: they were ways of taking up a relationship to culture, of making one's way through crises of action by means not of a "code" to serve as constant yardstick for every situation, but by means of a way of experiencing oneself, others, and the world (and the cosmos, as Hadot's posthumous dialogue with Foucault reminds us[46]) through practices that habituated oneself to be in a certain way, to, as Foucault tells it so well, have one's conduct emerge from the sort of learning that transcends moral codes.

Christian theology has its own duty to divest itself, through interrogation of its own history and practices, of—in principle—all claims to ahistoricity, first, and to uniqueness, second. The study of Christian spirituality, as exercises, should begin with a genealogical divestment for the sake of understanding what we have done, are doing, and might do to ourselves and others because of our exercises. And further, part of theology's therapy, or its penance, can be to help the theological, and religious, study of culture to understand itself as a self-involving and potentially self- and other-governing (in a word, subjectifying) pursuit, whether on the part of the scholar or of anyone willing to risk the demand to be (in the famous formulation of Bernard Lonergan) attentive, intelligent, reasonable, responsible, and loving.[47]

In other words, on one hand, Christianity (especially its sacramental tradition that prides itself on exercises) was wrong to think that how one interprets, studies, and teaches—that is, how one learns to read what they themselves are writing about culture—the most basic, say of scholarly exercises—derives from an inner-ecclesial history and can be practiced in ways that are *sui generis* Christian. On the contrary, every Christian exercise of making defensible sense of culture—interpretation, study, and teaching—is a releasement to "paganism," a reliance on ways of being and registering the world that represents a profound otherness already within (and which will take much more careful research to appreciate its complexity). On the other hand, Christianity (especially the sacramental tradition that prides itself on exercises) was right when it has held that how people interpret, study, and teach—that is, how they learn to read what they themselves are writing about culture—has an unavoidable importance for how people relate to themselves, to others, to culture, even to cosmos. Writing about the religious or spiritual significance of culture is in our day, especially in regard to pop culture, an obvious, and frequently quite openly, self-involving task. It is also necessarily social and political, raising the question of the exercises that form the scholar to make religious or spiritual sense of culture, and (another way of saying the same thing) of the exercise that religious or theological writing about culture *is*.

FOR FUTURE POPULAR CULTURE STUDIES

If popular culture changes the mind, soul, or perceptions of the individual scholars that are making the field, and if scholarship on popular culture can have that effect on people interested in the field, if indeed "we become what we read" (including our own writing), a turn to the ethics of learning to read one's own work and that of others in our discipline seems imperative, and thinking through exercises can be one way of beginning to approach that problem. Indeed, this chapter is intended as a contribution toward an ethics of theological and religious studies of popular culture. In taking the perspective of exercises, we may reconsider the very form of intellectual inquiry in the field, that is, beyond the problematization of theology "of," "or," "and" popular culture, to emerge into the ethical problem of theological and religious *writing* about popular culture.[48]

This perspective can be joined to the larger conversation about the self-involving character of the study of religion. Such work has criticized the study of religion as the covert advocacy of religiousness, lacking a sufficient criticality.[49] From the vantage of the present chapter, this concern can be interpreted as an involvement in religious questions as a form of spiritual exercise for the academic researcher. Hence the quality of "advocacy," which may be a displaced, indirect way of working on oneself, and an elliptical testament to such work on oneself.

One important anxiety about the self-involving character of our field is that it is susceptible to dilettantism.[50] One reason that dilettantism becomes a dirty word in pop culture studies is that it raises the specter that our inquiries are not entirely professional, academic, objective, or critical—generally accepted hallmarks of the modern study of religion. The objection to dilettantism is often a way of criticizing overly personalized interpretations published as scholarship. So Lynch criticizes analyses that "may be of personal interest to the author but have little impact on wider cultural analysis or criticism,"[51] and Miles self-effacingly writes of her "relation to 'the movies' [as] one that may not be shared by many readers."[52] While Lynch's point about the threat to sophistication in scholarship due to retreat into private analysis is apt, and Miles allows some access to her own personal history of investment in the power of film, these distinctions can be read as trading on a dichotomy between an individual scholar's desires and the level of the cultural in intellectual work that a turn to spiritual exercises would read as a problematic bifurcation. There is still room for developing a conviction like that of Karl Rahner in the field of popular culture studies: "I want to be a deeply thinking dilettante—and one who at the same time thinks deeply about his dilettantism and factors it into his thinking—but all with reference to theology's ultimately foundational questions."[53]

Dilettantes or not, theological or religious studies of culture are enactments of our relation to ourselves and others that re(in)habit the forms of experience that make us who we are. Letting through this politics of production of theological meaning can work as therapy—that is, thinking through the theological-religious government of self involved in the constitution of theological-religious interpretations of culture can bring the spiritual exercise that theology of culture already is into more critical, personal, and cultural perspective, an experience of the truth of theological interpretation of culture more efficacious for healing and insight because more available to conduction into the incomprehensible through which Christian faith thinks life practices.

This way of understanding the interpretation of culture is thus not finally selfish, or about "getting in touch with ourselves," nor about rehearsing a romantic autobiography, but about a critical releasement to who we have become and what we do to ourselves and other people. It is neither self-affirmation nor utopic social plan. Such analysis is a call to readiness for justice: "Many are those who are entirely absorbed in militant politics, in the preparation for the social revolution. Rare, very rare, are those who, in order to prepare for the revolution, wish to become worthy of it."[54] A different perspective on our interpretations of popular culture is given, through an ethics and politics of theological production.

For the future of religious and theological studies of popular culture, I would like to see this problem explored, which of course does not mean an uncritical repetition of the Hadotian or Foucauldian lines on these issues. In part, then, such exploration suggests an enrichment of our vocabulary, a defamiliarizing of our passions. But it is an enrichment about what is already going on, a matter of appropriating what is already happening in much of our writing: theological or religious analysis of culture as conscious, inchoate, or potentially indirect and retrospective figuration, refiguration, or—at the limit—transfiguration of the subjectivity of the author.

Learning how to read our works will be the first step into the future of the field. This, "one of the most difficult" spiritual exercises, according to Hadot, is the one Goethe himself recommended at the end of a life lived much longer and more richly than the brief history of our field: "Ordinary people don't know how much time and effort it takes to learn how to read. I've spent eighty years at it, and I still can't say that I've reached my goal."[55]

PART THREE

VOCATION

5

Reflections on Doing Practical Theology Today

FOUCAULT AS PHILOSOPHER OF PRACTICE

Foucault should be of particular interest to practical theologians, insofar as he himself was a philosopher of practice. I shall briefly give a theoretical characterization of that designation, without attempting to adequately specify every concern of his work that may be of potential relevance to theologians. I will then explain a few reasons why Foucault's theory matters for practical theologians.

The concern for practice is deeply bound up with a governing interest in Foucault's work, the question of subjectivity. Foucault wants to trace out the practices that constitute subjects as subjects. Foucault took up historical and philosophical investigations into categories of personal and social identity that were influential in the functioning of French culture, and that had helped form the ideological background against and through which a marginal space had been created for groups of people deemed outcastes.

Foucault argues that practices are the way we are governed and govern ourselves, because power circulates through how and what we can know about ourselves and our world, and that power circulates through practices (as distinct, for example, from just "ideas"), producing the world of identity, relationship, responsibility, and obedience that we then most often take to be simply given. In a deep sense, the very "organization of our practical knowledge,"[1] our forms of perception, the experience we have of ourselves and others, and the categories we employ for that experience, are historically constituted through power-saturated practices, making us subject to the institutions that support and are supported by regnant forms of knowledge in particular times and places.

Foucault politicized by historicizing the basic everyday categories that those he studied used to define and govern their humanity, to make sense of themselves and others. Such influential grids for subjectivity such as the reasonable and the mad, the homosexual and heterosexual, the normal and the abnormal, and the patient and the doctor, were seen to be implicated in cultural power relations, as dangerous weapons that have been used to ostracize the other, the strange, and the different. The history of those exclusions is part of the function of many of the historical forms of experiences that we presume are basic categories, and that we use to think through and govern our relationships. We are diminished by our inability to think through how our basic categories of self-understanding are caught up in past power relationships to which we no longer need be "subject."[2]

Constellations of practice, whether "religious," "psychological," "economic," or other, make us who we are by denying their own contingency, by denying that how we govern ourselves and are governed can always be fragilized, can always be interrogated with a question about its "historical *a priori*," its condition of possibility in a constellation of power-knowledge practices.[3] We are thus never done getting free of ourselves, and we are never able to finally assign blame to a perpetrator, a single institution, a guilty party whose expiation would presumably cleanse the system and lead us to our "true selves."[4] We must deal with cultural practices not as an intellectual luxury or possible correlate for a separately derived theologoumenon, but because we must strive to get free of ourselves (and not, or at least not only, to "interpret" ourselves).

We are "subject" to these forces in a double sense: first, of being positioned by them, experiencing what is possible, perceivable, normal, interpretable, or even thinkable for ourselves, as situated by these prior constellations of historical practices, and so our subjectivity is given to us historically and culturally; second, we are subject in the sense that we can fashion different relations to ourselves through a critical relationship to ourselves, through the courage to question how we became who we are and how the power we exercise in relation to others, or that is exercised over us, came to be given its present status. Catching up to ourselves, if you will, is the beginning of a spiritual indifference to who we have become, an indifference that requires active archaeology of who we have become through a critical historicizing of what seems most evident about the way we put our worlds and our lives together in our feelings, ideas, in short, in our "experience."

The constitution of subjectivity, in a strong sense, through historical practices that are caught up in power relations, means that subjectivity is always already tensioned, agonistic, strung up through competing discourses made of practices trying to form us in the truth of ourselves. The emphasis here is not on subjectivity as something *formed* pacifically by cultural practices, but something *contested* in and through them. Not an essentialist but rather an agonistic rendering of subjectivity, highlighting the ambiguity of all power-knowledge practices within even the most seemingly liberative subjectivities.

That does not mean agonistic subjectivity is always agonizing. To the contrary, we can assume the naturalness of the major forms of experience and concepts by which we understand ourselves only because the practices that make up those experiences and concepts present themselves as natural or essential. At the same time, Foucault's work can be read as a preferential option for the experience of agonized, particular, and marginalized subjectivities as a way of showing the agonistic character of subjectivity in general.[5] The attention in his research to the cultural practices that produced the criminal, the sodomite, the hermaphrodite, the madman, and the patient were born of Foucault's sympathy for the agonies present in the lives of those made to secure the power of the institutions of the police, pastorate, or psychologists by bearing the mark of the dangerous. Foucault was their advocate in what philosopher and Foucault student James Bernauer has called Foucault's "cry of spirit."[6]

From a Foucauldian orientation in theology, then, one theologizes because when we begin to think critically about whom we have been made to become as theologians and as persons, about what we have done, are doing, and can do to each other, we begin to experience the imperative to catch up with ourselves. This motivation for theologizing is distinct from the need for theology to be made intelligible or for social structures to be unmasked. Our identities and uses/abuses of power/knowledge are caught up in plural, ambiguous and historical cultural practices. A thoroughly "secular" practical theology[7] takes itself as itself, consents to its worldliness, not only factoring it in through a subsequent theological movement that enacts a methodologically rigorous solidarity with "the world," but as an always already project. Dealing with our power, on a Foucauldian reading, is one of the most pressing spiritual exercises, both intimate and social, personal and political. Given the significance of cultural practices for Foucault's philosophy, a Foucauldian "postmodern" theology is necessarily a practical theology, that is, making critical and reflexive sense of "the practice of ourselves" in faith and culture.

FOR PRACTICAL THEOLOGY

Personal Implications

Through a petition drafted in 2002, I helped advance a concise practical theological statement for Catholic theologians to sign in support of the right of Voice of the Faithful to meet, as a concrete response to episcopal efforts to forbid their organizing a national meeting in Boston. In the midst of my signature gathering, some influential and accomplished theologians said to me that the effort was misguided because it would not convince those who needed convincing, and that therefore these theologians would not sign a petition doomed to fail. In these conversations, I wondered at a certain presupposition: that the efficaciousness of theological activism and practical theological argument (here overlapping) was being located solely in practical results, and in a very specific understanding of what counts as "results": a basically instrumental and utilitarian way of evaluating a practical theological claim. This does not mean that these theologians did not take seriously the case being made. Indeed, they agreed "in theory" with most of the basic claims of the petition, but not with the petition itself as a practical theological action due to its limited chance for success.

It can of course be affirmed that rigorous and critical theory, on one hand, as well as an orientation to ecclesial-cultural change or transformation, on the other hand, are necessary figures of practical theology today. But the Foucauldian awareness raises a question: is there a third hand? These theologians' rejections of the case for the petition caused me to rethink my relationship to it and my understanding of the theological life. Is allowing oneself to share authorship in a theology that will "fail" worth doing at all? And what counts as failure for a practical theological production? Upon reflection, I considered that there could indeed be another way to understand the value of this exercise: how it could become part of theologians' work on their relationships to themselves and to others. In this case, one could see the value of the practical theology not only in terms of its theoretical sophistication (critically resourcing scripture and tradition with respect to a critically assessed present ecclesial need of lay involvement, for example), or its practical efficacy (how effectively this way of casting an argument is wedded to the petitional form of ecclesial intervention), or even the coherence between the two (how a Christian case for lay autonomy hangs together with the petition as a form of lay ecclesial responsibility and academic activism), but, who am I becoming through my engagement with this argument, how is my practical theological work a sort of work on myself, a sort of formation of my relation to myself and others? In attending to this possibility, one might see that committing oneself to this practical theological event (in its content and form) might involve questions like rethinking and repracticing the risk to which I am willing to put my academic status and resources by exposure to possibly punitive bishops, laity, colleagues, or tenure and promotion committees. Or questions like these: What is the relation between ecclesial or academic eminence and one's self-identity? How does one experience oneself as a theologian? How does one understand the ultimate value of academic work? These possibilities show how the definition of a "successful" practical theological argument can be enriched: not just whether practical theology is sophisticated theoretically, or relevant for ecclesial or social change, but is a vehicle for a changed relation to self and others on the part of the practical theologian him- or herself.

As a second example, the reception of my first book, *Virtual Faith*, raised some difficult theological questions for me. That book set itself the task of divining some important orienting theological sensibilities amidst my own generation by way of an interpretation of some forms of our popular media culture. Many readers said they had trouble with many of the particularities of the arguments, but nevertheless experienced a recognition of spiritual awareness through the reading of the book. They could not comfortably endorse many of the claims as strictly logical claims, but the forms of the argument helped them change their mode of relationship to the question of spirituality and popular culture, sometimes in significant ways. After many such conversations, I began to think that there was something at stake in practical theological argument other than the relative adequacy of the correlation or the liberational efficacy of the argument. I began to wonder whether the experience of adequacy of the correlation was itself not an effect of some other recognition, of consent to some other call. What if theology has a mystagogical effect on the reader but its arguments are "wrong" . . . or "not relatively adequate"? And, I began to think, what if those arguments of mine were rooted in my own mystagogy, were a spiritual exercise that I was performing on myself to change my relation to myself and others, and somehow rendering available in the writing for my readers? Without sacrificing any achievements of modern critical theology, then, how might we think critically about the spiritual-political effects of theology on theologians' relation to themselves and their auditors? Is a rigorous concern for method enough to establish creative direction for contemporary practical theology?

Through Foucault, as earlier indicated, I came to understand my practical theology across its many foci—pop culture, consumer society, generational ideologies, theological education, and the nature of practical theology itself—as a form of therapy. I began to see that a practical theological interpretation of culture can be an intellectual mode of working on one's convictions, perceptions, mode of existing in the world. Specifically, in my case, I have begun to see practical theology as a way of breaking out of the suburbs: the working-class and middle-class environments in which I was raised in the 1970s and 1980s, breaking out of these suburbs intellectually, emotionally, psychologically, spiritually, sexually, politically, physically, and most deeply, theologically. After, but rarely during, each theological project (essay, article, book, lecture, paper, syllabus), I am continually surprised to discover how my thought was and is protected and nourished by, as well as governed and positioned by, lower-middle socioeconomic class white Midwestern heterosexual assumptions. In coming to see my consent to God as bound up in changing my relationship to myself and others by breaking out of the suburbs, I have begun to discover one of the political tasks of practical theology, lodged at a surprising level in this theological discourse, the level of the theologian's own autobiography, not in a romantic sense, but understood through a critical postmodern account of subjectivity.

If these are not merely private or individual experiences but common effects, blessings, and even dangers of a theological vocation, what sort of approach will help us account for this significance in theology's practicality, of practical theology as a spiritual exercise?

Theoretical and Pedagogical Implications

I understand practical theology to be theology that focuses on the constitution of practice in a critical account of theological knowledge, for the sake of testing how theology can make critical and reflexive sense of practice in faith and culture. In this work, I also now see practical theology's deep importance for the larger theological world as a productive domain of contemporary theology that can hold and account for the practice of the subjectivity of the theologian.

The turn to practical theology, particularly in Catholic academia, is an opportunity to recover theological work as a spiritual exercise. This is not a romantic return to premodernity, but passes through the postmodern challenges placed by postmodern philosophies like those of Foucault. Practical theology is the approach that today is poised to make the importance of the theologian's relation to self for theologizing a topic of rigorous intellectual inquiry. Practical theologians can radicalize their practical turn all the way—back to themselves in their relationships, to the way theologians themselves practice their subjectivity through their research and writing, and deals with power, even perhaps including, in Foucault's characterization, our own internalized fascisms.[8]

Highlighting the way in which practical theology may be a form of theological therapy neither reduces theology to the "merely" therapeutic, nor cancels the contemporary plurality of truth games by which theologians validate their claims. It does not mean that we should stop thinking critically about each other's theologies, or that theology no longer can and must make a difference for the life of our specific ecclesial and social contexts. It does introduce a new domain of truth by which a theologian's theology can be evaluated. Or rather, it works into a name what for many of us is already going on.

We can use practical theological discourses to gain critical leverage on other approaches to theology by practicing theological work as a genealogy of theological production itself, showing that and how we use our intellectual work to "govern" ourselves, to foreground the ethical responsibility of the theologian that is the irreplaceable relation to oneself and others, something to which theologians from whatever station in life can have access (including my lower socioeconomic background students, too, as I will suggest). For, with the exception of the few of us who will write classic theological works, and perhaps even for them, too, we all eventually find that even our best theology begins to become brittle and fracture in the face of good criticism that shows how our claims to truth and interventions for freedom continually fall short, even working against our intentions. Yet even though we continually and creatively fail to fully represent the tradition, address the situation, or animate liberation, that does not mean, as we can become trained to think, that our theology is unimportant, irrelevant, unfaithful, uncritical, reactionary, or flat wrong. For we can also ask, and even be asked, how our theology is part of our work on ourselves and our readers, how it has helped change our modes of being and perception, of knowing and loving God and others.

As long as we are writing theology as human beings, we will have to deal with ourselves. It is one thing to leave this below consciousness in our psycho-spiritual life and untheorized in our intellectual life. Leaving it there means that it functions like a secret captain, guiding our thinking with a passion unhelpfully and unnecessarily unknown. It is another thing to slowly integrate one's relation to self into theological work, to make theology practical in this way, and thus to make of one's always already practical theology a spiritual exercise. Doing so offers a way not (only) to redeem what otherwise one might need to let go in one's theology as one moves on to other systems, problems, formulations, and questions, but proposes a way of retrieving the "subjective" investiture in and of theology, of mourning the loss of the imagined coherence of every formulation whose fictitiousness slowly and irremediably floats to the surface of every theological formulation. Using practical theology as the discourse of spiritual exercises can hold both the politics of cultural critique and interior adventures, journeys that are surely "individual but never individualist."[9]

Understanding practical theology as a spiritual exercise allows an expansion of the three publics to which David Tracy argues that North American theology addresses itself. His well-known and commonly employed tripartite formulation includes academy, society, and church as the addressees of theology, whose plausibility structures condition theological arguments. The present proposal, however, would widen the "public" of practical theology to include theologians themselves. This would be something different from the private-public opposition with which Tracy works, through the necessary public of oneself that is neither strictly private nor public, but a public privacy, a private publicity.[10] I hope that by now it is clear that this is neither merely a narrowly psychological claim nor a plea for a naïve theology designed only for personal devotion. It is to acknowledge that our own "relationality" is an addressee, is a "governable," in our intellectual work, that we theologians are addressees of our own authorship.

When practical theology is considered as spiritual exercise, that venerable task of the practical theologian called care of souls returns—refigured. For Schleiermacher, practical theology undertakes the "guidance of souls" in the church.[11] That formulation may now include that ambiguous phenomenon, the "soul" of theologians themselves, when theologians make interventions not only in and for the Christian other but in and for oneself as an other. In this way, practical theology is marshaled for the task of a "critical ontology of ourselves,"[12] to contend with every attempt in our culture and our discipline to exempt theologians' spiritual orientation from culpability in their theology, struggling against fabrications of our subjectivity that leave us as theologians separate from our productions, against a body-soul separation in the register of the textual body against the personal soul, with the former a surface effect of the vanishing latter, the docetic theologian. The care of souls includes, then, the concern that the theologian's soul does not become the prison of their body.[13]

TEACHING PRACTICAL THEOLOGY

If practical theology is the form of theology that foregrounds theological work as a spiritual exercise, then teaching our students not only about theology but how to be theologians, how to lead theological lives, seems critical. That theology is a way to work on oneself, a therapy (that does not necessarily need to buy into modern psychological presuppositions), will be attractive to many of our students, who often assume for various reasons that theology has nothing to say to them, and who at the same time are often comfortable with psychological or even psychagogical language in which to make sense of their lives and relationships.

Practical theology as a spiritual exercise means that disseminating theological power "from above" and recognizing the ways in which "from below" our students already are practically theological becomes very important. "Training" students to do theology as a spiritual exercise becomes a politically important act, a site for Christian creativity and resistance against powers in church and society—and academy—who under various banners seek to keep the unauthorized from theological power. It seems that this understanding of practical theology does not have an abundance of places to lay its head today, when a strong if undeclared separation of spirituality from theology encourages academic theologians to teach and write as if little is at stake personally in their or their students' theologizing. Such a stance risks becoming the anti-intellectualism it would otherwise condemn, insofar as it fails to integrate the spiritual context and motive for theology's intellectual work—at the very least, the ethics of the relation of the theologian to him- or herself—as a constitutive aspect of even the simplest attempt at theology.

Perhaps some of the resistance to teaching theology in this way is that it makes us vulnerable to our students, and that it suddenly puts us on a kind of equal terrain with them. They may not have our academic training in theology, but we rarely have to admit our inadequacies and uncertainties about our training. We may teach as if we have mastered certain intellectual maps. What we share with our students, uncomfortably, is the complicated and obscure travail of intimacy with God, the uncanny concrete individual knowledge of the divine whose logic Rahner insurgently encouraged us to respect,[14] the mysterious gift of desolation and consolation that not even the holiest among us can predict, our now passionate, now resigned, now outraged orientation to the uncontainable, the life of grace.

In my own practical theology course for undergraduates, the freshness of this approach lies also in its appeal to the liberty, subjectivity, and autobiography of my students: I encourage students to see the value of their work not only as a grade or a ticket to job, tenure, or access, but as a way of working on themselves, freeing themselves, becoming someone different from who they were before their theological attempt, in their own releasement to God. Even occasionally to deal with their "interior fascisms." I have had virtually no students who were not intrigued by this way of experiencing the practical theological life.

Many of them enjoy thinking about practical theology as a spiritual exercise, which in class we call "spiritually reviewing your theology," attending to how your own subjectivity as student theologian is at stake in your intellectual work. One wrote that such review is "completely critical in the practice of any spiritual or even simply intellectual person. If one is to truly understand anything, the first step must be the understanding of oneself, [because] the cage of the self . . . tints the world with the hue of past experience and expectation."[15]

Another offered that

> even though we are only learning [this review] now [at the end of the term], I believe that I have been subconsciously practicing [it] throughout the quarter. I have been using the practical theology that we have been exploring this quarter as a stimulus for deeper spiritual review. . . . In spiritually reviewing my group's Theology of Body-Shaping, I have really realized the relevance that it has in my life. Throughout high school and college I have been surrounded by cross country. It has been my true passion for the last eight years of my life. With this passion, however, comes the pressure to perform. Cross country has the second highest rate of eating disorders, just behind gymnastics. . . . In high school I, too, personally dealt with these issues. Runners' body issues are not as much body-shaping to try to reach an ideal appearance, but rather to reach an ideal performance. Regardless of the . . . motivation[,] I have come to realize through this course that depriving the body to reach a material goal is wrong. I have to avoid . . . letting running be motivated because of a desire to fit an ideal body image.[16]

Finally, another student wrote that theology "as a therapy is a very calming and encouraging way to view it . . . I believe that it is vital to seek happiness in this world because it is what we have for now, and though there may be an eternal life that is incomprehensibly more rewarding than this earth, there is still joy and peace to be found here."[17] Even though for many students the idea of practical theology as a spiritual exercise is at first surprising, even shocking, it quite quickly makes sense as a way of reading back onto the tradition in a way that encourages them to become theologians.

It is Foucault who helps us rediscover, in a newly critical way, the traditional Christian insight that Kierkegaard made famous, and which he addresses even to postmodern practical theologians: "Even in these relations [with the outside world] which we . . . so beautifully style the most intimate of all, do you remember that you have a still more intimate relation, namely, that in which you as an individual are related to yourself before God?"[18]

6

The Ethics of Characterizing Popular Faith

SCHOLARSHIP AND FANDOM

THE ETHICAL PLACEMENT OF THE SCHOLAR OF FAITH AND CULTURE

The serious attention given to "popular culture" in the study of religion and theology in the last two decades has generated a rich range of researches—from studies of the lived faith of nonelites, to erudite theological exegeses of media productions, to sophisticated sociological deconstructions of religious practices—and represents, at its best, diverse examples of the worthiest that an academic life concerned with religion can be: an intellectually serious engagement with everyday life, a deep curiosity and respect for the strangeness of sacrality as lived, an awareness of the necessarily political position of the scholar, or the creativity to test religious claims in the domains of the quotidian, the lay, the invisible, or, in the case of media, the often too simplistically visible, and even in this adjustment in the practice of the study of religion, to find the imagination to allow religious traditions themselves to be re-read as traditions of popular cultures.

Yet we have not fully appreciated how scholarship itself—in popular culture studies and beyond—can be understood as a kind of "popular culture." Scholars are learning that there are different kinds of ways of being made a "subject" through a specific popular culture, even for those who call the scholarly *habitus* their own. One example of a "fandom" recognizable in the lives of many younger scholars, if still generally unintegrated into academic identity, is that of the powerful pleasures of immersion in media culture so important for the last several decades since the ascendancy of a general electronic media culture in the West. Put more simply, lots of academics are also music, film, television, or sports fans. Appreciating the presence of such fandoms allows a curiosity about, and can be a propadeutic for, the more murky fandoms in the realm of scholarly life itself.

In aid of curiosity, I now provide my own example. In spring 2007, I attended a concert in Los Angeles of the rock band Winger, whose heyday was around 1989. As has been established in cultural studies, the "popular" dimension of everyday practice in such cases is not only registered through the concert itself, but also in the performances of fan behavior, including chatter about it afterward, and through that chatter conditioning the identities that people construct and deploy for the negotiation of everyday life. After the concert, part of my chatter was an e-mail to friends that, in part, said

> *[As for lead singer and bassist] Kip Winger—I can still bow down at this man's altar. His voice is somewhat addled by years of cigarettes and too much drinking, but he sounds fantastic nevertheless. You really have to give him props for a major league rock voice. He's not Mercury, Perry, or Plant, but he's just right for Winger, and he and Beach have added some extra oomph to their catalogue by making the songs rock even harder, adding frequent hiccups, odd times, and modulations in their songs, so that they keep you guessing about just how what they're playing is going to rock [. . .] And did I tell you that they were super, super, super loud? Ok, you retort, isn't Kip Winger (is this his real name?) the guy who is the poster child for the open E string? Yes, yes, that's true. On half of their songs, Kip tut-tutted his first and second fingers on the open E, and once in a while he even jumped onto the drum riser of Rod Morgenstein (=GOD). Yet I have rarely seen less musical rapport between bass and drums. How can Morgenstein stand to be so partnerless? The bass is now for Kip what it was in those [old music] videos: just an accessory to the more important things: the voice, the yearning, the 5 o'clock shadow. Having said all that, the man commanded attention.*
>
> *These guys must now be in their mid 40s or so, but they are playing at the top of their game. When they got to "Heading for a Heartbreak," the crowd was in the palm of Kip's many-ringed right hand. The place was filled with people mostly between 30 and 40 years old. Again and again, I recognized them as my people still, somehow, despite and because of the mullets and beer guts. And I think it is worth thinking about the spiritual significance of the ongoing presence of aging rockers in one's musical life. At critical points in my (our?) adolescence, this and other bands offered models of heroism, excellence, daring, success, masculinity, and escape from all that seemed small about the suburban spiritual captivity of my life, anyway. And now I catch up with these guys as they continue to tour into midlife, and what soul-functions do they and their music serve now? More than just nostalgia. Are they peculiarly intense reminders of the sort of free, experimental, even Dionysian relationship to reality that can still be had*

as an adult? Are they living symbols for establishing continuity between my teenage and late 30-something self? Are they witnesses to an ongoing disturbance about the things that I consider "settled" in life? Are they simply bittersweet reminders of the (rock and roll) road not taken? We who have the luxury of being witness to the aging of our rock heroes are in a unique position to consider such questions, especially if this music is not just diversion, but in some sense central to the project of our own lives. This is all another way of saying, watching Kip, Reb, and Rod, I was led easily, and with joy, into the consideration that the work that I do in theology is a conduction into the relation to self and others given by live rock music. I don't know which is more surprising: that I can still learn from aging rockers about what is at stake in a life well-lived, or that I still find pleasure in looking to them for such guidance in the first place. . . .

Yours for the salvation that rock alone can give . . .

In this example is condensed decades of immersion in rock and roll, a certain fandom that has, so far as I am aware, played a significant role in my personal identity, and is one important condition for my taking pleasure in life as a theologian today. The music of my ongoing formation were also part of a capitalist circulation of "corporate rock" in the 1980s packaged and sold to millions of boys like myself. My subjectivity has been striated by the forces of the American economy and the racial complexities of the poaching of black music by white artists and the music industry.[1] The cultural unconscious of race, economy, subjectivity, and more are there with my personal unconscious and the way in which male and female rock stars have been particular objects for my desire, projection, and consolation, and that likely have to do with my own formative childhood and adolescent experiences.

Few people are theologians moved by hard rock music, but is it not also the case that each of us has a strange mind—a residence of cultural and personal unconsciousnesses, catalyzing our involvement in the popular cultures we fancy, in relation to which we carry out our scholarship?

As I have argued elsewhere,[2] scholars who research faith and culture, and those whose lives are impacted by our scholarship, could benefit from paying more attention to learning what is going on when scholars write about popular culture and religion. Do we read our own works as having to do with subjectivity? (We most often do so negatively, when we want to explain someone else's motives for writing: as aggression, status-seeking, conciliation, ingratiation, or submission to authority.) How, indeed, have we learned to read our scholarly productions? Why do we so often only read them as scholarly interventions vis-à-vis a particular school, debate, or person, instead of also reading them as they relate to our own weirdness, the strangeness that we are made to be by our cultural and personal unconsciousnesses, and the different strangeness that we might be by attempting to let through and replace our histories, socially and individually? What politics of scholarly production prevent us from reading our writings as fictions, fantasies, daydreams, reports of desire and conflict, or *rapports à l'ésprit* yet unimagined?

Such questions turn us to the problem of the "government" of the ethical placement of the scholar as a cultural interpreter. Can we answer to what is "really going on" when scholars make religious or theological sense of the cultural practice of faith?[3]

WHEN SCHOLARS STUDY OTHERS' FAITH: *SOUL SEARCHING*

A case will serve to develop why a turn to the ethics of studies of faith and culture might be important. The recent volume *Soul Searching: The Religious and Spiritual Lives of American Teenagers* is a major sociological report about the faith lives of American adolescents.[4] In this book, the authors, Christian Smith and Melinda Lundquist Denton, present the results of the most comprehensive study of teenage faith ever attempted. Over 3,300 teens were surveyed by phone, and another 267 were subjects of personal follow-up interviews.

Through summary charts, brief biographical narratives, and rich quotations, the authors argue that a clear picture of contemporary teenage faith emerges. Far from being "spiritual but not religious" seekers, teens are surprisingly conventional in their faith. Indeed, they frequently profess to enjoy being religious, or at least lacking suspicion about it. Mostly, they end up believing what their parents believe. They affirm spiritual "seeking" in theory, but almost never do it in practice, and they do not bother to talk to each other in depth about faith. Nor are they generally concerned about what their professed traditions actually teach about faith and practice. Often treading cautiously among peers, they do not want to publicly offend anyone else's faith (or lack thereof). Rather, they seek to believe what "works" for them. And teens, the researchers discovered, want religion to provide them, above all, individual health and wealth: an American-style happiness.

Smith and Denton coin a phrase for this everyday teen faith: "Moralistic Therapeutic Deism."[5] By this they mean that teens like to make value judgments, but are highly inarticulate at defending them. They use their faith to further their own sense of individual entitlement, and they imagine God as indifferent to, or unable to be involved in, worldly affairs in general or their own moral decisions in particular. The teen credo that cuts across denominations is this: Believe what you need to believe in order to fulfill yourself. This is the contemporary teenage faith in the United States. Far from inventing this new religion, however, teenagers learned it from their culture, particularly through their moralistic, therapy-positive, functionally deist parents.

As any practical theologian must consider, this major study will have concrete effects in religious and academic environments. Those involved in the National Study of Youth and Religion (NSYR) have made numerous academic presentations of the findings, and there are multiple planned academic productions: some six more books, seventeen articles or chapters, and eight master's or doctoral theses presenting and interpreting the data.[6] Smith and Denton's authoritative interpretation has already been cause for handwringing in popular Christian periodicals, and their conclusions, along with presentations of the larger NSYR data, have been the stuff of dozens, perhaps now hundreds, of presentations to ministry professionals and church leaders.[7] Such use of this research also matters because of the resources being invested in "effective" youth and young adult ministries in the United States. The first new Catholic Catechism for the United States in over a century has recently been produced that was ostensibly written with reference to sociological data on young adult Catholic faith in America, signaling an interest in official Catholicism about studies of everyday faith.[8] Such a mobilization of scholars and presenters in academic and religious life reinforces and reflects the presumption, in most theological and ecclesial circles, that when sociologists present data on faith and culture, they are telling the more or less objective truth. Some questions and objections can be raised, however, about this research, that will set us within the theme for this chapter.

Soul Searching should be credited with and celebrated for many serious achievements in the study of American youth and religion.[9] My purpose here, however, is to underscore the problematic theological assumptions that seem to implicitly and explicitly guide the generation, classification, and reportage of this sociological data. These assumptions prevent this study from comprehending everyday faith in its specificity, that is, the ways in which everyday faith is amalgamated from multiple ways of operating in everyday life;[10] is practiced as "fragments," "side plots," and "tangents," more than theorized;[11] is irreducible to a "logical syllogism";[12] and is speakable only after something like "therapy."[13] None of these dimensions of faith as practiced is allowed in *Soul Searching,* except as a deformation of a supposed ideal form of faith.

This misreading of everyday faith stems from *Soul Searching's* conception of personal religious identity as derivative of official conceptions of identity. Institutions and their representatives get to define what counts as authentic faith, and it is these contemporary declarations against which teens' own declarations (narrowly understood, as will become evident) are measured. This misreading operates through four strategies in the analysis, which I shall delimit.

First, *teen faith is framed as a problem for the power of religious leaders.* Smith and Denton define institutional representatives as the "agents of religious socialization" and describe their ineffectiveness in contemporary American culture.[14] The authors presume, but do not defend, any theological ground for evangelical exhortations such as "there may be more than a few Catholic and Mormon leaders who may be justifiably concerned that roughly one in every seven of their teenagers are not even convinced that God exists."[15] They elsewhere write that "all religious groups seem at risk of losing teens to *nonreligious identities*,"[16] betokening a suspect theological assumption—that of an easy distinction between a religious and nonreligious identity. Such "top-down" analysis also lacks psychological-sociological curiosity regarding the ways in which "religious" identities may be necessarily related to "nonreligious" identities in a life or a social circle.

The authors imagine religious beliefs as starting from pure official teaching, stewarded by contemporary religious leaders, well or poorly, through official channels, such as programs of religious education. Beliefs that begin as given at the "top" are corrupted by American culture, sometimes with the assistance of weak delivery systems for education in faith. Thus, on one page, the study states three different times that teen faith has suffered significant "slippage" from the official doctrines of religious tradition and religious education.[17] They report with evident surprise that "a number of religious teenagers propounded theological views that are, according to the standards of their own religious traditions, simply not orthodox."[18]

This preoccupation with what slippage might actually reveal seems over the course of the book to be an anxiety regarding the maintenance of religious power. Typical evidence can be found in the survey question presented to teenagers regarding whether it is legitimate to pick and choose beliefs without having to accept the teachings of the faith as a whole.[19] Such a narrow question boxes teenagers in unnecessarily, adopting a "with us or against us" tone that lacks sophistication. No one, of course, can possibly know all the teachings, even all the "important" or "foundational" teachings, of a religious tradition. Moreover, as theology itself is discovering with ever greater complexity, the particular beliefs that are "sanctioned" by religious leadership, at any particular time and place, are deeply implicated in "nontheological" or "nonreligious" political, social, cultural, and economic factors. The very opposition between "picking and choosing" and "accepting the whole" is itself a recent way of imagining, often for the sake of an intended control, what the "options" for belief are today—much like the opposition between fundamentalism and enlightenment, or relativism and moral foundationalism. (Or, for the authors of *Soul Searching*, the dualism between inhabiting "morally significant" and "morally insignificant" worldviews.[20])

Part of the anxious defense of institutional religious authority happens through another dualism that runs through the study, between individualistic and communal faith. Individualism is cast as that which threatens the communal maintenance of traditional religious identity and convictions. But this bifurcation leaves important theological points in the study lacking nuance. For example, after discussing several examples of teenagers who say that they want to glorify God, live for God, have Christ in their heart, or give up old behaviors by being saved, the authors write that these teenagers "illustrate something of a departure from the individualistic instrumentalism that dominates U.S. teen religion by making God and not individuals the center of religious faith."[21] Or consider their contention that conservative Protestant and Mormon teenagers "tend to hold the most particularistic and exclusive views of religion and tend to be the least individualistic about faith and belief."[22] To the contrary, it is not evident that those who say such things have transcended "individualism" in their faith, nor whether the category of individualism allows a sufficiently rich screen through which to hear such statements. Such theological claims might well be heard in other ways: as self-serving affirmations, as testaments to surviving hardships, as ways of showing love or honor to the authorities from whom one learned such statements, or as phrases that cover a theological terrain very different from that intended by an "official" "theocentric" understanding. It could, indeed, be argued that a "conservative" theology can effectively be an individualist theology. The point is that an individualist/communal dichotomy fails to capture the richness and complexity of such statements to register the "rough ground"[23] of everyday life that makes American Christian faiths such interesting foci for study.

Second, *the authors accept religious—effectively, Christian—leaders' placing of the boundaries between religious traditions.* The study therefore employs the discourse of "eclecticism" or "syncretism" and, of course, comes out strongly critical of it, even as the alleged phenomenon rarely shows up in their study.

Smith and Denton claim that the "absolute historical centrality of the Protestant conviction about salvation by God's grace alone . . ." is "discarded" by many teens.[24] Such hyperbolic language as "absolute historical centrality" is already a clue that an ahistorical theological claim is being advanced. No such historical-ahistorical "conviction"—held by all (authoritative?) clergy, all (authoritative?) theologians, or even all "the faithful"—exists, as the turn to "historicism" in theology would expect, and as histories of Christianity, especially from "below," increasingly show.[25]

Further, no attempt is made to distinguish "eclecticism" from other attempts at plural faith inhabitations, including practices such as what theologians are presently naming "multiple religious belonging."[26] As it is, "eclecticism" is labeled as the domain of "religiously promiscuous faith mixers"[27]—a rhetorical dismissal of any potential case for a pluralistic holding by invocation of a sexually dangerous ("promiscuous") religious identification. According to the study, however, not many practice it anyway, since "almost all stick with one religious faith, if any."[28] This phrase, "one religious faith," is another problematic designation that the authors leave as a natural category. This seems especially worth questioning when the authors themselves find that 14 to 20 percent of five of their religious subgroups (black Protestant, Jewish, mainline Protestant, conservative Protestant, and Roman Catholic) attend services at more than one congregation.

Moreover, they set an unrealistically high academic bar for someone to be considered a spiritual seeker: those who truly qualify must satisfy at least a half-dozen conditions. They must be "self-directing and self-authenticating individuals pursuing an experimental and eclectic quest for personal spiritual meaning outside of historical religious traditions."[29] Not surprisingly, only 2 to 3 percent of teens do this, they report. However, this description sounds like a critique of a romanticized view of the Baby Boomer searching of a generation ago. How many adults would qualify as "seekers" under that description? While it seems unhelpful as a way of gauging spiritual bricolage today, it is consistent with the book's frequent segregation of "new age" from "biblical" views of God—without argument or rationale,[30] and the book's striking continual recourse to theistic terminology without a discussion of the limits of God references for theistic traditions themselves, or for teenagers in our culture. For example, references are made to survey questions designed to elicit views on "belief in God," "views of God," or of "God's judgment."[31]

Third, *Soul Searching accepts as unproblematic and self-evident many theological concepts, allowing them neither cultural context nor sociological-theological critique.* For example, the authors state that "two out of three teens profess to believe in something like the Bible's personal, historically active God."[32] This simplistic theological statement is made to sound common sensical regarding the Bible. On the contrary, it is far from evident that "the Bible" manifests an unproblematically "personal" and "historically active" God. The key phrase here is "something like," which allows the authors a zone of ambiguity regarding both the sociological and theological aspects of the claim: as if to say that lots of teenagers operate in a zone of belief that bears some affinity to a theological claim that may or may not be quite right, but it does not need to be justified, anyway, because the correlation is not being too tightly claimed. The very provisionality of the association between teens and the true meaning of the Bible is the rhetorical key, paradoxically, to the illusion of tight association/dissociation between the Bible and teens.

Smith and Denton also report that half of Roman Catholic youth believe in communicating with the dead, and proceed to group this belief with significant levels of Catholic teen belief in reincarnation, astrology, psychics, and fortune tellers.[33] These are portrayed as evidence of deficient religious education, and as a consequence, youth going over to magical or paranormal beliefs. The authors report this despite praying to the dead and the communion of saints being not only quite commonplace in Catholic teaching, but also part of the symbolic order of many churches and of home altars, especially for Hispanic/Latino Catholics. Further, the authors do not give any indication that what they term reincarnation, astrology, or divination has ever been seriously considered in, conceptually congenial toward, or an historical influence upon the Christian tradition.

Indeed, an ahistorical and idealized view of Christianity is evident throughout the analysis, such as in the statement that "the religion to which most [teens] appear to be referring seems significantly different in character from versions of the same faith in centuries past."[34] They then make theological judgments that rely on stock theological formulae: teen religion as practiced today is not orthodox, nor is it "revealed in truth by [a] holy and almighty God who calls all to a turning from self and a serving of God in gratitude, humility, and righteousness"; nor does it fashion teens "into a community of people embodying a historically rooted tradition of identity, practices, and ethics that define[s] their selfhood, loyalties, and commitments."[35] It does not witness to a "life-transformative, transcendent truth. . . ."[36] As a theologian, I wonder where, apart from experiences of the religious "ghetto"—if even there—such descriptions of [Christian?] religion's purpose really hold true. These idealizations structure the study throughout, perhaps most tellingly displayed in the important claim that "a significant part of Christianity in the United States is actually only tenuously Christian in any sense that is seriously connected to the *actual historical Christian tradition*."[37] As in "absolute historical centrality" earlier, the hyperbole is a clue to the anxiety of the power of religious authority underpinning the study. Readers then learn in a footnote the revealing claim that this "actual historical" tradition is given in Christianity by "creeds and confessions," a motley and contradictory Protestant and Catholic mix of which is then listed, presumably for the reader to sort out.[38]

Fourth, *the authors make their own a critique of teenage articulacy and inconsistency that becomes a characteristic form of moralizing.*

The authors note their discovery of the "apparent logical inconsistency of some teens in relating to God," and when teen "deists" report that they, too, feel close to God—the authors name this a "conceptual confusion"—and mockingly add, "go figure."[39] These criticisms indicate the lack of a creative sociological-theological research frame for the vicissitudes of everyday faith. Such criticisms make me wonder which religious, or even nonreligious, persons the authors would point to as models of logical consistency. (They seem surprised to report that it is "not easy to find someone who is clear and articulate about what [spiritual seeking] means,"[40] and they moralize about a seventeen-year old who lacks "solid grounding" for his "moral reasoning"[41]—something that has eluded even the best of our contemporary moral philosophers.[42])

It seems at least unfair, as well as theologically problematic, to overvalue what comes to teenagers' minds to say to an interviewer as a key to their deep moral commitments. That is why it is particularly striking to note the piling-on that the researchers do, salting their book with various moralizing comments whenever the topic of teen articulacy surfaces. It is characteristic of the way that sociology can rhetorically produce theological truths that the claim that "some" teenagers are "Machiavellian moral relativists" (never mind that Machiavelli was a sophisticated political philosopher who articulated his views as an adult) comes with disavowal of any interpretive action on the part of the scholar: after all, these teens "openly profess" it.[43] It is as if, to quote the old saying, their words go "from their lips to God's ears," with the sociological researcher having the divine clairaudience, the ear of the Other. It must be so: teens "profess" it, and "openly." The rhetoric of confession is precisely what a theological account of this study must protest.

After Foucault, we know too well the reasons for regarding confession as an unproblematic route to theological truth.

There are some acknowledgements of teen articulacy, but these tend to be swallowed by the study's moralizing approach. Interestingly, the authors claim that most teens are more articulate about sex or media than about their faith. However, they do not see these other kinds of literacy as bearing on teen faith, or as a way of articulating faith as such.[44] This seems to be part of a larger problem in the book of a lack of letting sociology be informed by scholarship on theological understandings of spirituality, such as research in spiritual direction and pastoral care and counseling.[45] (Theologian Donna Freitas has made a similar point in suggesting that in focusing on phone surveys and individual person-to-person interviews, a crucial theological resource has been left out of Smith and Denton's study: analysis of personal writings by youth and young adults about their faith lives.[46])

Such a lack of attention to theological perspectives on faith is evident throughout the book, as when the authors report that "One seventeen-year-old black conservative Protestant boy from New York . . . readily slid from discussing how religious faith influences him into how having faith *in himself* has been helpful: 'How is religious faith important? Well, like school. If I didn't have faith in myself, I wouldn't be going to school right now, wouldn't have the motivation.'"[47] The authors do not ask after the potential links between the two types of faith in self and God.

Despite all this, the simplest evidence for this moralizing is that *Soul Searching* never considers that contemporary teen belief may have something substantially spiritually constructive and new, not just alarming, to teach the larger church.

ON "MORALISTIC THERAPEUTIC DEISM" IN RELIGION RESEARCH

These four strategies of misreading teen faith may or may not be relativized by the authors' concession that "surveys cannot tell us everything or perhaps even the most important and interesting things there are to know about people and their lives. Surveys do have real limits . . . perhaps especially about the lives of adolescents and perhaps especially about faith and spiritual practices."[48] Unfortunately, this helpfully agnostic and even self-critical admission does not really shape their way of formulating the religious and spiritual lives of teenagers. Such a statement would need to have a structuring power in the survey and its classifications to have critical force, and not appear as an addendum to "keep in mind" while reading material otherwise voiced with a confidence both theological and sociological.

Their conclusion that American teens practice a religion of "moralistic therapeutic deism" turns out to be a promising skeleton key to their own portrayal of teen faith, as if teen beliefs about religion are being made to hold an array of disavowed beliefs present in the authors' discipline(s).

Moralistic

Soul Searching itself is "moralistic" through the simplistic categories that it uses to produce and then to classify teenage faith.[49] These categories—the orthodox and biblical against the new age, the individualistic against the communal, the particular against the general, the articulate against the inarticulate, the tutored against the untutored—are not just sociological but also moral categories, insofar as they gesture toward more and less worthy beliefs (that is, beliefs more in conformity with the identity generated out of a religion's prescribed subjectivities, its historically-grounded orthodoxies). To use Smith and Denton's own language, *Soul Searching* proposes a vision of sociologistic morality that is not "socially disruptive" for religions, and can function as "inclusive of most religions, which are presumed ultimately to stand for equivalent moral views" in their susceptibility to categories of institutional religious authority, such as texts and creeds, internally consistent worldviews and clearly specified classical faith characteristics.[50]

Therapeutic

This study is also "therapeutic"—again, using its own language—insofar as it provides "therapeutic benefits to its adherents,"[51] that is, a healing discourse for American religions (for which Christianity is taken as a model), wherein religion can be shown how—through the very words, as it were, of the teens who loosely inhabit these religions—that religious leaders' difficult situation is both their fault and not their fault, providing leaders with a sociological container or frame in which their complex situation can be held and understood, and therapeutic goals suggested (particularly in a "Concluding Unscientific Postscript," treating of implications for "Religious Communities and Youth Workers").

Deism

Finally, *Soul Searching* is "deist" in that a natural law has been inscribed in the world by a deity who now leaves the world to us to interpret, and to change. That natural law is the sociological chastity, discipline, *askesis*, that earns for itself the tools to apprehend, but not to advocate, religious belief; a social-scientific approach that can register how an encounter with a "biblical," "personal," "commanding," "transforming," "transcendent" God does or does not appear in the professed faith of teenagers. Here, a disciplinary law of inquiry stands between revelation and autonomy: on one hand, it will not question that a benevolent power exists and wants the best for us all—so no questioning of the motives, texts, or claims of religions themselves; on the other hand, it will question what teenagers say about their own religious quests, which is an interrogation and problematization of our autonomy in face of the traditions of revelation. The deism of the study means that sociology cannot try to be in relation "directly" with God—because that would involve it more explicitly in theological discussions, possibly allowing on board questions about the theological structuring of such a study.

The sociology of teen belief cannot, therefore (and unfortunately) be imagined richly as a new front for theological encounter among sociologists and between "theology" and "sociology."

If "Moralistic Therapeutic Deism" is finally a religion that, for Smith and Denton, inserts teenagers more deeply into the economies of American life,[52] the moralistic therapeutic deism that positions the analyses of this Moralistic Therapeutic Deism invites the authors and readers more deeply into the economies of power in social science and religion: the peculiar power to tell people the truth about themselves in a way that will be useable for the reauthorization of the practices of religious authorities in *academia* and *ecclesia*.

This is nowhere more clear than in the book's "Brief Excursus," which is a meditation on another dualism, "On Living in Morally Significant and Insignificant Universes."[53] The term *excursus* serves to suggest that it will illuminate some larger philosophical issues raised by the research, while bracketing off the discussion as a temporary indulgence, a little sidelight philosophizing that is a departure from the primary social-scientific methodology with which the main text is preoccupied. But the excursus, in its break with the text's internal genre, its self-conscious parenthesizing, and its very naming of its task, calls attention to itself as a knowing digression, a time-out zone in which, freed from the need for social-scientific rhetoric, an aside can be uttered that will now be taken with the seriousness of earned and learned insight, all of which suggest that this excursus may well contain the book's message in germ, and like the motif in travel writing of the excursus/excursion that succinctly symbolizes a more expansive sojourn, this excursus can be read not as a detour, or pauseful speculation, but as a parable for the trip itself, that is, a searching account of the soul of this study's moral and moralizing performance.

The excursus' fundamental distinction between "morally significant" and "morally insignificant" worlds marks, according to the authors, a difference between finding oneself caught up in a larger meaningful story that is not of one's own invention, a plausible and finally cosmically coherent *Weltanschauung*, over against finding oneself left with "only" this world in its finitude, implausibility, and incoherence. It is the difference between how and why one lives having a resonance beyond one's narrow personal goals or desires, on one hand, and being beset by the stringency of needs and interests that are only too familiar, culturally embedded, and finally narcissistic, on the other hand. Comprehending what it means to take up habitation either in a world of deep meaning, or of nihilism, they suggest, matters for their study because, while "many teenagers" live in a "morally significant" world, "some" teenagers do not.[54]

It is difficult to see the value of this distinction, even as a purely heuristic one. Philosophically, it seems too simplistic, and theologically, it seems difficult to support. The distinction extrapolates too readily from a particular series of discrete statements to the general positing of a "moral universe." It overindividualizes moral commitment. It makes of the individual will a too determining force. It neglects the forces of nurture, environment, and upbringing in general. And it fails to register that many contemporary—and deeply moral—philosophical theologies or philosophies of religion take their stand in what the authors consider "morally insignificant universes": that is, understandings of the world that privilege the "specific people, pains, pleasures, and opportunities concretely before a person, [with] no demons tempting or angels watching over anyone, no natural law or world-historic struggles and achievements. . . ."[55] This is close to the very definition of a postmodern understanding of the world, and one in which many important ethical conversations are happening in contemporary philosophy of religion, yet the study shows no awareness of this. In other words, the difference between morally significant and morally insignificant universes reads more like a moralism than a concept that illuminates the practice of faith in culture today.

What *Soul Searching* offers, then, is an example of academic study that generates, while seeming to reflect, a stabilized discourse about faith. This discourse is a result of the indulgence of the power of the disciplines of sociology and theology to tell the truth about younger generations, that is to say, to be able to assign a truth to younger generations and their faith, to include populations of young adults in social-scientific and religio-theological discourses of truth. The dream of a stabilized discourse concerning young people's faith is the fevered dream of marketing religion in America.[56] Young people's faith must be stabilized in order to be put in motion in the economy of American morality and religion, to safeguard the proprietors of the tradition, including those theologians who think that faith identity moves from a pure "above" to a messy "below."

The book's forced disclosures about teen faith are like weights that give shape to the book, throw weights that condition, but do not determine, where and how the book will land. The book is weighted, but not fated for, assimilation to the institutional goals of American religious life, through its pull toward the shutting down of creative inquiry about the faith lives of American teenagers. This stabilizing of teen faith is this kind of throw weight. It will take an intellectual *agere contra*, acting against the pitch, to do something different with the work.

PRACTICAL-THEOLOGICAL INTERVENTIONS IN EVERYDAY FAITH

This study raises difficult questions for the study of faith and contemporary culture. How do scholars get clear about what are commonly called our "biases" or "presuppositions"? Or, as I would rather state it, how do we get clearer about the register in which we are writing or reading accounts of faith and culture?

What we have here in a sociological register is what is often also seen in a theological register: writing about popular beliefs in a way that makes them assimilable to institutions, academic and ecclesial, that attempt to govern religious belief. This is one reason the results have been greeted so welcomingly and with the natural agreement of a commonsense confirmation—a sense of "of course that's right"—and also received, as delivered, with the force of a moral and missionary charge, by scholars, educators, and ministers in the United States.[57]

As I have suggested, several important aspects of the theological judgments and language used in the study would have benefited from an historical registration, on two levels: first, a more critical historical account of the theological categories used to study the popular faith of adolescents, and second, a more critical historical and "subjective" account of why such categories are the ones available and attractive for the carrying through of the study. Theologian Don Browning had some awareness of such issues fifteen years ago when he was studying the lived faith of Christians in several Chicago churches for his groundbreaking book *Fundamental Practical Theology*.[58] One need not completely accept his hermeneutical orientation for thinking about how faith gets lived in culture in order to appreciate that the "preunderstandings" or the subjectivity of the researcher must be somehow accounted in the study itself and be critically shown to one from various perspectives. Further (and with Browning) from a theological perspective, one must be willing to let go of, in principle, any specific theological concept or claim to truth in face of what one learns from specific situations of lived faith. I take this to mean not only the "contents" of Christian faith itself, but also the conceptual "forms" that organize those contents, such as what "orthodox," "biblical," "creedal," or "fundamental" might mean. Historical research on Christianity increasingly shows the contingency of the categories that often set the stage for framing the religious questions in studies of faith and culture.[59]

In the spirit of Browning's work, I would like to emphasize a practical-theological reason for drafting my critique of *Soul Searching*: it is already having effects on American churches through presentations, studies, and sponsored conversations at multiple levels of church governance, including youth workers, bishops, religious educators, parents, and academics who work on youth issues. It is likely that this study and the many other reports from the NSYR data (previously noted) will play a significant role in pastoral studies across denominations and religious traditions in the United States in coming years. Being able, therefore, to wisely locate this study in its theological and sociological perspectives on the nature and practice of faith identity, being able to locate the theological suppositions that structure and are structured by the sociological work, such tasks are intrinsic to knowing what can be done, and appreciating what will be attempted, with this study in ministry, in ecclesial planning, in academic elaboration, and in the everyday spiritual lives of Americans and, at least as importantly, all those affected by what happens in American religious and spiritual life.

In the midst of its achievements, what can also be learned from *Soul Searching* is its lack of a complex enough awareness that it is sociologists, with apparent assistance from theologians and theological models, who are really doing the "soul searching," that is, the exploration of the soul of and for American youth. To the extent that the study remains unreflexive and beyond serious theological critique, and to the extent that the study becomes a truth-bearing influence on the development of sociology and theology, of religious education curricula, ministry programs, or everyday self-definition on the part of teens or those who interact with them, to that extent we ought well mind Foucault's claim, that "the soul" can be, and often enough "is the prison of the body."[60]

THE RELEVANCE OF POPULAR CULTURE STUDIES

Although this study does not show evidence that the authors are fans of the teen culture that they study—perhaps just the opposite—the authors of *Soul Searching* nonetheless seem to be fans of a different sort: of a certain academic approach to studying faith and culture. It is the fandoms that help structure academic identity that run deeper than the study results themselves, and to which I shall return below. If the case of *Soul Searching* is not an isolated example, if this book and its reception are not the only exhibits of an argument in analysis of faith and culture needing an ethical-theological critique, there may be larger points for those who are concerned about how our academic work on such topics is a part of our lives and the lives of others, how thinking and writing these concerns function as interventions in our own lives and in the lives of our readers, and thus of all those influenced by our living.

Indeed, the present analysis of *Soul Searching* raises the ethical question whether the turn to popular practice in religious and theological studies will repeat the habits of the academic life, or whether it will interrupt and refigure those habits. And I mean an interruption and refiguring not just in a change of topics or a refinement of methods, but in our relationship to ourselves as scholars, to each other, and to our work. I mean an exploration of what it means to live the life in which these questions find a home in the first place: what it means to live a theological life, a sociological life, a professorial life.

As has been shown in musical studies of religion and culture, immersion into new performance can change an ethical orientation—as Sharon Welch, Jeremy Begbie, and Robert Beckford, in very different ways, have argued.[61] Asking what performances constellate potential scholarly lives in the study of faith and culture will require an ethics of academic identity, and I suggest that the task includes at least two moves: First, attending to the complexities of the subjectivity of the scholar in the writing and reading—in short, the "study"—of faith and culture, what for myself means accounting for what is already going on in the autobiography of the scholar (including the workings of our psychological and cultural unconsciousnesses) in their relation to what we study.[62] (Rather than recommending one method above others, my present argument is that the ethical question of the composition of the place of the scholar in regard to such studies is a basic exercise that can be approached through a legitimate pluralism of methods.) And second, there will then be the ethical question of changing the functioning of academic life to accommodate this different understanding of scholarship, of a professorial, scholarly, theological, or sociological life. That is, how do we allow what we are learning about our involvement in our scholarship to be read back onto the way that academic life as such functions in our respective institutions? Here, I mean such considerations as learning to think about our motives for doing what we do, about the relationship of academic to everyday life, about academic understandings of religion contrasted with everyday understandings of religion, about the scale of values in academic life compared with the scale of values in our personal lives and the lives of those we study. This question already exists as a broader problem of the ethics of academic practice, a realm identified by ethicist James Keenan as one of two important realms in contemporary Western life where ethical questions have not been posed with the necessary depth and complexity that their work requires. (The other realm is the internal life of the church.)[63]

REFLEXIVITY AS ETHICAL TASK: POP CULTURE ACADEMICS AS FANS—OF THE ACADEMY?

Scholars committed to this problematization of the ethics of scholarship can look to popular culture studies for assistance in talking about the cultural dynamics of formation for advocacy, and attendant developments of forms of governing methods of interpretation, texts, and membership: the subdiscipline of fan studies.

Making fan studies into a reflexive discourse for the work of scholars in faith and culture, that is, raising the question of the ways in which "we academics" are fans of our own disciplines, gives a "nonreligious" language for the problematizing at hand. I suggest a popular cultural analysis of the practices that constitute the study, and studiers, of popular culture. This is to ask not only whether and how academics are fans of the cultures and their sacreds about which we write, but how we are fans of the academic disciplines and practices through which we are subjectified. Such a focus may allow us to read our research not only as a valorization of the freedom of the everyday, or as the effect of social forces exposed by the scholar, or some combination of these ("habitus," "reflexivity," etc.), but to read our work and its constitutive practices as exercises of what could be called academic fandom.

Cultural studies theorist Matt Hills has come to a similar conclusion in his recent synoptic account of fan studies, *Fan Cultures*.[64] Hills makes two points of relevance for present purposes. First, he specifies how fans of media culture, and academics, are often the "others" of each other's discourses. Both communities operate within "imagined subjectivities" over against the other: the academic is rational, committed to argument, adopts a broad-minded view, and has the authority to decode the discourses of others. The fan, by contrast, is intense and passionate, an expert in the minutiae of the frivolous, a fantasizer whose primary associations with like-minded individuals fosters an irrational way of relating, grounded in fetishistic returns to venerated superficial objects. The fan has an immediate relation to pop culture; the academic, a discerning and learned distance. This binary is even kept in place, Hills observes, by well-meaning fan studies in "reception" or "audience" theory that privilege fan creativity and resistance, insofar as the fan becomes theorized as something of an academic without portfolio, decoding media culture with pleasure, just as politically savvy popular culture literate professors imagine themselves doing.

As Hills pays attention to this influential binarity in media and cultural studies, he shows how, within fan cultures, fans do their own kind of theorizing that borrows from, but reworks, academic theorizing, by the way that they practice their relation to each other and to their cultural objects. Fan knowledge is situated within and across binaries: it is consumption as well as resistance, both communal and hierarchical, concerned both with displaying knowledge as well as justifying it, inhabiting worlds of both fantasy and reality, existing as both cult and culture, being both "textual" and "extratextual." By looking at material practices with an awareness of the seductions of binary, moralizing, or valorizing thinking, fan cultures can be appreciated on their own complex and ambiguous terms. They are spaces of contradictory values whose very contradictions are essential to their workings.

Included in Hills' account is a development of the idea of fandom as the personal tending of "secondary transitional objects." Hills works this idea out from his reading of ambiguities in D.W. Winnicott's psychoanalytic account of primary transitional objects. Hills argues that Winnicott allows that primary objects can and must dissipate over time, back into the cultural milieu from which they came (and, Hills, points out with reference to research on consumer culture, may more likely happen when those objects come from a plastic culture of disposability, as does so much of Western youth culture). But "faded" objects do not lose all affective importance in the project of developing a self, Hills observes. Secondary objects are those objects that retain significance less intensely after serving as a primary object, that are less affectively operative and available in the inner life of subjectivity, but not altogether absent. In United States society, childhood toys and television characters, along with pop stars from pubescence, may continue to bear emotional resonance for us and help us constellate our identities. They are more susceptible to being conditioned by culture and its governing powers than are primary objects. Hills' research goes a long way toward dispelling the idea of the fan as needing to be split along a binary: either passive or active, creative or consumptive, childish or mature, and the like. His account shows how these dualities do not need to be valorized on one side or the other but rather that their interplay constitutes the creativity of fan life.

Hills' philosophy of fandom leads him to a suggestion that co-inhabits the ethical space of the present chapter. He recommends that fan studies take up investigations that "look beyond cultural groups which self-identify . . . or which have . . . been described as 'fans'; groups, for example, such as academic subcultures,"[65] the subcultures of the very academics who study fan culture, who focus their scholarly work on the passions of others. I take Hills and myself to be saying something similar: that we join the emerging discourses about "reflexivity" as scholars, and this is even an ethical next step for our fields.[66] I agree with Hills that an "approach to fandom *within* the academy [will] continue to tease out the many ways in which fan attachments, affects, and passions permeate 'academic' work, institutions and the *embodied*, rather than imagined, subjectivities of academia."[67]

There are some difficulties with bringing such an analysis to the way academics relate to their disciplines as fans. On one hand, the emergence of a system of "academic stars," the fetishization of the monograph, and other hallmarks of the hierarchical economies of the "corporate university," offer analogues to the media culture fandoms described in fan studies, and show how academia has innovated an economy of "popular culture" of its own, yet not so different from those who fancy television or video games.[68] On the other hand, academics have been typically inured to thinking of themselves as fans of anything, whether of media culture or of elements of their own academic culture. To allow oneself to be considered a fan is to be assumed to surrender the critical faculties that academic life purportedly works so hard to instill (and the politics of which fan studies in media culture have been so successful at problematizing). Yet this academic resistance might need to give way. As social theorist John B. Thompson has argued, "[B]eing a fan is an altogether ordinary and routine aspect of everyday life," insofar as it "organize[s] one's daily life in such a way that following a certain activity . . . becomes a central preoccupation of the self and serves to govern a significant part of one's activity and interaction with others." As such, fandom is a "way of developing the project of the self through the reflexive incorporation of the symbolic forms associated with fandom."[69]

While there is scarce work on academics as fans of their own academic cultures or disciplines, this is where my present itinerary following the dynamics of research into "other people's faith" has led me. It has made me consider that there may be an unacknowledged, or more strongly, disavowed fandom that the scholar has toward their own discipline, or more likely, of an "object" within it, such as a specific method, field, problem, community of inquiry, or better, a person who can represent any of these. It has already been argued, apart from fan studies, that academics can be usefully understood as defenders of "tribes" and "territories,"[70] and that when we think we are initiating students into our disciplines, we may be playing out an unacknowledged narcissism.[71] These clues to disavowed fandoms in academic life gain greater traction when we appreciate the contingent and contradictory, even "dangerous," character of a very specific scholarly telling of other people's faith like *Soul Searching*.

This approach contrasts with the principle of conscious identification that guides much research in fan studies: that intrinsic to the value of studying fan cultures is that fans own their fandom; that is, that there are people who delight, at various levels of self-awareness, in being "fanatics" about a music group, celebrity, or comic book series, who take pride in their partisanship toward what the rest of society considers quaint, ephemeral, juvenile, or even repulsive. Fan studies and the turn to studies of culture "from below" have typically gone together, with the former being one extension of the latter. But what of academics who are, almost by definition, not given to "fanaticism"? It is just here that I believe inquiry opens onto a space of a disavowed fandom. This fandom will be an attenuated form of the more self-conscious fandoms of popular culture in which the contestation of fan identity is often a part of the constitution of fan identity. Hence, it will not necessarily bear the relative creative richness present in some accounts of fan culture. It must be a fandom by disavowal, because passionate attachments, dwellings in the artificial and mass-produced, pleasure in mere assertions of value, and arguments that primarily justify emotional investments are not phenomena that can typically be publicly allowed in academic spaces. This disavowal will most typically be unconscious, and as "repressed," will likely manifest itself in conceptual contradiction, claims that exceed evidence, and minute enactments of the relationships between knowledge and power that pertain to the discipline in question. There is no need here to choose superficially between, say, "Freud" and "Foucault": This space of disavowal is a convergence of a personal and cultural unconscious: personal because confabulated out of the affections of the scholar's mind in having cathected a scholarly identity out of psychic conflicts rooted in (most often early) life experience, and cultural because the meaningful forms of intellectual experience in the scholar's history and in their scholarly productions will be historically constellated in relations of truth, subjectivity, and power. Such disavowed fandoms in the scholarly life seem inordinately resistant to disentanglement, which is why I prefer to focus on a specific text, in the hope that the specificity of analysis can link up to other such studies of the ethical emplacement of researchers in religion, in aid of ethical theories of academic "motivation" and production—and academic life together.

THE DIFFERENCE A FANDOM CONSCIOUSNESS INTRODUCES

It is possible to give a brief indication of the difference that attention to academic work as a kind of fandom could make with regard to the construction of a study like *Soul Searching*.

We can think of fandom as a kind of caughtness in objects, in the multiple sense of "catching" and "being caught." It is a way of catching cultural objects, in the negative sense of something that has worked its way into oneself: catching a cold, catching a disease; and the positive sense of catching a thrown object, like a ball: aligning oneself with an incoming object, an active kind of receptivity in face of something given. It is also a way of being caught by cultural objects. This has the positive sense of having one's attention arrested, a summons from a surprising entry into our awareness. It also has the negative sense of being dragged along unwillingly and abrasively, in the way a branch is caught in the undercarriage of a car.

Hills' Winnicottian object-relations perspective suggests that objects of fandom are both taken by persons in some measure of freedom to balance off their interior and exterior realities, and also afforded or denominated by the culture in which the person attaches to objects. One could thus see fandom as a way of catching and being caught, in the complexity of registers of "caughtness" noted previously, by objects that promise the working through of consent to lived reality. These objects are "owned" in the "passion" of the fan as striated by the passions available discursively in a cultural setting. We become fans of objects that help us "come to terms," but only with the palette of objects available. This caughtness of our caughtness should lead us into a genealogy of ourselves, which is why theologies of everyday life and sociological inquiries into everyday faith demand both radical critique in and of their claims about, and productions regarding the truth of, "external" reality: society, history, and culture; and "internal" reality: psyche, mind, soul, and conscience. A theology of this sort needs, in other words, both a critical genealogical consciousness and a critical psychoanalytic consciousness. These seem essential for comprehending both the fandoms at work in everyday life and faith, and the (everyday academic) fandoms that inform academic study of these (everyday nonacademic) fandoms.

The band Winger has been part of a wider rock-and-roll *vade mecum* that began in my early adolescence and continues through the present. I have been schooled in, that is, caught in, the ambiguous feelings, images, and performances of power, masculinity, sexuality, and more. The exercise that this music has been for me has been my profoundest aesthetic education, my longest lasting instruction in form, for what my theology can be, as exercise for others. My caughtness in rock seems synchronous with the ambiguity of the Christian theological tradition, a series of "tunes" I am similarly caught within. And just as my twenty plus years of electric bass playing is an attempt to play with, against, and back on the rock soundtrack that animates my everyday life, to take it and leave it by playing with it, so this sort of education which prepared me for a theological life has made me want to have theology be such an exercise for myself, for my readers, for my students. My rock fandom conducts me into a theological fandom (which returns me to rock fandom). Both are objects for change and control, for governance of self and others in ways thoroughly ambiguous, but also sites of promise for training in wisdom.

Admittedly, it is not easy to make the shift from media fan cultures to academic fan cultures. The heterogeneity intrinsic to media "cults"— admitting "no final and absolute classification [because] many new 'media cults' produce further recombinations of family attributes, or even the generation of new 'basic' traits"[72]—ought to caution against a predilection for homogeneity in other fan cultures. Still, some similarities in rhetoric of identity between media fan cultures and the form of research reported in *Soul Searching* opens up ways of thinking about academic work as a kind of fandom.

Soul Searching indicates a fandom whose subjective provenance is difficult to identify, given that the work was written by a primary author (Smith) as well as secondary author (Denton), and was the product of a consultation with dozens of scholars over several years.[73] And in the absence of material that would provide more personal access to the authors, such an approach must be tentative. But given what I have argued, it seems reasonable to suggest that their study exhibits a fannish caughtness in the adequacy of sociology of religion to everyday faith. The method of the study, the truth value of the objective comprehension of young people's faith, so often discussed, defended, and rearticulated in the pages of the book, is a strong candidate for an object of fandom. Such overinvestment in method may, according to sociologist Nancy Ammerman's recent review of research in lived religion, be common. "The concerns of sociologists [of religion] have been shaped both by our theoretical preoccupation with secularization and by the survey methodology that has been our dominant epistemological technology."[74]

This fandom is not without dialectic; as noted, the authors occasionally avow the limits of their method. However, if we take the method as the object of fandom of the authors, the disclosure of their own unadmitted ethical orientation that I have attempted to piece together, their own moralistic therapeutic deism, makes more sense. The sociological approach to religion for which they are fans stands as a "secondary object" through which they are seeking to balance (with who knows how much of "Denton" and how much of "Smith") "internal" drives to moralize (in the judgment of others' practices), to give or receive therapy (in the shoring up of their identities), to struggle with deism (in calibrating God's indifference), and "external" learning of objective methods for measuring everyday belief. Whether "Smith and Denton" were drawn to methods that stabilize young people as the conduits for a new civil religion and as objects for a possible institutional management, or whether the methods employed taught them to understand faith as susceptible to their study, the social-scientific methods employed can be understood as both created and found—a key quality of primary and secondary objects—by them. The basic and even passionate trust in the method, the obligatory rhetorical gestures stating its limits, the shoring up of colleagues who do similar work, the marshaling of a scholarly community to tell and retell the NSYR story from various angles—all of this suggests a fandom at work. We can speculate, and no more than that, that the method both allows and closes off a possible balancing of "interior" and "exterior" for that problematic category of academic production: "the authors."

Intrinsic to fandom in our culture is an obstinacy about the superiority of one's chosen objects.[75] Because the authors cannot imagine themselves, in the writing, as fans, they cannot appreciate fandom as a practice that they have in common with the teens they study. Thus they cannot see "inarticulacy" as having any positive meaning. But seeing teens themselves as fans of belief systems would enrich their analysis. As Hills reminds us, "the ethnographic process of 'asking the audience,' although useful in many cases, constitutes a potentially reductive approach. It assumes that cultural activities can be adequately accounted for in terms of language and 'discourse.'"[76] Indeed, thinking through what we know of fans could illuminate what happened in the *Soul Searching* study: "Addressing the question 'why are you a fan of this particular text?,' it seems that fans typically register some confusion or difficulty in responding, before then falling back immediately on their particular fandom's discursive mantra."[77] We can learn, then, that when researchers ask teens to explain and justify their beliefs, they are constructing an image of a "teen believer" (or "teen unbeliever") that from the outset cannot comprehend the affective complexities of faith, the positive significance for teen life and faith of what looks to scholars like "inarticulacy," and the ways in which teen faith may be registered indirectly through other "nontheological" interests, questions, even fandoms. In other words, if scholars who research faith and culture could think through their own fandoms, this would invite a rethinking of the moralizing categorization of teenage inarticulacy.

Academic fandom does not make Smith and Denton's *Soul Searching* unique; such fandom stands only as a symbol for a process as typical in academic life as it is underappreciated and undertheorized. In Hills' formulation,

> We are, perhaps, *all* "stuck" on something, whether that thing is the dogma of Lacanian lack, sociological anti-subjectivism, Deleuzian philosophy, or the dogma of a specific fandom. I would suggest that it is whether or not our "stuckness" can act as a personal and good enough "third space" for affective play that is significant. . . .[78]

Acknowledging academic fandom is a move against disavowal—of the "other" of academic reasonability as described by Hills, and of the governance of affective investments that induce us into uses of academic power in the interpretation of others. The "disavowal" I mean here is not a narrowly personal, much less intentional, kind of denial. It is a historical and social phenomenon, a way of having been fashioned by the constellation of cultural forces that shape perception in the study of religion in particular and Western academic life in general. It is a living absence in the scholar, "a practice forgotten in its origins and its meaning, but always used and always present,"[79] the mark of the precluding of forms of attention in the history that produced our present academic truths for religious and theological studies. At the same time, it is also a personal kind of denial, in two senses. First, insofar as our academic subjectivities, so bound up with our individual hopes and plans, are given in prespecified histories and cultures, as the critical study of academic life increasingly shows.[80] Second, because many of us in academic life already know better at some level—that we are in more or less active disavowal about our disavowed fandoms, aware that there are unexamined scenes backstage of all our smartest writing and most rigorous thinking, backstage scenes of misrecognized and unfulfilled desire, unrequited and unworthy love, unrecompensed losses, malevolence. In this sense, the fandoms of the scholars are made of personal objects, once known and now mostly disowned, in Matt Hills' Winnicottian sense—objects that may run the gamut from a compelling "Protestantism in sociology of religion" per se,[81] to a relation to an advisor, *Doktorvater*, book, or other person or object who was "transitional" for the scholar. It is the domain specified by overlaying, say, a "Freudian" creative individual repression and a "Foucauldian" historical unconscious.[82]

THEOLOGY'S CONTRIBUTION TO THE ETHICAL QUESTION

Limning the ethical placement of the scholar of faith and culture is one way to bring Christian theology, and its tradition of spiritual exercises, to bear on a multidisciplinary conversation. One relevance of Christian theology for cultural analysis is found in Christianity's already being so deeply embedded in much of Western culture and its popular culture, on one hand, and the potentially "humanizing" contributions that theology can make to multidisciplinary considerations of culture, on the other hand. Giving theology a place at the scholarly table can thus be a recognition of Christian power in all its ambiguities, and an opportunity for theology to test what can be said about reality in face of other people of good will, including sociological colleagues, who have understood something of reality that is far from the minds of theologians.[83] Theological engagements of culture show not only how complicated it is to talk about lived faith in contemporary culture, but these engagements also make themselves visitors in practices, disciplines, and debates they may not recognize, thereby risking their claims to truth in a contemplative kind of traveling-through, learning and shedding along the way. Theologians in cultural studies thus are themselves residents of their own popular culture, and sociologists, religionists, and other scholars make "us" take up many strategies that we find in those we study: resistance, assimilation, refiguring, *bricolage*, experimentation, and beyond.

From the perspective of a concern for spiritual exercises, then, and as a theologian who must inhabit the agonisms of academic subjectivities, I agree with Matt Hills, and have tried to indicate here, that self- and communal examination of our ignored "power relationships," our "others," our "moral dualisms" is an ethical task for scholars who want to speak on behalf of other people's faith. This is not to simplistically try to prize ourselves apart from the ways in which we are fans of our studies, methods, disciplines, networks, or institutions and the cultural practices that place us in these fandoms, but it is to ask us to let through a richer ethical conversation about the cost of the stability of the scholar in our studies, in favor of "academic commitment which is modeled on fan commitment," for "impassioned thought rather than the parroting of academic . . . mantras [and] for an 'affective reflexivity' " which can contemplate our "own fandoms," and the ways we give ourselves as fans to our academic studies.[84] Is it possible that, on this point, theologians may be able to dialogue with other scholars of religion, to not only continue the slow revolution in the turn to the religious every day, but also to make ourselves more worthy of it?[85]

PART FOUR

CHRISTIAN LIFE

7

I Was Imprisoned by Subjectivity and You Visited Me

BONHOEFFER AND FOUCAULT ON THE WAY TO A POSTMODERN CHRISTIAN SELF

INTRODUCTION

One of the most important stakes in the church's mission is what the church encourages or allows young adults in particular, and Catholic adults in general, to think about themselves; how the church teaches that we should interpret our lives and order our relationships with others. Not only is it observable that on such issues ministry to young adults often stands or falls, but it is also the case that the meaning of one's own life and relationship with others is at the very heart of the way of Jesus. Due to the margin of freedom that many young adults, in particular, claim with respect to personal and spiritual development and church affiliation, and given the power that the church can and does attempt to exercise over the lives of adults, a great deal hinges for both on what the church communicates about what is important about adult lives and how we order our relationships with others. What exactly the church should be preaching and practicing about self-identity is a complicated question, both in principle and in the actual situation of many of our churches today. Each of us practicing theology or ministry does so with at least an implicit understanding of what constitutes a Christian self. Fortuitously, and as shown throughout the present volume, subjectivity has come in for serious questioning in much postmodern philosophy and theology. The time is opportune for an intentional reappraisal of how we construe Christian subjectivity.

In service of such a reappraisal, the purpose of this essay is to engage Dietrich Bonhoeffer, by way of Michel Foucault, for the task of reinterpreting the Christian self in our present. The rethinking of subjectivity going on in postmodern theories and theologies affords an opportunity to revisit a classic Christian text, through a postmodern lens, for the sake of gathering up intellectual resources for ministry today. It is not a matter of forcing Bonhoeffer's work to take responsibility for *our* questions or our answers, but rather of culling what is useful for Christian subjectivity today from the Christian tradition.

I come to Bonhoeffer's work, in the words of Michel de Certeau, to "poach" it,[1] to read it for contemporary needs, putting it to use for a theology of the present. Such a project was not foreign to Bonhoeffer, who remarked in an early lecture that out of "love for this contemporary world of ours, [e]very word is to be spoken out of the present for the present."[2] This poaching delimits my task in giving to our understanding of a theology of the cultures of younger generations further tools in service of what Foucault called the "undefined work of freedom."[3] Thus, when an idea struck me as useful in Bonhoeffer's work, I adopted his fiancée Maria von Wedemeyer's tactic: "I purloined it and bore it off."[4] My style of interpreting Bonhoeffer is also a matter of honoring a chief characteristic of Bonhoeffer's own theological style, of which Eberhard Bethge has written, "Bonhoeffer did not let himself be deterred from applying his subjective contemporary experience to an eclectic examination of texts."[5]

I admit a certain hesitation in writing about Bonhoeffer, first, as a Roman Catholic and, second, as decidedly not a "Bonhoeffer scholar." Can anything new be said of this man, or can anything said of old be deployed for a new freedom? My task here is to ask, with respect to an ethic of the self, not what Bonhoeffer himself necessarily saw. Instead, it is to ask what his work allows us to see today. There can be no question here of an attempt at comprehensiveness with respect to Bonhoeffer's *oeuvre.* Although it is important to associate my question within ever-widening circles of his other works, of interpretations of the Christianity of his day, of interpretations of the self in the traditions to which he was heir, none of these tasks can be accomplished here. At the risk of parochialism, I shall restrict myself as much as possible to the prison letters, fixing their coordinates for this question as an initial movement in a larger project for a postmodern theological attention to subjectivity.

One challenge of this topic is that its evidence is scattered like so much chad over the gaps, repetitions, miscommunications, and interruptions intrinsic to letter writing. Some sort of tentative whole must be made, risking Theodor Adorno's warning that "the whole is the false."[6] Threads joining fragments together will have to be sewn into the text, and artificial limbs affixed. While this is true of an interpretation of any text, it is more readily evidenced in a project such as this. I shall begin with Foucault to furnish a running start into Bonhoeffer: sketching the self in Foucault, looking at the self in Bonhoeffer's letters, and drawing implications for theology and ministry today. In this way, I hope to develop one small piece of the groundwork of a problematic that will serve the church's mission to young adults.

THE SELF IN FOUCAULT

One of the most fruitful construals of the self in "postmodern" philosophy has come from Michel Foucault. Instead of surveying his work, I shall attempt here to merely introduce the logic of one strand of his thought about the self. This work attempts to demonstrate and provoke critical thought about the meaning of subjectivity. Foucault privileges a rigorously historical approach that seeks to remove subjectivity from the realm of the natural, the transcendental, and the ahistorical, and strives to demarcate the historicity of subjectivity itself. In principle, this is not an inscrutable method of inquiry: honesty in the face of historical consciousness would demand that we observe that people in different times and places have understood themselves, and what it is about themselves that they share with other human beings, quite differently; they have valued very different qualities about themselves; they have appealed to a wide range of authorities to interpret themselves; they have imagined in very different ways what it means to say "I," indeed have innovated very different terms to refer to the entity who is the author of his or her actions. Even today, what it means to be or to have a "self" manifests quite significant variations according to one's geographic place, economic situation, race, sex, gender, and educational background.

One distinguishing characteristic of Foucault's approach is that he refuses to unite the differences present in the history of subjectivity through an appeal to a transcendental subjectivity, on the one hand, or through privileging the modern, Western, "enlightened," individual, rational Christian self as the summit of selfhood, on the other. The latter is one particular historical configuration of subjectivity whose superiority to other historical periods or places cannot be assumed. Who are we *today,* and how is it exactly that we have come to know who we are? Do we dare to historicize not only our political structures, cultural forms, and religions, but our very selves? For the sake of our own freedom, Foucault says, we must do so, else we are bound to the histories of our subjectivity, instead of taking up a critical relation to ourselves through confronting the history of selfhood. Once this line of inquiry is opened, a flood of questions is released, and the attempt to think critically about subjectivity necessitates not only a rigorous historicity, but an inquiry into the subtle functioning of power and knowledge in that historicity: How does the modern Western self come to recognize itself *as* a self, or to be recognized as a self by our cultural authorities? When we recognize ourselves as subjects, what is it exactly that we are recognizing or knowing about ourselves, and what was the historical process that created the conditions for such a recognition or knowledge? What exclusions were enacted in that very historical process? What options and possibilities for relating to ourselves have been denied in order to secure the history of the subjects that we are today?

In the West today, we call upon experiential categories of subjectivity readily familiar to the formally educated classes, allowed us by forced structurations of reality that Foucault called discourses, propagated through specific ensembles of practices. For example, many of us are positioned to recognize ourselves in the terms of a certain constellation of psychological discourses (e.g., as a hothouse of unfinished childhood business and secret sexual desires; as a Myers-Briggs classification such as "INTJ"); in Christian religious discourses (e.g., as sinful, graced, saved, lost; concepts even former Christians or people who have never been Christian employ); in sex and gender discourses (e.g., as masculine, feminine, gay, lesbian, bisexual, transgendered, straight); in racial discourses (e.g., as European, African American, Hispanic/Latino, Indian, Asian); and in economic discourses (e.g., as productive or unproductive; heard in the common undergraduate wonderment, "What will I do with my college degree?" or "My dad says a religious studies degree is not worthy of his $150,000 for my college education."). The way we live or practice each of these ingredients of Western subjectivity is bound up with authorities that have power to tell us the truth about ourselves.

It is precisely those qualities that we take to be most natural about ourselves that Foucault placed radically into question as historically constituted. It is those aspects of being a self that we think are transcendentally given or ahistorical that Foucault unearthed and whose history he wanted to trace. At the points at which we are most certain about our identities, Foucault wants to ask how, why, and at what cost that point of assurance came to be associated with truth and that truth with subjectivity. He suspends "human nature" in quotation marks. He forces the daunting question about the medical, psychological, economic, theological, and pedagogical "discourses" in which our understandings of ourselves are implicated.

In this approach to subjectivity, no aspect of modern selfhood gets a free pass. If the glory of modernity was its celebration of the progress of a scientific understanding of the world and the self, the Foucauldian logic struggles to recover the secret imprisonments that are the untold history not only of our past but of our present. In Foucault's studies, he did this by attending to the creation of new dimensions of the self in modernity associated with truth: insanity, criminality, and sexual identity. "The 'Enlightenment,' which discovered the *liberties*, also invented the *disciplines*."[7] It is characteristic of his work that Foucault refuses to disassociate the former from the latter. Psychology, religion, sexuality, and medicine all have both freed *and* imprisoned us in new categories of self-definition. This logic of subjectivity redirects our thought about ourselves: What new forms of thought are occluded by our contemporary understandings of the difference between reason and unreason? What economic or social order benefits from the institutionalization of a class of people called criminals? What pleasures and forms of relationship to oneself and others are denied us by the rigidity of modern confessions of sexual identity? In short, what freedoms are denied to human self-creation by accepting as natural, given, and freeing, the aspects of self that are themselves historically constituted and continually reinforced in our lives? Foucauldian thought forces us to begin to confront the vertigo of the radically historical character of our identities. The purpose of this logic is twofold: first, to refuse the contingent and historical limits on what we can be, limits that are reinforced by institutions and traditions that benefit from fixing one historical configuration of the self as the eternal or natural self; second, to create new ways of practicing ourselves, of more varied and creative freedoms in our present.

The critical interrogation of how we have come to be ourselves is the task of what Foucault understands by ethics. The most basic question of ethics for Foucault is what relation do we take up to ourselves—a relation to self both under the control of external forces and under our own authority. How do we come to know the truth of ourselves? What are the practices by which we constitute ourselves as the subjects of our own moral action, our own thinking and doing?

To analyze one's relationship to oneself, Foucault breaks this relationship into four primary dimensions.[8] First is the "ethical substance," that area of oneself that is understood to be the relevant domain for ethical judgment. Second is "the self-forming activity," or "ascetics." This is work that you do on yourself to turn yourself into an ethical subject. Third is the "mode of subjection." This is the way in which the person sets up their relationship to a particular moral code or rule of conduct. Fourth is the "telos." This is the endpoint of ethical work, the mode of being at which one is aiming. Searching out the content of these four aspects, and the way they relate to one another—in any particular place and time—discloses how the self is constituted in that place and time. Ethics, in sum, critically examines how the self relates to itself, how the self participates in

> a process in which the individual delimits that part of himself that will form the object of his moral practice, defines his position relative to the precept he will follow, and decides on a certain mode of being that will serve as his moral goal. And this requires him to act upon himself, to monitor, test, improve and transform himself.[9]

It would be a mistake to think of Foucault's work as simply antimodern or anti-Enlightenment. The degree to which he prizes human freedom and makes use of, while reformulating, tools of historical consciousness and critical theory block such a judgment. Late in his life, he associated his work with a new stage of the Kantian project—not repudiating but reformulating Kant. As James Bernauer argues, Foucault took Kant's three great questions and inverted them by "denaturalizing" and "historicizing" them:

> Not "What can I know?" but rather, "How have my questions been produced? How has the path of my knowing been determined?" Not

> "What ought I to do?," but rather, "How have I been situated to experience the real? How have exclusions operated in delineating the realm of obligation for me?" Not "What may I hope for?," but rather, "What are the struggles in which I am engaged? How have the parameters for my aspirations been defined?"[10]

Foucault's work challenges us to ask how we take up new relationships to ourselves, and so to others, that rely on less dominative strategies, that give over less of our bodies, intellects, and freedom to institutions, traditions, and governments that do not serve the critical practices of human flourishing. What relations to ourselves remain to be created?

In service of these questions, he called for a new aesthetics of the self, new "technologies of self" that

> permit individuals to effect by their own means or with the help of others a certain number of operations on their own bodies and souls, thoughts, conduct, and way of being, so as to transform themselves in order to attain a certain state of happiness, purity, wisdom, perfection, or immortality.[11]

Technologies of self are intermeshed with technologies of power. The latter seek to distort subjectivity by setting up relations of domination to oneself and to others, through a violence of psycho-socio-spiritual restraint or coercion that rarely reaches the level of explicit physical compulsion. Foucault enumerated technologies of power as varied as medical-psychological-scientific discourses, pedagogical institutions, religious traditions, and penal systems. Technologies of power, for all their heterogeneity, share the common strategy of an attempted control over the actual and potential freedom of the subject to realize his or her own capacities. Technologies of self are acts of power over one's relation to oneself and others; power is not something to be either accepted or rejected for Foucault. It is to be used to expand the margin of freedom for oneself and others, while at the same time holding permanently open the final meaning and content of that freedom.

The technologies of power by disciplines, traditions, and institutions often attempt to govern us and our relation to ourselves in the name of liberation: liberation of our essence, our identity, our interior, our secrets, our sex, and our soul. Through our participation in their discourses of liberation, they instill in us a "positive" content of self-knowledge that binds us to discourses, practices, institutions, and histories that compromise, restrict, and domesticate the possibilities of freedom. Foucault's notion of technology presses the question: how did we come to identify with the truth of ourselves, and how did that truth come to be identified with a particular biological, sexual, therapeutic, moral, or religious content?[12] Who or what produced this within us?[13]

I find Foucault's notion of ethics as relation to self helpful for the ways it provides conceptual tools in service of problematizing human liberation, and thus as a significant apparatus for Christian theology. It views subjectivity as a historically particular technology, enmeshed in competing discourses of power and knowledge. The technology of self is not an ahistorical idea of oneself but a set of practices of relating to oneself and others, practices that are dangerous because they have been shaped by institutions and traditions that not only form but also deform the self. It is necessary, precisely on Christian grounds, to rigorously examine Christian technologies of power and to elaborate more adequate Christian technologies of self. One approach to elaborating such an argument can, I believe, be derived from Bonhoeffer's prison letters.

Theology and ministry need to develop Christian technologies of self to contest technologies of power operative inside the church and in the larger culture. In Christian ministry and in the larger culture, technologies of power can be particularly pernicious and destructive, because they are so immersed in regimes of knowledge about the self they are reinforced by pastoral and institutional power—so often today deployed under various banners of liberation. I have in mind here medical-psychological-sexual discourses about the truth of human identity, and religio-economic discourses about the identity of the Christian vis-à-vis the larger economic and political structures of society. More specifically, I have in mind: the way the church deploys shame and guilt, healing, and reconciliation, and confession; what the church preaches and models about taking up a relationship to the prevalent economic and political structures of one's time; in short, the various forms of normalization attempted by the church: over the proper form of one's relationships and family, over the way one relates to "culture," over the proper disposition of one's soul, over the proper value and use of one's money.

How will our Christian traditions think through the ways they may help to free younger generations through specifically Christian technologies of self for our present? We may look to Christians who dared to develop new technologies of the self. It is here that Bonhoeffer is a companion.

THE SELF IN BONHOEFFER'S *LETTERS AND PAPERS*

I am turning to Bonhoeffer's prison letters because I am interested in testing their adequacy as a theological resource for a new generation, and because they record an intensified relation to self from a man whose life struggle was the Christian meaning of freedom. As I read the prison letters, I see a man who had the courage to take up a new relationship to himself in prison out of his desire to practice a more deeply freeing Christian life. I hope not only to show this, but also to indicate that he trod some ground that his twenty-first century readers may productively retill, for the sake of contesting the technologies of power today. In retrieving a classic Christian resource, my presumption is that theology constantly reinterprets, reuses, ruses, its own past in seeking to answer problems of the present situation.

One must read the letters carefully for traces of Bonhoeffer's changing relation to himself and its theological overtones. He does not announce it through a bullhorn; nor was it part of his family's tradition to speak openly and easily of intimate matters. Such a fact should remind us that his relation to himself in prison was embedded in the history of the life he had led up to 1943. While one may establish certain lines of continuity between his academic work and his prison life, this is no easy task, because the letters themselves contain varying degrees of self-revelation. Due among other things to the demands of the censor, or rather many censors, internal and external, they include both disclosure and concealment, revelation and deception.[14] This is a first clue to the nature of these texts: they always threaten to trick the reader, disavowing their originary referent in a lonely solitary prison cell. As skillful a letter writer as he was a musician, his correspondence is full of musical tricks: he often merely suggests the resolution of chords, modulates unexpectedly, de-tunes in the midst of performance. In the letters, he mutes the notes. We are not like the guards to whom Bonhoeffer entrusts the letters; averting our eyes because they were not written for us. We are more like the censors passing his letters under our scrutinizing eyes; yet they still were not written for us. We read them as through a telescope backwards: the deceptively wide optic yielding only a very tiny window onto the one who is practicing himself in prison. Though the most consistently frank letters seem to be written to his friend Eberhard Bethge and less often to his fiancée Maria von Wedemeyer, this should not keep us from reading all the letters for clues about our question. They lead us to an incarcerated "*ratio*—a way of thinking invested in a way of acting."[15]

They are fragmentary; they are incomplete; often, they are mere undated phrases. There are a variety of literary forms within them. We must stitch them together if we are to take them from two to three dimensions, from text to sculpture. I offer, then, a provisional thesis: Bonhoeffer's letters reveal fragments for a Christian technology of self funding an apophatic relation to self. I shall attempt to gather those fragments in what follows.

His prison correspondence reveals fundamental dimensions of his practice of self. These include what we might call various "techniques" by which he constructed a relation to himself. These techniques include (1) giving himself to feelings of existential separation; (2) acknowledging a felt indebtedness to others; (3) practicing an active memory with regard to his own history; and (4) finding solidarity with the sufferings of others and with his own suffering. These four techniques are central to his relation to himself in the letters. I shall give brief examples of each.

First Technique: Releasement to Feelings of Existential Separation

In the letters we see scattered notes that regard the "experience of time as experience of separation." He then mentions several separations, from God and from marriage, and from the past and the future.[16] The pain of separation from best friend Eberhard and fiancée Maria in particular was ever-present to him. The contiguity of meditations on time as separation and an anticipatory sense of death may suggest that the relationship he took up to himself in prison was experienced as a slow separation from life, a proleptic death, a radical palpable timeliness about his life both threatened and borne by an impinging timelessness. "Flight before the experience of time in dreams . . . future, timeless," he muses.[17] Projecting his present into a definitive end to this life was already evident when he had written on the verge of prison that "fundamentally we feel that we really belong to death already, and that every new day is a miracle."[18] And in some undated prison notes, we find a fragment that reads "suicide, not because of consciousness of guilt but because basically I am already dead."[19]

Second Technique: Acknowledging a Felt Indebtedness to Others

In prison he admits that he is "so completely dependent on other people."[20] For the necessities of protection, food, and health care, such as it was, he relies on the prison staff. For the "luxury" items of books, paper, clean clothes, and extra food he is utterly dependent on his family and friends. As a result, he showed great gratitude for visitors. In one letter he christologizes such experiences through Matthew 25:36, "I was in prison and you visited me."[21] He relates that Luke 17:11–17, "about gratitude—is one of those which I love and treasure most."[22]

For an *eros* newly discovered, thrown roughly into sharp relief by an engagement experienced in separation, he relies on Maria. "I rejoice at every word from her. . . . Seeing Maria—an indescribable surprise and joy."[23]

> That I need not torment myself when thinking of you, that my longing to be with you need not distress me in any way, but that I can think of you and long for you with quiet confidence and joy—that is what I owe to you. . . .[24]

For the most life-giving of his writing relationships, to Eberhard, he is completely reliant on guards to smuggle the letters back and forth. Though it is a challenge to his independence, he gives himself to this dependence, and as I will indicate later, thinks theologically through this experience.

Third Technique: Practicing Active Memory Regarding His Own History

He writes of the utter "need to bring before me my own past" in the face of a "situation that could so easily seem 'empty' and 'wasted.'"[25] In another letter he writes that "I am forced to live from the past."[26] This bringing before him his own past was a recollection of spiritual trials, musical pleasures, personal relationships, and travels—even the significance of an attraction to a woman in his twenties that he reveals to Wedemeyer as "part of the story of my life."[27] This technique became quite prominent in his regular routine. He writes that a "*dialogue* with the past, the attempt to *hold on* to it and *recover* it, and above all, the fear of *losing* it, is the almost daily accompaniment of my life here."[28] This dialogue occurred through writing letters, plays, poetry, and fiction, enabling him to regularly reintroduce himself to his own history, to the facticity of a past, we could even say: to take up a relationship to his own concrete history of sin and grace,[29] to associate the meaning of his life in the present with a constant retilling of that history, and in attention to his history of grace, to find reasons to hope for a graceful future. (In this, he shares a strong similarity on the importance of memory with his contemporary, who served in the German army during World War II, the Roman Catholic theologian Johannes Baptist Metz.) Bonhoeffer dedicates a whole poem to the image of his relationship to his past as one constantly threatened by the inability to retrieve it; it is restored by God in prayer as a history of forgiveness and grace.[30]

Fourth Technique: Finding Solidarity with His Own and Others' Suffering

His knowledge of himself is given in part by his experience of solidarity with the concrete suffering of fellow prisoners.[31] His "Report on Experiences During Alerts" is one example.[32] In it he details the inadequacies of the prison in dealing with the psychological and physical needs of prisoners during and after bombing attacks. And in an aside to Bethge, "My cell is being cleaned out for me, and while it's being done, I can give the cleaner something to eat."[33] He wrote angrily of the harsh guards who were "petty tormentors . . . unjustly shout[ing] at and insult[ing]" prisoners. In response, he remarks that "two or three times I've given [the guards] a quite colossal dressing down. . . ."[34] He was also confronted with his own significant suffering, including rheumatism, influenza, and stomach problems: "A short time ago my rheumatism was so bad that for a few hours I couldn't get up from my chair without help, or even lift my hands to feed myself."[35] In his "Who Am I?" poem, he writes of himself as

> restless and longing and sick . . . struggling for breath . . . yearning for colours . . . trembling with anger at despotisms and petty humiliation . . . weary and empty at praying, at thinking, at making, / faint, and ready to say farewell to it all.[36]

Even though he downplays his suffering to almost everyone else, he admits it to Bethge on December 15, 1943:

> in spite of everything that I've written so far, things here are revolting, [and] my grim experiences often pursue me into the night and that I can shake them off only by reciting one hymn after another, [and] I'm apt to wake up with a sigh rather than with a hymn of praise to God . . . everything I see and hear is putting years on me, and I'm often finding the world nauseating and burdensome.[37]

It is difficult to speak clearly of Bonhoeffer's acceptance of, or "solidarity with," his own suffering due to the fact that he reveals it rarely, and then only to Eberhard Bethge or to Maria von Wedemeyer. He disliked others focusing on it,[38] and he advocated "taking seriously, not our own sufferings, but those of God in the world. . . ."[39] However, an acknowledgement of his own suffering does appear in the same letter in which a fragment for a new technology of self appears, as I will note in a moment, allowing us to associate it with his practice of self.

AN APOPHATIC SELF

Having briefly suggested four concrete techniques that fed Bonhoeffer's relation to himself, I shall argue that what we see in the letters from prison is the emergence, through these techniques, of an apophatic self. This apophatic self is, in short, a christomorphic separation from, or suspension of, all positive contents of the self.

One way in comes from a provocative reference to his understanding of himself, from the December 15, 1943 letter just referenced.

> I often wonder who I really am . . . I know less than ever about myself, and I'm no longer attaching any importance to it. . . . There is something more at stake than self-knowledge.[40]

In the famous poem "Who Am I?" that he sent to Bethge on July 8, 1944, Bonhoeffer renders poetically the vertigo of his self-identity:

> Who am I? This or the other?
> Am I one person today, and tomorrow another?
> Am I both at once? A hypocrite before others,
> and before myself a contemptibly woebegone weakling?
> Or is something within me still like a beaten army,
> fleeing in disorder from victory already achieved?
> Who am I? They mock me, these lonely questions of mine.
> Whoever I am, thou knowest, O God, I am thine.[41]

What are we to do with these striking passages, which suggest an agnosticism, even an apophaticism, about the self? How did he get from these four techniques to this understanding of himself? While there can be no question of certainty here, our inquiry must become constructive, joining together the scraps of paper from the four techniques: feeling of separation, acknowledgement of indebtedness, acceptance of one's history, and risking solidarity with the suffering. I offer three theses.

First thesis: *These four techniques may be read as funding a christomorphic practice of self.* In Bonhoeffer's letters, self-knowledge seems to be a sort of *poiesis*. It is an active care for the suffering of others that, in the very practice of it, produces two effects. The first effect is an experience of history-death-separation in the disorientation to the world produced by suffering; and a giving of that suffering to be shared with another, not interpreted for them in that moment of suffering. The second effect is that the self takes on the irreducible vertigo of the suffering of another as its very own; this vertiginous helplessness introduces a rupture into one's subjectivity, opening a new groundlessness by binding self-identity to the experience of that suffering.

Francis Schüssler Fiorenza calls suffering an experience at the "seam of interpretation."[42] That is to say, it is a human experience resistant to hermeneutical analysis. Suffering's meaning cannot be exhausted in the grids of hermeneutics, does not yield up a final "meaning," however much it is influenced by cultural norms. We each suffer "in single file,"[43] in a way that relies on a certain interpretation given to experience while breaking every stranglehold of hermeneutics in the pure givenness of pain.

For Bonhoeffer, in the binding of self-identity to the vertiginous helplessness of the suffering other, the self is taken, ever more, to a dissolution of self-apprehension, and in this very movement, recognizes in Jesus the limit and condition of all authentic self-relation because Jesus is the limit and condition of all authentic other-relation. "The center of our own lives is outside ourselves":[44] a statement lived so definitively by Jesus is provoked, in the letter of September 5, 1943, by Bonhoeffer's experience of losing students or colleagues to the war. This center that is outside ourselves was also provoked concretely in Bonhoeffer's reflection about his reliance on others, in particular on Eberhard Bethge: "What we owe to others belongs to ourselves and is a part of our own lives."[45] We allow our indebtedness and our solidarity to hollow out whatever has been placing itself at the center of our lives by recentering us continually beyond ourselves.

Second thesis: *This christomorphic practice of self yields fragments of an apophatics of self.*[46] "I know less than ever about myself. . . . There is something more at stake than self-knowledge."[47] A technology of self that manifests the incarnation must point to its own dissolution in a constant displacement of the truth of oneself. This construal of a historically contingent, precariously free self may in the terms of Bonhoeffer's letters be understood as a "penultimate" self. "One cannot and must not speak the last word before the last but one. We *live in* the last but one and *believe* the last. . . ."[48] The penultimate self hopes and trusts, through the action of discipleship, that a christomorphic self, in which the truth of one's self is released to crucifixion, will be endorsed by God, and indeed already has been insofar as this has happened in the technology of self lived by the incarnate Word. On this reading, this is why we may "seek the past . . . only with God."[49] In meditating on Eccles 3:1, Bonhoeffer writes to Bethge that "nothing that is past is lost, that God gathers up again with us our past, which belongs to us."[50] God in Jesus is the God who is experienced in the commitment to the history that is our first and only domain for fullness of Christian life. That is, only the God manifest in the self-dispersing, concretely historical, alienated, indebted, solidaritied Jesus "guarantees"—eschatologically—the coherence-in-incoherence of the christomorphic self that releases itself to the vertigo of concrete risk, to defining itself by unpopular, inglorious service of causes that defy every definition of success imposed by contemporary technologies of power in church or culture.

The fragments of an apophatic self in historical action and through our very historicity are also present in another form. On July 8, 1944, Bonhoeffer writes a few pages to Bethge that open a line of criticism against "religious blackmail." Several aspects are important here. First, Bonhoeffer criticizes a tendency of ministers (and theologians) in modernity to locate God in ever more remote recesses of human interiority. The "range of [one's] intimate life . . . [has] become the hunting-ground of modern pastoral workers."[51] Second, these regions of interiority may not be "natural," but historical productions. Bonhoeffer briefly intimates his thinking here, suggesting that "the discovery of the so-called inner life dates from the Renaissance, probably from Petrarch."[52] This discovery, in his opinion, is abetted somewhat insidiously by existential philosophy and psychotherapy.[53] To all this he contrasts what he calls a biblical conception of the whole person, not easily separable into an inner and outer life. Here Bonhoeffer uses this concept of the whole person to block any attempt to elevate an historical region of inquiry into an essential aspect of human self-identity. He did not take the next step and suspend the notion of the whole person in historical quotation marks, or examine the varieties of whole persons in the scripture or Christian tradition. Yet the fragment here is provocative enough to gather up for postmodern Christian selfhood.[54]

One of Bonhoeffer's most-cited scripture particles in the letters is Jeremiah 45:5. Pressed under the weight of this apophatic reading of the christomorphic self, we may read a new imprint on the letters in this verse, translated in the standard English edition of *Letters and Papers* as "I will give you your life as a prize of war." In the letter to Bethge of February 23, 1944, Bonhoeffer returns to it after a discussion of the fragmentary quality of the life of his generation. His reflections recall the penultimate self culled from his letters earlier, but add a new note. When one confronts the partial and incomplete nature of almost every aspect of existence, Bonhoeffer seems to say, in the final analysis only God can make of these fragments something that may definitively and irreversibly be called "a life." The only task then is to gather up diverse experiences and render them as an aesthetic work through human living, "accumulat[ing] . . . a wealth of themes and weld[ing] them into a harmony in which the great counterpoint is maintained from start to finish."[55] He imagines our lives as Bachian "Arts of Fugue." Styled by each of us, from fragmentary experience, into our best effort at holism. The blessing of such an aesthetic momentum is a divine gift, a life of fragments beautifully rendered whose "completion can only be a matter for God."[56] Thus Jeremiah 45:5 can be read as God's final blessing on this life of fragments straining toward harmony in a daring exercise of human freedom. Out of the great contestation of human subjectivity disseminated by historical vertigo, God gives "a life," finally, a coherent and eternally satisfying relation to oneself and to God, as a prize from this "war" for subjectivity. (Here we see interesting parallels between Bonhoeffer's *Art of Fugue*-ish fragmentary self, and Foucault's turn to an ethics as aesthetics of existence, in which the self must take responsibility for its own self-fashioning.) Knowing this, according to Bonhoeffer, allows us "not [to] bemoan the fragmentariness of our life, but rather rejoice in it."[57]

Thus, we have gained a vantage point from which to interpret the fact that at the summit of his radical thinking in the summer of 1944, Bonhoeffer declares his ignorance about his identity. His "Who Am I?" poem,[58] on this reading, is not an aberration or a failure of nerve, not a momentary psychological crisis rendered poetically. It is instead an intermediate stage in a battle against technologies of power—namely the state and the state church—that sought to domesticate the freedom of Christian selfhood. The battle did not reach a conclusive stage before his death; its skirmishes are scattered throughout his letters. In the end, there is indeed "something more at stake than self-knowledge"—in the poem's last line, "*Whoever* I am, thou knowest, O God, I am thine."[59] This poem is Bonhoeffer's rewriting of his cell in Tegel as the Garden of Gethsemane. The outwardly strong man for others reduced to absolute self-doubt, crowned with internal division, mocked by his own uncertainty, stripped of self-presence. The Garden is the ultimate penultimate, where decision in the struggle for the center of one's life must be made. The Garden is the intensification of the everyday Christian self-fashioning that struggles to release itself to accept a life as a prize of war, risking an apophatics of existence.

The "Who am I?" poem is the implicit correlate of the question Bonhoeffer raised a few months earlier, about "Who Christ really is, for us today."[60] "Who is Christ today?" and "Who am I today?" are bound together for the Christian in his letters. Indeed, the last fragment to consider in this apophatic christomorphism is the possibility of an anthropological analogue for the famous notion of "religionless Christianity."[61] We could call such an analogue "humanismless humanity." It may be that one cannot have the former without the latter. For like the state, "Christian religion" can impose intolerable technologies of the self. Indeed, the question of a radically historicized subject lurks throughout the famous April 30, 1944, letter. Bonhoeffer wonders whether a human "religious a priori" is not itself a historically contingent aspect of human experience—and not a transcendental given of human identity. Doing "without religion" means "without the temporally conditioned presuppositions of metaphysics, inwardness, and so on."[62] Here we may see a glimpse of his rethinking of Christianity rooted in his practice of an apophatic self—of seeing the necessity of displacing and reconstructing his own relationship to himself. A "humanismless humanity" bonded to a "religionless Christianity," both animated by the principle of the radically historically particular character of the incarnation, and its manifestation in history-cross-death-separation-solidarity. An apophatic trajectory, "inwardly revert[ing] to the simplest aspects of existence,"[63] and risking even those.

Third, *these fragments of an apophatic christomorphism fund a Christian technology of self, contesting our contemporary technologies of power.* What is at issue in a contemporary reading of Bonhoeffer's fragments as an apophatic christomorphism is the mutual imbrications of the incarnation and postmodern subjectivity.

Bonhoeffer's letters show how the incarnation becomes practicable through a certain technology of self. For these texts, a Christian technology of self is a refusal of reified subjectivity, a willingness to leave a blank there, to not know, and a solidarity with those in need, a "being caught up into the messianic sufferings of God in Jesus Christ," or a "participation in the powerlessness of God in the world."[64] This Christian technology of the self posits a relation to self that always passes through separation, historicity, indebtedness, and solidarity. "Drinking this world to the dregs," in Bonhoeffer's choice phrase, is the rigorous displacement of any transcendental subjectivity that refuses transfiguration through a cruciform anthropology. "One must completely abandon any attempt to make something of oneself."[65] Who am I? I cannot and must not render a definitive answer that evades my responsibility for the demand that I can and must render a present action. This Christian technology of self joins a rigorous ecstatic apophatics of self to concrete and historical solidarity with those in pain.

These fragments from the letters give us a sense of what a Christian technology of self might look like, with respect to the four dimensions given by Foucault: (1) First is the "ethical substance," that area of oneself that is understood to be the relevant domain for ethical judgment. In these texts this ethical substance is the direction one gives to a capacity for self-commitment. (2) Second is "the self-forming activity," or "ascetics." This is work that one does on oneself to turn oneself into an ethical subject. These are the techniques of feeling separation and acknowledging indebtedness, accepting one's concrete and absolutely specific history through the practice of memory, and risking solidarity. (3) Third is the "mode of subjection." This is the way in which the subject sets up their relationship to a particular moral code or rule of conduct. The subject here seeks to make of these techniques a *habitus* as both end and means. (4) Fourth is the "telos." This is the endpoint of ethical work, the mode of being at which one is aiming: In these fragments, the subject is guided by the releasement of self to a center to one's existence that it cannot control, because it does not lie within the subject, and so the subject is released to discover a being claimed: ". . . participation in the sufferings of God in the secular life . . . being caught up into the way of Jesus Christ, into the messianic event. . . ."[66] Redemption lies in fashioning this christomorphic relation to self, the practice of displacing every idol that stakes a claim to tell the truth about the center of one's life.

To be sure, Bonhoeffer wrote "To be a Christian does not mean to *make something of oneself* . . . on the basis of some method or other, but to be a [human], not a type of [human], but the [human] that Christ creates in us."[67] Knowledge of truth and knowledge of self is a dialectical, relational praxis. Only by fully living in one's present, with a full-bodied "yes" to it, controlled by solidarity with those suffering in that present, does one say yes performatively to Jesus. And only in the redemptively and concretely historically suffering Jesus, for Bonhoeffer's letters, can that "yes" be practiced Christianly with a believable hope. The relation to self whose fragments I am gathering here, that I am also calling a work of poiesis, is not a narcissistic or undialectical "making something of oneself," as if we self-sufficiently create ourselves. It is, however, a self-fashioning, insofar as it is a relationship one takes up to Christ through one's releasement from oneself in the practice of the four techniques. It is a spiritual exercise.[68]

FOUCAULT AND BONHOEFFER: SUMMATION

These fragments from Bonhoeffer bear an isomorphism to Foucault's own thinking about the self after his study of early Christian practices of the self. This isomorphism helps us see these Bonhoefferian fragments as more than isolated wisps of radical Christian thought, but associated with an ancient Christian tradition of relation to, precisely through renunciation of, self.

Foucault argued that the early church encouraged a "publication" of oneself: the self becomes public as a sinner. Christianity imposes a "truth obligation," namely that "each person has the duty to know who he is,"

> that is, to try to know what is happening inside him, to acknowledge faults, to recognize temptations, to locate desires, and everyone is obliged to disclose these things either to God or to others in the community and hence to bear public or private witness against oneself.[69]

This publication, the "demonstration of [one's] particular truth,"[70] is not originally confession as the church later knew it, although it does continue into confessional practices. It is "the dramatic recognition of one's status as a penitent."[71]

Penitence becomes an early Christian technology of self: The penitent is "the aggregate of manifested penitential behavior, or self-punishment as well as of self-revelation. The acts by which he punishes himself are indistinguishable from the acts by which he reveals himself."[72] This publication of self is "not a way for the sinner to explain his sins but a way to present himself as a sinner."[73] It is an "everyday death" that is the effect of a unique Christian "relation of oneself to oneself."[74] There is a "permanent hermeneutics of oneself"[75] for early Christianity—a deciphering of one's soul that is a continual attempt to interpret oneself for the ways one is held hostage to sin. The Christian self is a text dense and legible.

This hermeneutics of the self is for the sake of a repudiation of oneself. In this experience, there was no discourse of truth to guide one didactically.

Instead, there was self-presentation to the bishop or community. One manifested penitence to *repudiate* oneself, *not* to get at a positive anthropology of oneself. "Penitence of sin doesn't have as its target the establishing of an identity but serves instead to mark the refusal of the self, the breaking away from self. . . . It represents a break with one's past identity. . . . Self-revelation is at the same time self-destruction."[76] The truth of the self is manifest in the ritual martyrdom of penitence. In the words of James Bernauer, for early Christianity,

> all truth about the self is tied to the sacrifice of that same self[,] and the Christian experience of subjectivity declares itself most clearly in the sounds of a rupture with oneself, of an admission that "I am not who I am."[77]

Mark Vernon argues that these words are "not only the historical declaration of the neophyte emerging from the waters of death in baptism to new life, but [are] the core of a contemporary Foucauldian ethic."[78] Do we not also hear these words in the Bonhoefferian fragments?

Manifesting his debt to this early Christian technology of self in *The Use of Pleasure,* Foucault wrote of the practice of separating from oneself, getting free of one's "self," of one's "subjectivity," in an "effort to think one's own history."[79] He thought through attempts to "render oneself permanently capable of self-detachment."[80] This is an attempt to create new possibilities of selfhood by way of an ethic that is an aesthetic, an artistic self-fashioning, perhaps an art of fugue. This is an ethic not for the sake of stepping out of history itself, or the history of ourselves, but to step anew, and to step always historically, particularly, contingently, but indeed to step, to shift into a new space that eludes—however momentarily—prior determinations. Foucault writes of the importance of his rendering of this Christian technology of self "to liberate us both from the state and from the type of individualization which is linked to the state . . . [for] new forms of subjectivity."[81] "What are we and what could we be? What forms of new subjectivity can we create that will not originate in subjection?"[82]

Several decades before Foucault's disorienting destabilizing of modern "subjectivity," Bonhoeffer sensed the lack of ground under his feet, and his responsibility in this groundless situation. It goes without saying that Bonhoeffer's historical situation was very different from Foucault's. Foucault was not fighting a fascism of the exterior but of the interior. He attempted to innovate historical and philosophical tools to break free of every moralizing domestication of his self-identity, including rejecting the essentialisms impinging his identity as a gay man. Despite their different historical situations, Foucault, like Bonhoeffer, struggled to articulate an apophatics of the self: "I don't feel that it is necessary to know exactly what I am. The main interest in life and work is to become someone else that you were not in the beginning."[83] For both, this insight and its practice were animated by an engagement with

Christian discourses; this can be admitted without attempting to reduce Foucault's later work on ethics to a simple rehearsal of traditional Christian theology, nor reducing Bonhoeffer to a proto-Foucauldian.

Bonhoeffer's struggle was certainly against a fascism of the external political world. But was the technology of self he was beginning to develop not also a struggle against an internal political world, an interior fascism? In the words of Foucault, do we not hear the fragments of Bonhoeffer's Christian technology of self struggling to "ferret out . . . the fascism in us all, in our heads and in our everyday behavior, the fascism that causes us to love power, to desire the very thing that dominates and exploits us"?[84] This technology of self helped him displace what Foucault termed the "political technology of individuals" or the "technology of government."[85] This is a technology of the self organized by the state that leads people "to recognize themselves as a society, as a part of a social entity,"[86] and "makes of the *individual* a significant element for the state."[87] Thus Bonhoeffer's displacement of the practices of obedience so bound to German national identity. The "legitimate self-distrust" in the German tradition of obedience to call could become a "self-sacrifice [that] could be exploited for evil ends."[88] In the letters we witness a subterranean conflict over the questions: Who will tell me the truth about myself? Who will control the practices and discourses producing this truth, and what will they be?

These are two very different thinkers, working out of different struggles.[89] What David Tracy remarked of the thinkers that inhabit Jean-Luc Marion's *God without Being* may well be true of Bonhoeffer and Foucault: "They clearly do not mean the same, but . . . their differences can co-inhabit a new space of reflection."[90] Both delineated the intolerability of a pastorate that reified historical constructions of the self and its inner life, and that then exploited this reification to its own advantage. Both find intolerable the church's creation and maintenance and control of human interiority—of the "truth" of our inner lives: Bonhoeffer by the relegation of God into the ever-receding depths of human interiority where human knowledge fails; Foucault by the discursive production of human depths where the powers of prevailing morality make their nefarious nest. And in response to this intolerable situation, both, in different ways, schematized something like an apophatics of the self that requires the aesthetic fashioning of a technology of self. For both Bonhoeffer and Foucault, the most radical constructive possibilities of these insights occurred toward the end of their lives. That the works of both reveal subjectivity itself as a potential prison qualifies them as postmodern. Bonhoeffer's way out, a christomorphic self, riffs on Matthew 25:36: my subjectivity was a prison, and Jesus visited me.

What James Bernauer says of Foucault is also true, if in a different way, for the Bonhoefferian fragments: they "bear witness to the capacity for an ecstatic transcendence of any history that asserts its necessity."[91] Would it be inappropriate to speak of ecstatic transcendence in Bonhoeffer? His thought and life bear witness to the capacity for idoloclastic suspension of "any history that asserts its necessity," through acknowledging debt to and separation from others, accepting one's history, and risking solidarity. There is an ecstasy here, in the sense of ecstasis, the self's relation to itself as an ongoing displacement of the center not into an apolitical idealism but political solidarity; the self as an intrinsically risky practice.

IMPLICATIONS: THE CHURCH AND POWER

It is certainly not a matter of suggesting that the church's mission advocate a fundamentalist repetition of Bonhoeffer's life or technology of self today. Perhaps when Bonhoeffer's resistance to the fascism of the outside seems distant, it may be appropriated today as a Christian technology of self that deflects every essentialism that threatens to become another interior fascism. Here we begin to see more clearly what is at stake in "gather[ing] the fragments left over, so that nothing will be wasted" (John 6:12) from Foucault, Bonhoeffer, and elsewhere, in constructing an adequate Christian relation to self in our present.

Can the church present itself to young adults as the bearers of a less dominative relationship to themselves and others? Can the church innovate Christian technologies of self that would enable young adults—to quote Bonhoeffer outside the letters and out of "context"—"not so much to tolerate and maintain in responsible fashion what already existed, as to create, as a result of radical criticism, their own form of life"?[92] Or in the words of Foucault, "to show people that they are much freer than they feel, that people accept as truth, as evidence, some themes which have been built up at a certain moment during history, and that this so-called evidence can be criticized and destroyed . . . [in order to] show which space of freedom we can still enjoy and how many changes can still be made."[93]

Young adults experience a variety of interlaced technologies of power as the powers and principalities of our lives today. They are often positioned to accept various trinitarianesque doctrines: the seemingly unbreakable bondage of truth-self-desirable body, truth-self-sex, truth-self-productivity, truth-self-race, and truth-self-tradition. These dogmas may be found in both "liberal" and "conservative" secular and religious environments. These doctrines become more tempting as forms of retreatism in postmodernity, in the face of increasing ethnic, religious, sexual pluralism, functioning as a new reification of subjectivity, a new pietism of self. The fundamentalist self is one of postmodernity's prime temptations, and not only within traditionalist communities. Our culture of options, whether in church or society, remains too often a culture of normalization.

The church will serve young adults when it skills young adults to undertake practices of self-examination, to archive their own relationships to the technologies of power in their life, to take up a critical distance from these technologies of power and reestablish technologies of self that will help them resist. This means the church will have to confront its own technologies of power that attempt to control subjectivity through a certain moralizing, a certain pietism, control of access to sacraments, demand of confession, misuse of power relationships in the church community, undialectical acceptance of secular theories of selfhood, or any other dominative effects of the church's not unnecessary attempts to make interventions in the subjectivity of young adults.

Bonhoeffer's fragments help clear the way for a recovery of the place in Christian tradition of the eschatological character of truth. Bearing this postmodern cross means re-confronting the gap in John 18:38: In the face of Pilate's question "What is truth?" Jesus is silent, a silence so silent that John does not bother to pause to note the silence. Perhaps we have not fully entered Jesus' silence. It is a magnetic force toward which all of our theological claims are drawn. We must strive again and again to face his silence, which in a practical way means radical and unending critique, and not an access to the truth of ourselves because it has been verbalized, even by an authority like the Son of God (who himself refused to do so). It means living the irresolvable tension between the examination of truth as a practice, and the seeking of God's freedom for us.

Can the church resist the slumber of an ahistorical subjectivity and teach vigilance about the self, a continual self-criticism? This project is important if the church is to empower a new generation to say amen to their present, and by developing a Christian apophatic self inspired by Bonhoeffer, to say yes to the twenty-first century.

8

The Struggle to Speak Truthfully

INTRODUCTION

Among the people I have most respected in my life—whose impression on me has been of a sacramental sort, in that I keep unpacking their presence well after I am no longer physically around them, their memory rehearsing my availability to being available—are those who are able to speak wisely as a matter of course, about all topics, who find everything that is happening a kind of invitation, who are like guitarists who can play by ear with any ensemble and who can retune their strings while they are playing, an improvising that is the fruit of many years of moderating the urge to improvise, people about whom I feel everything they say is interesting, people that a less self-conscious age might have called holy, or at least wise.

That does not mean that such people are right about everything, but that they seem to have arrived at a way of making sense of the world through an often unasked for coming to terms with themselves. Such people seem to have accepted that there is nothing they can communicate about their sense of the way things are that could be a danger to themselves. Or, maybe I should say, that there is nothing they can communicate about their sense of the way things are that could be an *unacceptable* danger to themselves, because these are people who accept that trying to tell the truth, to speak honestly, to represent oneself with the spacious maturity of an adulthood lived and understood, and at the same time an unrepeatable perspective-taking that escapes banalities about tolerance, maturity, and adulthood. These people seem to accept that telling the truth goes along with representing oneself publicly, goes along with that now too easily uttered postmodern codeword "contingency": that what any of us knows, about our favorite subjects, about our loves, about ourselves, is painfully small, never complete enough, and our lives match our knowledge in their incompleteness.

How often have we had the experience like that of the Road Runner cartoon where Wile E. Coyote is running quickly and confidently, only to notice too late that there is no ground under his feet and he is already over the cliff? But certain people seem to be able to live with that fragmentariness, and to accept that when they relate to others, they are putting themselves in the arena of potential transformation, they are putting themselves in the hands of a test they cannot control, and therefore trying to tell the truth is wrapped up with speaking frankly, and that there is always a danger. Who can have the courage of the daily decision to lead a truthful life, and make such decisions in security? Only the sort of people for whom being known as honest, truthful, and frank is more important than exposure to the vertigo involved in the everyday ambiguities that belong to wanting to be honest, truthful, or frank—or if not wanting to be, at least wanting to want to be.

And wanting to be valued as honest, truthful, and frank is one Christian temptation, especially for those involved in ministry. The people I have known who are deeply "self-appropriated," to use Bernard Lonergan's language, have a combination of humility and courage that is always patterned unrepeatably, seem always aware that they wager themselves in how they witness in their everyday life. And the remarkable, refreshing, and hopeful thing to me, every time, is remembering that this happens among some people who learned how to live this way, and now they do it as a simple way of being, as a *habitus*, as a native speaker of a language won through facing life, through, as friends in recovery say, "dealing with life on life's terms." Some get there through an education that was a vital risk, through suffering that took away a treasured story about oneself or one's family, through the innumerable ways we have of consenting to the deepening of soul that can happen when we have to figure out if we want to live in reality, and then, if we *can* live in it, if we can love it.

Occasionally, I meet people like this, and one of Catholicism's best-kept secrets is that many women and men are like this not despite, but because of, their Catholic commitments, because of their Catholic struggles, Catholic questions, Catholic sacrifices, and all the relational tournaments that go with dealing with a faith tradition and community, its exercises, and teachings. There are many mentors in trying to live and to make possible an experience of being alive, for myself and others. Many of these teachers of mine have been Catholic priests and Catholic sisters. Is there a church in modernity that has done a more remarkable job of producing people who creatively imagine the possibilities of a flourishing human life, and thoughtfully question the everyday economies of exploitation that make our society work, than the Catholic Church?

And at the same time, is there a church in modernity that has done a more remarkable job of exploiting people than the Catholic Church? Still, I would like to someday become a Catholic who tells the truth, who speaks frankly, who represents himself at some risk, who knows what he can do, and do joyfully, with his faith and his suffering and the world's suffering, or who at least knows, joyfully, that he does not know what to do with his faith and his suffering and the world's suffering.

Now that I have rhapsodized about what sort of personhood religion can have a hand in forming, let me go back to my comment about Catholicism as a tradition that produces a remarkable amount of exploitation. We can name any of the well-known grievances with the church, or some that are not yet well-enough known, and most of these problems are related to Catholicism's problems with truth and with frankness. This seems to be the case whether one says the major difficulty in the church is that Catholic women give their lives for a church that cannot bring itself to work out the implications of gospel equality; or the major difficulty is not only that remarkably harsh and even hateful language in church teaching about gay and lesbian people exists and has become a prominent part of the public face of the church in America, but also that this teaching is articulated and defended even by some gay priests and bishops; or the major difficulty is that the laity, especially Catholics from those families who overestimate the value of the "American dream," are not willing to take on the hard teachings of the church, seeing the church as a community of convenience for themselves; or the major difficulty is that a remarkable indifference to the actual beliefs and faith practices of young people keeps the larger church incredibly out of touch with some of the deep challenges of being Christian today; or the major difficulty is that the vision of the bishops at their conferences as a sea of mostly aging white men presents no problems for a church that is more multiracial, multiethnic, and multicolored than ever; or the major difficulty is that Catholicism for the first time in its entire history is having to deal with a massive number of believers, a great many of whom are well-educated and not willing to renounce their adulthood, in a church that has as a matter of course depended on the renunciation of intellectual and spiritual adulthood for the laity in order to maintain its authority; or the major difficulty is the deep rot of Catholic power exposed by the sexual abuse of at least eleven thousand individuals by at least four and a half thousand priests over the past fifty years, and the enabling cover-up by any number of church authorities; or the major difficulty is simply and profoundly the innumerable slights, insults, condescension, and acts of disrespect caused by those who in the name of the church act in a willfully antidemocratic way—a string-pulling, backdoor-dealing, Eucharist-politicizing, house of self-worship. "For centuries," Foucault reminds us, "religion could not bear having its history told."[1] And the more we learn about the history of our religion, we see why that history has not been told: it is a history, among other things, of our failure to be truthful people.

Is there any doubt that today the Catholic Church is seen by many people on the inside and the outside as a place where people have trouble telling the truth, have difficulty speaking frankly, as a place where there is a premium on shoring up power over an ever-smaller circle of people who actually care, who attend church on a regular basis, and participate actively in its ministries? Yet sexual abuse and episcopal malfeasance represent just the front end of troubles. There are other notable silences: regarding the changing ethnic and racial face of Catholicism within the United States; regarding the high tuition in Catholic higher education that makes an excellent Catholic college education into a financial millstone for many if not most middle-class families; regarding a still-incredible lack of investment in youth and youth ministry, leading the biggest study ever of the faith of American teenagers to conclude that young Catholics are the least deeply connected to their faith among American denominations because the Catholic Church alone among the major traditions consistently makes youth ministry a minor focus for resources, and never gauges its own health and success by the spiritual situation of Catholic youth.[2] To these and so many other concerns, where are the identifiable public Catholics who speak frankly of the truth of these situations?

What is left for a prophetic ministry today? Learning to speak frankly to each other and the outside world about who we are, what's gone on, and where we would like to go. Perhaps even learning to speak frankly about what, really, "we believe."

PARRHESIA IN ANCIENT THOUGHT

The notion of a way of speaking that is both frank and truthful is not foreign to the Christian tradition. However, like a good many theological ideas, it needs to be given the patient respect of a searching curiosity that can be hard to muster when we are encouraged to plot our ministry around well-established points on the catechetical-theological compass. There is always a potentially new orientational center for Christian ministry, whose place in relation to Jesus of Nazareth must always be investigated afresh. And it is one of the basic precepts of practical theology that it is usually our roadblocks in practice, our crises of action, that occasion clarifications in faith, or even the constitution of new spiritual centers for Christian life, or the respect for multiple centers, polycentrism, in Christian faith.[3] I propose that speaking openly, *parrhesia*, is one of those possible Christian practices that might prove enlivening for our present situation in the church.

The Greek term *parrhesia* means "saying everything" (*pan-rhema*). And although it sometimes has a negative connotation of a blabber-mouthing that is useless, careless, or dangerous, it was also valorized in antiquity for the way it could disclose the truth. When it is used in this socially substantial sense, it is variously translated as speaking frankly, truthfully, openly, fearlessly, and boldly. Early Christianity found it useful for transcribing the significance of Jesus, poaching the nomenclature from ancient Greek literature and philosophy. As is true of so much of what goes on in early Christianity, including the texts that became the New Testament, a familiarity with Greek social and intellectual life allows some perspective about which ideas and practices Christian writers might have intercepted, however consciously, from their cultural environment. Indeed, it is only through historical study of the unruly stew that Christianity made of Greek, Roman, and Jewish philosophy, culture, and religion, that we can hope to gain some freeing perspective on how Christianity might relate to philosophies, cultures, and religions in our own day. In what follows, I limit myself to one tiny sample of a notion that overlays ancient Greek philosophy and ancient Christianity: *parrhesia.*

Michel Foucault has given a study of *parrhesia* in ancient philosophy,[4] and it will aid our practical theological task if I can summarize Foucault's basic points. He argues that in the ancient world, *parrhesia* had several qualities.

First, this way of speaking is frank insofar as it represents as directly as possible what someone believes. One is not to hide behind the veil of someone else's authority or a set of learned rhetorical feints. *Parrhesia* is first-person speech. Second, it is not enough to merely speak frankly about whatever comes to mind. We all know people who go around trying to "tell it like it is," who take some pleasure in expressing themselves about every intuition, impulse, feeling, or opinion. That is why Foucault highlights the second quality of *parrhesia*: truth. The *parrhesiastes* is one who speaks truth directly. And this speaking of truth is bound up with the sort of person one is, not only with what one knows. The *parrhesiastes* is someone who has become able to tell the truth because of their formation.

But if it is not enough to speak frankly, neither is it enough to speak the truth frankly in order to practice *parrhesia.* One must risk something in one's frank and truthful speech. *Parrhesia* is not comfortable speech that secures the power and authority of the speaker (Foucault mentions that for those who have no risk in speaking, like a king or tyrant, there can be no *parrhesia*).[5] Foucault highlights this third quality, danger, not to suggest that it is a kind of masochism or death wish one has when one speaks. It is rather a matter of being faithful to yourself, to who you have become, with a certain indifference to the cost. You have become someone who cannot not speak truth frankly. One who uses *parrhesia* does so because that person "prefers [one]self as a truth-teller rather than as a living being who is false to [one]self."[6] You have to speak to keep on being yourself. You have to speak to live with yourself, a stake which comes clearer when speaking threatens your well-being.

This quality is closely related to the fourth quality, duty. One who uses *parrhesia* does so because they are exercising their own freedom, not because they have been told to do so, or because they are under external compulsion. One could do otherwise, but one chooses to speak anyway. Foucault is saying that the free decision to speak becomes part of one's ongoing formation as someone who in speaking freely also makes oneself ready again to so decide in the future. Speaking frankly is work on oneself, because one's relation to oneself and to others is in play.

The fifth and final quality is criticism. *Parrhesia* requires that there be an edge, a questioning, a suspension and interrogation of a situation. So this speech that is frank, free, courageous, and truthful is also directed at change of a personal or social situation. This speech cannot come from one who is more powerful than another in order to be *parrhesia.* It must come from someone who does not have the luxury of criticizing with impunity.

"The *parrhesiastes* is always less powerful than the one with whom [one] speaks."[7] Foucault gives examples of particular interest to theology:

> [T]he advice that the interlocutor should behave in a certain way, or that [they] are wrong in what [they] think, or in the way [they] act, and so on. Or the *parrhesia* may be a confession of what the speaker . . . has done insofar as [one] makes this confession to someone who exercises power over [them], and is able to censure or punish [them] for what [they] have done.[8]

In other words, *parrhesia* can also be self-criticism or speaking with candor the truth about oneself, one's family, and one's community in a way that makes one vulnerable.

FEARLESS CHRISTIAN SPEECH

I would like to pause on ancient Christian thought and indicate some theological meanings of *parrhesia* before going on to consider limits and possibilities for *parrhesia* in the church today.

Stanley Marrow has written a rich summary article on *parrhesia* in the scriptures.[9] He argues that the Bible appropriates Greek *parrhesia* and that the New Testament develops a "specific Christian *parrhesia*," which, following biblical scholar Heinrich Schlier, he calls a Christian's evangelical "openness" with other persons and with God.[10]

By this gospel openness, Marrow seems to mean the confidence Christians have, in faith, that allows them to be forthright about *what* they trust to be real, and their *relationship* to what they trust to be real. It is a courage that is not solitary, but is the kind of transformative courage one is given by being in the presence of others who free us to live and to represent ourselves without fear. It is the courage of a bold living that becomes bold because of Jesus' boldness before Christians, within Christians, alongside Christians. Discipleship involves our buoyancy in God that finds expression in a "blessed assurance," in the words of the old hymn, a blessed assurance in dealing frankly and truthfully with God and others.

Marrow outlines several meanings of *parrhesia* in the early Christian theology contained in the Christian scriptures. Here I will note and develop them a little bit.

First, there is *parrhesia* as the "Christian's ready access to God."[11] In 1 John, Marrow observes a "confidence before God" with respect to God's judgment and with respect to prayer. 1 John 4:17 tells of "confidence for the day of judgment," and 5:14 speaks of the "confidence which we have in him, that if we ask anything according to his will he hears us." And in Hebrews, Marrow finds an "altogether new element" in *parrhesia* when access to God is founded on the mediating sacrifice of Jesus: "[W]e have confidence to enter the sanctuary by the blood of Jesus, by the new and living way which he opened for us . . . through his flesh" (Heb 10:19–20). Here, Jesus' sacrifice is given as cause for assurance in faith and "confession of hope without wavering" (10:22–23).[12]

Second, there is Jesus himself as *parrhesiastes*. John 7:4 has Jesus' friends telling him (and the reader) that "no one works in secret if they seek to be known openly [*en parrhesia*]." In 7:26, we find Jesus and *parrhesia*: "Here he is, speaking openly [*parrhesia lalei*]," and then, John adds with an understatement that I take to be droll humor, "they say nothing to him." When Jesus talks "plainly about the Father" (16:25), his friends credit him with "speaking plainly, not in a figure" (1:29).

Jesus is known, of course, most famously for speaking in parables, even if the parabolic form was something he himself borrowed from the Jewish teaching traditions of his day. Speaking thus allusively, "in figures" (John 16:29), is contrasted in the New Testament with Jesus' frank, plain or bold speech that takes place once the passion narratives begin. Once the final scenes of Jesus' life begin to play out, the parables stop and the frank speaking takes over. John 18:20 has Jesus saying to the high priest: "I have spoken openly [*parrhesia lelaleika*] to the world. . . ."[13] Marrow summarizes masterfully the importance of this characterization:

> These words of Jesus, at the hour of his trial, are as compendious a statement of the meaning of *parrhesia* as any we can find in the Fourth Gospel. It is a fearless, open (not hidden), and clear (not in parables) testimony in every sense of the word.[14]

Third in the Christian scriptures' senses of *parrhesia*, there is the church as parrhesiastic community. Marrow notes a fascinating framing in the book of Acts, a book which Christians often read as the charter document of the church. He observes an *inclusio*, that is, an opening and closing motif, or set of parentheses, that provide the frame in which the story of the church's birth is told. From Peter to Paul, Marrow points out, *parrhesia* is the basic theme. The opening parenthesis is Acts 2:29, Peter's speech at Pentecost, in which he begins by relating that "I say to you with boldness [*meta parrhesias*]. . . ." And the closing parenthesis in 28:31 concerns Paul, teaching about Jesus and the kingdom "openly and unhindered [*pases parrhesias akolutos*]." What Marrow seems to be suggesting is that the church itself is founded on *parrhesia*, implying that Christians today are part of the continuing story of the church when we practice confidence in God and before others, when we speak freely the truth to which we are related, when we practice Christian *parrhesia*.

Finally, Marrow draws attention to writings attributed to Paul as being masterpieces of early Christian *parrhesia*. On one hand, it is Paul's entire style that is parrhesiastic: his boldness, candor, frankness, his almost showy, pushy, and assertive or aggressive (depending on your perspective) way of putting forward his sense of what is and ought to be—especially, for example, in the

Corinthian correspondence. But in addition to his overall style, there is a basic theological point that Marrow argues animates Paul's *parrhesia*: access to God given by Christ's "lifting of the veil" (2 Cor 3:14), making Paul bold in being with others. For Paul, Christ has won a freeing relationship with God characterized by and grounding freeing relations with others.

Marrow draws strong contrasts between Greek and Christian *parrhesia*. In Marrow's judgment, the New Testament "use of *parrhesia* and its verb reflects none of the meanings current in the Gentile world, though, of course, the term itself does maintain the basic meaning of saying everything freely and openly."[15] The concept travels from the civil to the spiritual realm, or in Marrow's words, making a "transit from the secular sphere to the religious."[16] Moreover, he suggests that "the Apostles, no less than the Christian community itself, knew all too well that this *parrhesia* is a divine gift to be prayed for, and not some moral virtue to be attained by dint of personal application, or acquired by repeated exercise."[17] Like many such blanket and bifurcatory declarations separating pagan from Christian assumptions, or grace from works theologies, this sounds a little polemical. Theologically understood, there need be no necessary separation presumed between exercises and giftedness, between moral virtue and gracious bestowal, between "personal application" and unmerited infusion. This is precisely why, as is increasingly recognized, spiritual exercises were able to be taken over from Greek philosophy into early Christian theology, especially in the monastic, mystical, ascetic traditions. But I wish here only to make a simple point, to flag the difficulty of thinking about *parrhesia* in dichotomies of "secular" against "religious," "exercise" against "grace," "gift" against "attainment."

Some of the difficulties involved already stick out like unruly hairs on the head of Marrow's otherwise well-coifed argument. We can return to a key sentence just cited. After Marrow proposes that there are no contemporaneous "Gentile" meanings manifest in the New Testament usage of *parrhesia*, he then takes this claim back in a significant degree by writing, "of course, the term itself does maintain the basic meaning of saying everything freely and openly."[18] This is not a minor "of course," of course. That someone could say something, anything, or "everything freely and openly" is a particular way of living, a sort of style of governing oneself, and that relates to how one is governed by others, that is not natural, easy, or socially neutral. This was a way of speaking that was typically the preserve of male citizens in antiquity, those who had a duty to speak openly for the good of the city or, later, in the more circumscribed sphere of personal relationships, especially friendships. That this kind of speech is philosophically and politically available and is called upon by some Christians to communicate the character of Christian freedom in relation to God is significant politically and spiritually.

Parrhesia is a political technology, a certain kind of relationship to self, others, and to truth, in the ancient world. It is not just a random, socially neutral idea that can be picked up and used without many strings or social repercussions attached to the idea or to its claimant. Foucault is aware of this because of his interest in ancient spiritual exercises and techniques of the self; thus his analysis highlights the qualities that make up this parrhesiastic practice. But insofar as Jesus becomes symbol for Christians' relations to themselves, others, and the truth, *parrhesia* becomes potentially radically "democratized," and not only the preserve of some privileged segments of society, but rather a form of life in which all Christians can engage—a mystical and political orientation for everyday life. When Christians represent ourselves in courage, for truth, at some risk, being critical or self-critical, and freely, we may be practicing gospel confidence in God and with others. We are learning to live more freely. *Parrhesia* can become a spiritual exercise, one of the most important for Catholics today.

FRANK SPEECH, CONFESSION, AND ECCLESIASTICAL POWER

Consider the space for frank speech in the Catholic Church today. Are there sanctioned spaces in which free and frank speech happens, in which it is more than tolerated, and even welcomed? To my mind, such a space does exist: the distinctively Catholic box, the confessional—a little-used space today, to be sure, but a telling space nonetheless.

In recently published lectures, Foucault remarks almost offhandedly, *à propos* of his study of the history of confession, that the Catholic confessional, a "small" but crucial spiritual and political "piece of furniture," is a space with certain distinctive qualities.[19] I would like to summarize Foucault's discussion and elaborate on it.

Foucault comes to discuss the confessional as a way of explaining what happened to penance in the Western Catholic tradition: how penance became bound up with practices of confession, and those practices then situated in the official ecclesial language of "sacrament," and as a result, penance becomes a way that the power of the church was exercised over the faithful. In other words, the ancient Christian practice of penance becomes, with the Council of Trent, the site for an extension of "ecclesiastical power" over the faithful, over their souls, desires, and bodies. Such an extension and concentration of power needed not only a juridical interlocking of Eucharist and confession. It required also a material space in which to symbolize this power and to practically allow it its reach. The confessional became such a space. As Foucault argues, the confessional was "the material crystallization of all the rules that characterize both the qualification and the power of the confessor. . . ."[20]

Foucault notes the following about the confessional: First, it is within the church itself; second, it is an "open" space; third, it is "anonymous"; and fourth it is "public" (what he terms a "public place within the church").[21] I think Foucault's remarks open onto a way of parsing Catholic power and its relation to Catholic frank speech, and I would like to expand on his suggestive ideas, going further into more theological considerations.

The confessional is like a miniature public square, a peculiarly Catholic public square. One should say what one really thinks, one should speak freely in the presence of another. Depending on how formulaic the script followed with the individual confessor, penitents witness to the depths of what seems to be happening in their life, without censorship. They speak freely, frankly, of what is taken to be the truth, and always in their own name. No one can go to confession for anyone else; no one can witness to the conscience of another. Penitents must always speak in the first person.

The confessional is public because it demands communication with another, with all the attendant concerns for intelligibility, rhetoric, or cultural differences, that any public interaction has. This public space is "open" insofar as in principle no speech is forbidden. It is "anonymous" precisely for the protection of free and frank speech. The confidence of a mutual trust is essential. This is true whether the old-style confessional screens (which still exist in many places in the United States and throughout the world) are there, or whether a face-to-face arrangement is available.

That this practice takes place within the church suggests that free and frank speech is part of the church's modern way of proceeding, intrinsic to its way of being. Here is a place where one really wants to witness to what is the case in one's life, witness that publicly, and it is striking that that practice of "keeping it real" simply *cannot be outsourced*. Theologically, it seems to suggest that it is not just that penance/confession/reconciliation is sacramental in the traditional sense of essential ways of being initiated more deeply into the life of God and thus freed to live a courageous everyday life in the Spirit; it is also theologically significant insofar as frank and free speech is being acknowledged as a churchly practice. Living with God and each other requires provision for spaces wherein we are honest with God and each other.

The paradox of the confessional is that by installing a quite restricted space in which no more and no less than two people can ever participate at one time, the church installs "openly" within itself frank speech, installs within itself training in speaking frankly. This training in speaking frankly ought to be registered as "sacramental" for the *church* as much as the personal confession is counted as "sacramental" for the *individual*.

So the confessional is a fascinating greenhouse for the insurgent Christian spirituality that frank speech can and must allow. Its very presence is like a Lewisian wardrobe that not only reminds us that another deeper world of spiritual drama underpins our everyday life, but also actually teaches us how to talk honestly to another member of the church, and to the church as an institution.

But what kind of free and frank speech is this, after all? The fact that Catholicism has the confessional as its one hallowed zone of frank speech means that we have to confront the profound ambiguity of Catholic free and frank speech.

Foucault argues that what has counted historically in the confessional is a fairly selective, restrictive, and specific set of contents that play into ecclesiastical power by inciting in the penitent an unending inventorying and recitation of bodily pleasures, desires, temptations, aspirations, and suspicions—movements of the flesh. These are to be found not only in one's present but also over the course of an entire life. An endless self-inspection became the content about which one must speak frankly.[22] So it turns out that speech that looks frank, feels frank, and is accounted as frank, turns out not to be all that frank. We get the pleasures of frankness, without its truth. Or rather—here is the Foucauldian nub—we get an experience of it being true, which is an experience born of a certain kind of social-ecclesial power.

You are perhaps familiar with the "free speech zones" that have been erected by purportedly democratic institutions in the last several years to keep demonstrators from participants at controversial events such as the World Trade Organization meetings or American political conventions. I taught at a Catholic university that even had a "free speech zone" in which students were expected to remain as they registered whatever complaint they dared to raise. Like the confessional, they were hemmed in on all sides with a guarantee that they could say what they want, and also that it would be heard somehow by a representative of the institution who was presumed present but not often seen. The confessional is just such a free speech zone in the church; it is a peculiarly Catholic frank speech zone.

Very few students overtly questioned the need for a restricted free speech zone; most were just impressed when anyone showed up for any expression of speech or assembly. Those who come to college knowing nothing of social questioning other than the free speech zone assumed that these zones are a natural part of the college experience, like other special spaces set aside for the exhibition of collegiate behaviors: fraternity and sorority houses, dining halls, and high-tech classrooms, each with codes of speech and appropriate behavior. Similarly, how many Catholics want to allow the radical side of confessional practice "outside the box" and into the church's liturgy, governance, or religious education? It is true that everything can be said in the confessional. But as Foucault reminds us, "one must say *everything*, but one must *only* say it *here* and to *this* person."[23]

It is no surprise, then, that the Catholics who *can* take the rules and powers of confession outside the confessional have been, too often, clerics who are the ones invested with the ecclesiastical power of the confessional. Think of one of the many harrowing statements to come out of the sex abuse—or episcopal authority—crisis. I am talking about a statement attributed to Cardinal Bernard Law, which he allegedly made to one victim of abuse:

> *[O]n April 24, 1989, at the funeral of Father Joseph Birmingham in Boston[,] Tom Blanchette saw Cardinal Law sipping coffee alone. "There's a lot of young men in the diocese who will need counseling in the wake of their relationship with Father Birmingham," Blanchette*

> *told him. He confided how the priest had molested him, his four brothers, other young men. Law drew him aside and asked him to return to the church. "Bishop Banks is handling this, and I want you to make an appointment."*
>
> *Placing his hand on Blanchette's head, the cardinal prayed in silence. Then he said; "I bind you by the power of the confessional never to speak about this to anyone else."*[24]

Or consider the witness of Aiden Doyle, who tells of being sexually assaulted in Ireland by a priest, and who recalls being given this as a response when he went to tell another priest about it:

> "I'm going to apply the seal of confession to you, so that you must never talk about this, and it will be kept secret."[25]

If Catholics can bear having "our history told," these disturbing relations of power make us confront the deep problem: Is it a contradiction when modern institutions who represent themselves as egalitarian establish zones for free and frank speech that have the effect of keeping free and frank speech offstage? Or is it a fulfillment of the kind of modern power that runs through and organizes both the modern church and the modern state? For all our asserted Catholic distinctiveness, whether of the liberal or traditionalist sort, does the power that creates free speech zones not create them in both church and state?

Why is fearless speech not, after all, among the recognizable virtues of Catholic formation today?

PARRHESIA TODAY?

It is my experience of having been addressed openly and candidly in my life that has made me want to learn more about *parrhesia*, about how that attitude is formed, and about how one does so as a Christian. What is it that makes such mature people also so humble, open, curious, and spacious? Perhaps it is because they are not being bold about just anything, but they are (in the words of Ephesians 6:19) trying to "boldly proclaim the mystery." Thus, frank speech is not merely reportage about what is true and false, appropriate and inappropriate, actionable or inactionable, but is a way of becoming available through how one talks and what one says to the mystery with and for others. We are caught up in a relationship to an incomprehensible truth.

And so the questions face the Catholic Church in its present numbness: Where does the church have trouble speaking frankly? Where do church workers have trouble speaking the truth frankly? What is one truth that needs to be spoken more frankly in your ministry or your life? What sorts of preparations are you and I undertaking to be parrhesiastic Christians?

In the courage to ask such questions, and to follow Jesus in his fearless speech, we can invoke the witness and intercession of one of our most important examples of Christian *parrhesia*, Teresa of Avila. It is she who assures us that "God is the friend and lover of courageous souls, so long as they proceed humbly and without trust in themselves [alone]."[26]

9

Faith and Apocalypse

DISORIENTATIONS IN THE LIFE OF FAITH

In Catholic pastoral ministry, I have been struck by how frequently our imaginations of the spiritual life are built around models of ongoing and irreversible trajectories of growth. We preach, teach, and counsel people about maturation, development, deepening adulthood, continual progress in faith, everything as a "learning experience," and God "leading" us forward, "right where He wants us." It had been my intuition that such ways of thinking about the life of faith were hard to reconcile with people who had undergone traumas in faith and life—deep disorderings/reorderings of meaning and commitment. I also found it difficult to reconcile with the complexities of interreligious life today, that is, with Catholics whose lives are also substantially bound up with other religions (whether through their own personal religious practice or through their intimate relationships), like Judaism or Buddhism, but who are continually encouraged to think of faith in these progressive terms, instead of seeing "progress" itself as needing to be rethought through what happens when the commitments of a religion beyond Christianity take up residence inside oneself. Can one still simply speak of maturing, continual growing in faith? Under what conditions ought we begin to think about faith being replaced, or re-placed? It was, then, with much interest that I discovered the traditions of apocalyptic spirituality and theology, first and most influentially, for me, in the work of Johannes Baptist Metz. This apocalyptic perspective is more curious about the defining character of the tragic and fragmentary experiences we have, and more respectful of the resistance in "postmodern" philosophies to being defined—even and perhaps especially in faith—by metaphors of progress.

As J. Matthew Ashley has so thoroughly shown, Metz uses the notion of "interruptions" as an interpretive lens for the Bible, for everyday experience, and for the history of modern catastrophes, most importantly the Holocaust.[1] For Metz, an interruption is an unexpected, utterly unforeseen, and unasked for experience of destabilization of one's (or a people's) narrative, memories, and hope. One of the key points is that for Metz, the problem of God is the problem of the interruption: whether and what kind of God can still be believed in despite the negative interruptions of human history, and whether modern Christians have a faith that will allow God to interrupt their settled stories, explanations, and expectations. Theology is, fundamentally, theodicy. And he argues that what scripture and theological history offer is that there is no access to God unless it is the God of and through the interruption. Not the God who "causes" interruptions in a naive sense, but the God the stories about whom can only be "real" insofar as they consent to the interruption, by allowing the suffering of the interrupted other to disorient the privileged modern stories about God, to launch us into hope. Interruptions are those experiences that demand a new story about our faith, such that a failure to consent to the reality of the suffering involved in the interruption prevents us from truly hoping for this God, a God who can be encountered in and through apocalypse as revelation. I hasten to add that this does not mean creating Branch-Davidian scenarios in order to call on God. That would not be apocalypse, because it would be something foreseen, planned out, and strategized.

DEVELOPMENT AND APOCALYPSE

In Catholic pastoral life, two major metaphorics of development are regularly invoked. Both of these structures are called into question by an apocalyptic spirituality. These metaphorics are influential templates for how faith makes its way through the history of the individual in the form of deep personal meaning, and the history of the Catholic tradition in the form of doctrine. These two metaphorics are "faith development" and "development of doctrine."

First, from the vantage point of apocalyptic spirituality, we can see that the notion of "faith development" appears as an interpretation of faith suited for the educated privileged Westerner. This theory, articulated in the highly original and justly famous *Stages of Faith* by James Fowler,[2] and defended countless times afterward in pastoral and religious-educational circles, holds that individual faith develops in stages, on the model of moral-psychological development over phases of the life span, and through movements of deepening ethical maturity. As is well known, Fowler outlines six potential stages of faith, from "intuitive-projective faith" all the way through to "universalizing faith." What I want to highlight about this approach is that the full flourishing of faith in stage six is characterized by deep immersion in a single religious tradition as a precondition for faith maturity. Fowler calls this the "absoluteness of the particular."[3] By this, he means that one has taken with radical seriousness a commitment to a specific story, symbol, and path to a "faith relationship characterized by total trust in and loyalty to the principle of being."[4] In other words, Fowler suggests that the highest kind of faith we can practice is that which proceeds from the irreparably finite character of revelation and, in a sense, our ascetic restriction to it—our willingness to submit to the particular precisely as a gateway to the universal.

One difficulty raised from the perspective of an apocalyptic spirituality starts with a challenge to thinking that we can apprehend what Fowler calls a "predictable sequence of formally describable stages in the life of faith."[5] Against this, apocalypticism foregrounds unpredictability, resisting the closures of faith and potential enclosures of God that go with the developmental stage theory. From this viewpoint, stage theory is its own kind of theodicy for Christians in our society. This theodicy, in effect, says that one can and must devote oneself to a specific faith tradition and community in order to have access to what is true for all the "lasting great religious traditions."[6] Moreover, insofar as one is able to do so, one can hope for progression or development in faith that is "predictable," moves in "sequence," and is "formally describable." But, apocalyptic spirituality might protest, what of the interruption one finds again and again today in the form of "religious pluralism," particularly the phenomenon of "multiple religious belonging"?[7] What if one can and now must, particularly as a result of a profound dislocation, be dispersed across—be multiply located through—plural religious identities?[8] The disruption of the absolute-particular dichotomy is one of the most helpful conceptual challenges of this phenomenon today. Faith development theory, at least as we have known and used it now for a quarter century, has given people reasons to stay with traditions, but through this theodicy it has blocked the apocalyptic experience of being "converted" to multiple religious traditions (and nontraditions) at once, or even to being interrupted into departures from religion, from faith. But before I take this up, let me mention another form of development.

The Catholic notion of the "development of doctrine" is central to debates about the modern character of Roman Catholic teaching and theology. As is well known, John Henry Newman's genius energized the deployment of the idea in the nineteenth century.[9] He proposed that doctrine could unfold over time as understandings of the deposit of faith unfold over time, guided by the Spirit, and through the magisterium, and understood according to specific notes of authenticity. This understanding is seen by many theologians as compatible with, and itself developed in, the Second Vatican Council's understanding of revelation, and much subsequent church teaching and Catholic theology. Indeed whether seen as elaborations of statements that are logical corollaries to earlier teachings, or as further refinements of understanding of the mystery of Christ in new sociocultural situations, doctrine is held, occasional official Roman protestations notwithstanding, by and large by Catholic theology today, to develop.

These two theologies of development, if you will, both of personal faith and of ecclesial doctrines, have become a refuge for Catholic progressives. At the same time, it is difficult not to see these theologies as ambiguous and problematic attempts to govern, through producing, the narrative of a spiritual life for Christian faithful, with the coherence of the continued unfolding faith of the individual or the church being a way to solder Christians to Christianity. Positioned in this way, the notion of development of doctrine, particularly as enshrined in official ecclesial documents, becomes a way for Catholic faith to be superintended by the management of Catholic history—as a history essentially, and despite everything, of consensus, continuity, and organic growth that unfolds over time under the finally irenic direction of the Spirit. Regardless of the tension or outright contradictions one finds in teachings over time and across space,[10] it is said, do not refer these seeming discrepancies to any other development than development itself. To do so would be to betray the Spirit, and would be to betray the official history of revelation. Pneumatology, then, often becomes the element through which this progressive, theological-ecclesial power as a setting of the meaning of history is exercised.

DEPARTURE

But has Catholic theology admitted "development" as a secret theodicy for stabilizing Catholic identity? If it has not yet, can we hear the dislocations going on within pastoral life as more than stages in development, but as interruptions? Hear, for example, the lament of Mark Jordan regarding the treatment of queer Catholics by the church:

> The longer the sacraments are withheld, the more inadequate merely speaking out seems. For Catholic Christians, the practice of the faith requires regular participation in the celebration of the Eucharist. It demands membership, in a very strong sense, within a community that revolves around the sacraments. So if a Catholic Christian is consistently denied access to the sacraments by a church organization, the person must decide to go elsewhere. Life without the sacraments is not Catholic life. When you speak out against members of the hierarchy for failing to provide sacraments and they ignore you; when the same hierarchy teaches that you should not come forward to receive the sacraments without repenting of any full expression of your sexuality; when you may be denied access to the Eucharist for identifying yourself as lesbian or gay—then, precisely as a Catholic, you need to deliberate about going to another eucharistic table. You must, in short, ask whether you shouldn't leave the Catholic Church in order to live as a Catholic.[11]

The implosion of the Catholic sacramental system, caused by the emplacement of the sacraments in distorted thinking about normal sexuality, can induce a departure from Catholicism for the sake of Catholicity: Catholic reasons for leaving Catholicism.

Jordan speaks a Catholic language I can understand. Being a "pilgrim" in faith, as Saint Ignatius called himself, being a member of a "pilgrim" church, as Vatican II referred to Catholics, suggests Christian life as exploration, rootlessness, readiness for departure in the face of new apocalypses that detach us, or detach those whose burdens we shoulder, from false readings of our Christian narratives, and that even can detach us from a comprehension of what makes a narrative Christian in the first place.

Even though I sometimes blanch when I meet people who describe themselves as "recovering Catholics," I sense that our lives share many overlapping stretches of road.[12] Many people who call themselves "recovering Catholics" do so because the apocalypses to which they were witness—physical, psychological, intellectual, and spiritual—were not able to be located on the map of the faith they had been taught. And contrary to many Catholic apologists (including my earlier self), this does not necessarily mean that they had a deficient religious education. Many "recovering Catholics" know as much of what Catholicism at its best is about, as many of those who still choose the Catholic Church. Many of "them" are trying to honor the interruption by keeping moving, desiring something more, something else, something other, something bigger, something that feels more "real," with a richer map for experience. I think "practicing Catholics" might be helped by allowing ourselves into such "recovery," by stopping trying to contain the tectonic shifts to which they have borne witness, whether the theological prescription serving the containment is "Christ, the same yesterday, today and tomorrow" for traditionalists, or "Faith needs to be able to doubt" for progressives. Both can be ways of a domesticated voicing of that refrain from the old Christian spiritual, "Let the church roll on!"

But there can be no prescription for apocalyptic spirituality; it remains more unsettled disposition than settled position. Following through such a perspective would imply even needing to let Metz go a little, to let what Metz calls "suffering unto God" become, when it must, a questioning of what Christianity itself means, and whether Christianity "in its essence" makes sense. And for this, I must go beyond Metz, to Michel de Certeau, for whom departure is the available and even necessary spiritual orientation for those who would try to deal with faith in the midst of the collapse of all attempts of religion to justify the truth of its claims by its exclusion of otherness. It is just here that Certeau finds the ongoing manifestation of the mystical way, in its radical risk of exposure in love with that unnameable and untameable beyond, which Christians with increasingly recognized radical inadequacy call "God."

> He or she is mystic who cannot stop walking and, with the certainty of what is lacking, knows of every place and object that it is *not that*; one cannot stay *there* nor be content with *that*. Desire creates an excess. Places are exceeded, passed, lost behind it. It makes one go further, elsewhere. It lives nowhere.[13]

It is apocalypse that opens us to that which has the "power to induce a departure,"[14] and perhaps even, most apocalyptically, a "movement of perpetual departure."[15]

QUESTIONS FOR A CONCLUSION

Where do Christians overrely on stories of stability and success in the life of faith, of the life of faith of family, church, or other community? What deep questions or even negations have been put to those stories? What experiences have you and your community undergone, in the face of which repeating the old stories no longer worked? What have been the upendings, interruptions, unbraidings, dislocations, disorientations, and apocalypses? And what effect has this had on your ministry?

The basic question is an utterly central one if theology is finally concerned with making faith-sense of life in the face of suffering, especially the suffering of the other; and the question of how apocalypses have conditioned ministry is utterly central if, as the developmentalists have pointed out, there is such a thing as *adult* faith, and yet if, as apocalyptic charges, the very adult quality of faith can never be a matter of an ethically neutral curriculum for "growth," "literacy," or "outcomes," but must always be an unpredictable experiment undergone with God through the world—and not a scientific experiment but a risk, a test, an ordeal of discipleship as departure, in hope, from every unsettlement to which we are subject.

From an apocalyptic perspective, "growth" in faith is not a quest to make all the pieces fit,[16] but to abandon oneself to reality, a reality preferentially narrated by those who are the victims of the narratives of the theologically healthy, normal, traditional, and appropriate. What was it about Jesus that, in Mark, the earliest and the most apocalyptic of the gospels, allowed him to go to God not as the one who had it all figured out, not as the enlightened one, but as totally unhinged (Mark 15:24)?

Are there people in our midst who need us to respect an experience that cannot easily be digested into "who we are as church," who "God is," and what Jesus "came for"?

Luke 5:27–28 reads, "[H]e went out and saw a tax collector named Levi, sitting at the tax booth; and he said to him, 'Follow me.' And he got up, left everything, and followed him." One section of verse 28 in the Greek reads "and leaving everything, he got up. . . ." The verb form of "got up," *anastas*, is taken from the same verb that Luke uses to describe Jesus rising from the dead later in this gospel. Levi, in other words, is only able to "rise," physically and spiritually, as he is able to be "leaving everything." The Greek puts the "leaving everything" before the "getting up," unlike the English, which wants Levi to rise first and then dispense with all things. There is no resurrection—here with Levi, in the midst of everyday life, "sitting at the tax booth"—without letting go of . . . everything?

What does Luke leave out of this account? What goes on inside Levi in this "leaving [of] everything"? Resurrection is glorious, but isn't it also painful? Especially when it is not the big *R* of Resurrection but the little *r* of resurrection in everyday life, like Levi's. Still, in using *anastas*, Luke's text suggests that we read everyday resurrection as a participation in Jesus' Resurrection as the *askesis* of "leaving everything." It may indeed be that for some, faith moves through a "predictable sequence of formally describable stages" that end up being rooted finally in one home of faith. But can Catholics also admit "perpetual departure," leaving Christian spaces for Christian reasons, as one way of dealing with Christian faith and the apocalypses in which it shares?

Conclusion

Witness to Dispossession

ON THE WAY TO A PRE-CHRISTIAN CATHOLIC THEOLOGY

"From this philosophy comes the movement through which, not without effort and fumblings, dreams and illusions, one detaches oneself from what are the received truths and seeks other rules of the game. From philosophy comes the displacement and transformations of the limits of thought, the modification of received values and all the work done to think otherwise, to do something else, to become other than one is."
—Michel Foucault[1]

". . . glorious bewilderment . . . cannot comprehend what it understands, it understands by not understanding [and] can only be gained by abandoning everything. . . ."
—Teresa of Avila[2]

The importance for Christianity of the genealogizing historical and philosophical research carried out by, with, and after Foucault is potentially far-reaching. It allows Christianity to become witness to dispossession, to be schooled in its being what it can be in the present by offering up everything about itself to be handed over, away from the theological suppositions, still so important today, of uniqueness, essences, and givenness.

There have been attempts to screen Christianity from a genealogical unmaking, but such attempts always strike a note too romantic to be believed, describing a faith that existed only in the mourning minds of those retrojecting it onto sites in the tradition that seem hospitable to fantasies: past concepts, communities, or charisms that somehow, if we only pay deep enough attention, will light the way for the present. This sort of past qualifies as history, as the manifestation of a "historical consciousness," but only in an attenuated sense, because these theologies portray no Christian past as truly an *historical* past, but only an *amiable* past: that is, a past that teaches us like a schoolmaster, alternately reprimanding and encouraging us, but finally a past that belongs to us, as a "forerunner in faith."

This need for a familial, amiable past is also present in theologies that accept the grief committed by and against Christianity. These theologies take with sober seriousness history as violence to the faith, as corruption of the original vision (in which history tells of the slow overweighting of the original body of revelation), and as site of danger for the true believer (in which history is a martyrological scene, a confirmation of faith by the examples of its being misunderstood, ostracized, or attacked).

Theologies that attempt to be historical thus play on the essence/accretion dyad, and history gets told in that dialectical mode. But what if everything Christian is "accretion," all accretion, all essences candescences, flashpoints caused by the meeting not only of "Christian" and "non-Christian" ideas and practices, but "non-Christian" and "non-Christian"? What if the strangenesses out of which Christianities were made continue to strangeness Christianities? This must be so if the heart of what is taken to be "the faith" must undergo a genealogizing that is experimental, radical, and necessary for "credibility" today—by which I mean entering unreservedly and critically into the rhetoric of credibility. I mean, for example, a genealogizing that is experimental and radical regarding christologies; regarding soteriological models; regarding elemental concepts of the faith such as "body," "Lord," "spirit," "sacrament," "confession," and "ecclesia"; regarding traditional structuring practices such as "spiritual exercises" or "liturgy."

There Christian theology is left—with what? Empty hands? Hands, rather, that become Christian hands by how and what they give away. Hands that are witnesses to dispossession. Hands that become the risk of a possible future Christianity by practicing dispossession. Including the giving up of Christianity itself. Hands that must give up Christianity are hands that have learned to let through Christianity's promises: to let them through in the sense of cooperating with their release from Christian ownership, handing over even as they are being taken away, a cooperative dispossession; and letting through in the sense of this dispossession being ingredient to Christianity's self-regard—that is, Christianity runs through Christians when they let its component histories run through their hands. In so doing, the hand's bearing teaches us what Christianity was, "after all," about.[3] After what we thought of as Christianity are hands that have learned to let go. This is one of the few ways left for being Christian in the present: learning to participate in handing it over. Or better, learning how to rehearse through the hands what has already been given over.

SECRET DISCIPLINE

The modern liberal and liberationist Christian theologies that have, often at uncountable cost, taken the disinherited as their subjects, constituents, and addressees, almost always thought that in doing so, Christian theology must—as if it were a shadow of the capitalism against which such theologies often operate—keep possession of, secure against terrorism, its own private property: whether that property be the liberating christologies, the liturgy of the world, the Trinitarian community that God is, or the sacrament of solidarity (and any number of less "progressive" theological ideas). It is this anxiety—that one must launch a critical theology from a "firm foundation" in relation to which liberation takes place—that animates much of even the most liberal of contemporary, especially Catholic, theology. It is rarely considered that the dispossession of Christian theology's own power and content might be more than enough stability for the kind of liberating that is possible today.

One learns dispossession in diverse ways: from abandoning advantage on behalf of a loving gratitude for existence expressed as risk for another here and now; from learning about how Christian ideas about self, other, world, and God came to be considered Christian through a checkered history that includes violence and abuses of power. Both paths are ways of giving up security, and both are ways of learning to live a life of departure, an abandoning life, which can be both the fruit of and preparation for the sort of political spirituality that our best critical philosophy and Christian theology allow.

This abandoning life can be our way of living Christianity as a "secret discipline." Dietrich Bonhoeffer's *Letters and Papers* of the 1940s brought this notion from ancient Christian theology into the incubation of an anti-Nazi christology. In a world come of age, characterized by religionlessness, the mysteries of the faith would need to be treasured inwardly, suggested Bonhoeffer, by those willing to commit themselves to prayer and righteous action for others, to share secular culture's joys and grief, "belonging wholly to the world," and to become one who "must drink the earthly cup to the dregs."[4] This Christianity would not be a public performance of religious rituals meant to showcase alliances, perform a public apologetics, or curry favor with brokers of culture, but instead a way of being whose fidelities, texts, worries, and patterns of formation would be a private sign of God's "weakness" in the secular world, and a time of waiting for a more resounding and bracing disclosure of the faith for contemporary society. To have passed through postmodern researches, to live in postmodern culture, is to find our own reasons to sympathize in our own ways with Bonhoeffer's wonderment "whether there have ever before in human history been people with so little ground under their feet."[5] While we can share with Bonhoeffer the conviction that the church has conceded vision and policy to the nation, we are beyond Bonhoeffer in feeling also a profound loss of ground in the radical turns of postmodern theories: of history, gender, sexuality, language, and above all, culture.

What this notion can mean for postmodern Christians, witnesses to dispossession, is that faith be known as *discipline*, in all the ambiguities of the meaning of *askesis*; moreover, faith retains the character of secret, because there are no more correlations on the level of intellectual coherence, and no more stable pushes for a specific public politics. It is a secret discipline, then, because it is an *askesis* that is uninterpretable to oneself and to the world because it is constantly being unmade by attention to the power/knowledge/subjectivity formations that have positioned it for our affect and intellect. It is a secret discipline, in the sense of an *askesis* of unknowing, an exercise into what must be secret even for Christians, even to those on the "inside." Faith, in its cognitive contents and its felt attractiveness, in what we can know of it and why it keeps hold on us, holds its secrets from the believer. A postmodern Christian faith can never be sure what its faith is, or what it means to have faith, preventing its public registration in the ways that publicness wants in the American context. It is not talking more about Christian faith in "the public square" that will help heal social divisions, on the one hand, or allow an authentic prophetic distinctive voice its own-most moment, on the other. It is, instead, learning to question the injunction to speak as a Christian that will feel a way toward a new path to "preserve our souls . . . from the burning building" that is Christianity today.[6]

This is not so much Bonhoeffer's protecting the truths of the faith from "profanation"[7] as it is testing the profane roots and uses of the sacred, or beyond that, the disassembling of the sacred/profane, pure/syncretism defensiveness of Christianity. We are not in a situation, under the challenge of the strong postmodern challenges to theology implied in the religious research on the genealogy of the Western subject and its complexly secular placement, to have the confidence of Bonhoeffer in a secret discipline fastened on "maintaining the distinction between [Christianity] and complete secularity."[8] A postmodern secret discipline, rather, would instantiate the hope that there is meaning in departing from Christian certitudes, in being witness to dispossession, and its secrecy registers the necessarily "internal" and "personal" character of this dispossession. It is a secret discipline because Christians need time to learn to be postmodern, and so cannot publicize a coherent Christian worldview; because it will be the finding of an *askesis* as much as a purely intellectual achievement; and because it unwinds so profoundly the history of Christian thought *about* Christian thought that, like a wound must be tended over time by a caring community. Even if the wound is the wound of love that mystics talk about as the painful-joyful conversion of the soul, this wound is most generously and patiently tended privately, in communion with others who are willing to learn what submission and witnessing to dispossession mean.

And yet this descent into secret discipline does not merely repeat the dichotomies that we would think are familiar for Bonhoeffer or he might think are familiar for us: secret versus disclosed, discipline versus unruliness. This descent into a secret discipline shows how such dichotomies that guard the traditional understanding cannot be maintained, insofar as a postmodern secret discipline becomes also its "opposite," a disclosed indiscipline, or to borrow other current theological cognates, "indiscretion" or "indecency."[9] The secret discipline becomes at the same time a disclosed indiscipline because the secret to be protected is always already not the property of the whisperer; the maintenance of the mystery is a hedging of and against the mystery itself, is a giving shape to the mystery, and the only discipline that could try to maintain that mystery would be a discipline that would be Foucault's negative sense of *subjectification*, the government, in the name of truth, of individuals who can know the truth. The postmodern Christian secret discipline must also be the reckoning with the disclosure of indiscipline, which is another way of saying that a secret discipline today will itself witness to the dispossession that is Christianity's gift and task, its present.

"MY LONGING FOR ROME IS DEEPLY NEUROTIC"[10]

One monument for thinking Catholics, in particular, who are in such dispossession, will be the venerable Roman temple, the Pantheon. The second-century architectural wonder, an amalgam of temple porch and massive rotunda, is a Catholic Church, known as Santa Maria ad Martyres.[11] But it is a church indwelled by a thoroughgoing "paganism." There is a circular hole, 30 feet across, set in the domed ceiling, 150 feet up from the floor. Through this oculus, rain and light pour down into the building; basic elements of the universe, air, light, and water, spill in and join the interior to the heavens. The oculus, orifice of spirit, hovers between grasping and receiving, both permitting and inviting the celestial materials. Arrayed around the circumference of the great circular floor are sixteen positions, niches and tabernacles, originally intended for the display of divine statues. There are floors traversed by centuries of worshipers honoring deities heard and unheard of by Christ and his followers.[12] When mass is said in the Pantheon, one is placed, wittingly or not, outside all religious categories familiar and comfortable, housed spiritually in the house of "all gods." Today, one still speaks of Jesus there, and of worship in "God's house," but the bewildered question, once the physics of the place are incorporated theologically, makes itself finally, intemperately, unavoidable: *Whose house are we in?*

To say that this place is claimed for and by Christ, as has been possible ever since its conversion to a church by Boniface IV in the early seventh century, is to underestimate what happens psychically and culturally when Christian claims are arranged through historically and culturally non-Christian materials. Here, in this place, is Christ positioned as much as positioner.[13] Christ, as if by contamination of a pagan structure whose "difference" from Christianity foregrounds its constructedness, himself becomes available to be seen as a built structure, a work of Pantheonic architecture. Christ, literally, is placed, and therefore, displaced, by "pagan" gods, present despite their physical absence in the very construction of the religious space. How ought such a(n) (im)pediment of Christian theology be read? The original temple of all gods carries out its multitheistic orientating even when the statues themselves have been carried out. The spatial and spiritual orientations remain, making it possible to honor Christ as God, but only so long as this God resides among the space of the gods—into untidy surrenders of dominion, as if the reach of the very idea of the Pantheon must exceed the attempt to tidy it up imperially, whether that empire is geographic (Roman) or theological (Catholic).

Fourteen hundred years of being functionally defunct as a "pagan" temple, after all, does not change the disposure of the bodies of the faithful within the Pantheon's cosmically containing volume. Inside the Pantheon, attention goes up and down, on a vertical axis, rather than back and forth, on a horizontal axis. The Pantheon's cylinder and dome, rising up majestically on all sides upon passing from the porch through the doors, take perception up, again and again, to the oculus, and its illumination of all interior space, shifting its shadows as the hours of the day pass. As MacDonald observes, this spatial orientation is different from what would become that of Christian basilicas and their horizontality of attention, their back and forth, fore and aft self-presentation through cruciform structures.[14] While Christians may feel some familiarity upon stepping onto the front porch because they are expecting an axis of longitude to continue forward inside the Pantheon, once they step through the doors at the back of the porch and into the giant cylindrical space of the rotunda behind, that promise of what a Christian would expect to be a basilica-like axis is immediately revoked, dispossessed, "dissipated and lost in an incommensurable void," in MacDonald's elegant architectural language.[15] Indeed, the ancient Vitruvian conviction, made famous for modernity by da Vinci's drawing, regarding a deep consanguinity between circle and square architecture, such as the vaulted form of the Pantheon, and the naturally extended upright human body, suggest that it is no accident that humans feel both dwarfed and taken up inside the Pantheon, because they feel a fundamental fit between the body's erect frame and the shape of the container that is the rotunda. The body is invited to recognize its dimensions because of the proportionality of this tremendous container to the body. It may be part of what gives the Pantheon the sense of communicating being at home in the cosmos.[16] The verticality may be presumed to be claimed for Christ when Christians pray in the Pantheon, but the nature of that claiming is not that of a fresh restarting, but rather of a co-inhabiting of a disavowed "paganism." Edmund Thomas has written of the pagan "theological speculations" embodied in the interior of the Pantheon, a subdivision into "sixteen sectors correspond[ing] to the division of the sky in Etruscan religious thought," along with a vertical "arrangement of twenty-eight divisions below five rows of coffering below the oculus [which] can readily be interpreted as a representation of the moon and the sun and the five other planets between them."[17] The very sunlight itself, which spills through the oculus, descending through the vertical space, was there as "Zeus-Jupiter-Helios, the supreme god allied with the Great Sun . . . epiphanized in light. Above all, it is the garment of light worn by the rotunda which connects the individual with the heavens, and which, appearing in movement on the architecture, bridges the intangible and the tangible."[18] To have been taken into light was to be present to the "eye of Zeus."[19]

What gets named a Christian space is a specific conglomeration of cultural artifacts, monuments to power, whose order orders any logic that can be read in them. Worshiping the Christian God in such a space as the Pantheon is implicitly to venerate all the gods who once lined the walls and whose visages were the purpose for the very arc of the walls, cut of the stone, access to the sky.

> Its forms record an attempt to describe something of the awe in which [humans have] always held the universe, visible and invisible. . . . It is truly a building of immanence, of no firmly held and dogmatically expressed religious belief.[20]

A Christian is necessarily a religious pluralist—internally: she is inhabited in her soul, in her arc, cut, and access, by Judaisms, Stoicisms, Epicureanisms, Skepticisms; in her walls, stone, and sky by Olympus as well as Sinai, Plato as well as Paul.[21] If the God presenced in the house of God is experienced through and with the structure, if the built, historical space of God is accepted and cathected in the worship of God, then in consenting to God in the Pantheon, one at the same time consents, however unwittingly and unwillingly, to *pantheon*. And the Pantheon then becomes the church of churches, because it is the model for how to be dispossessed in Christian worship in any space made for God by cultural materials, any church.

But the Pantheon as temple-church cannot be understood only as a religious space with secondary political implications for the practice of Christian theology. It was also designed to be a political space as such. It seems likely that visitors to the Pantheon in antiquity would have seen an imperial eagle, wings spread, on the face of the pediment, or tympanum, just above the porch, a kind of ancient branding, "well-known in the iconography of Roman dominion."[22] MacDonald has observed that the shapes of circles and squares on the floor of the Pantheon bear a striking resemblance to a "Roman surveyor's plan for a town," and that that pattern is reflected above in the coffering of the dome, "up in the zone of the mysteries of the heavens," emphasizing that divine order and Roman order were of a single cosmic cloth.[23] And while it is unclear which gods were actually arrayed around the inside,[24] the gods represented the breadth of the Roman empire, their arrangement as points on a compass of great circumference a symbol of the empire's extraordinarily encompassing geographical circumference. Indeed, the visitor to the Pantheon might well have conceptually overlaid Roman containment of all gods under a spherical dome with the government of the spherically domed cosmos itself, a palimpsest showing the heavens themselves to be Roman. Constructed by Hadrian, the temple was an imperial building project from the outset, and a statue of the deified Julius Caesar was likely inside, with statues of Augustus and Agrippa just outside the rotunda, adorning the back part of the adjoining porch. The "all gods" which the Pantheon's very name invokes meant, practically, all gods *for* Rome.[25] The spiritual majesty of the Pantheon is entangled with Roman empire, a constitutive paradox hardly relieved by the controlling authority passing to the Roman Church. Indeed, this political dimension of the power to show the divine approaching in space, to show, in principle, access to "all gods," is a reminder of the Roman power still circulating in Catholic churches and theology.

In the disassembling of Catholic character enacted by the Pantheon, a new and different experience of the local Catholic Church is suggested, as well. Taking the Pantheon as a symbolic Catholic map for houses of faith renders every local church a potential pantheon. It also opens for imagination a way of inhabiting the Vatican itself as a pantheonic space. It is bracing to remember that Bramante's building of St. Peter's in the sixteenth century included a plan to top the structure with a replica of the Pantheon's dome. Theologically vitalizing, too, is the memory that Michelangelo, when his turn at continuing the construction came along, proposed a porch in the shape of a temple-front that would have made St. Peter's something of a mirror image of the Pantheon;[26] the grand church of the keys to the kingdom would live in constant referral to that ambiguous site of consent to all gods and baptism into Roman authority. Matthew 16:18 ("You are Peter, and on this rock I will build my church") would be relativized architecturally as mere commentary on the earlier "Roman Catholicism" down the street.

An illustration of the move from the ecclesial symbology of St. Peter's to the Pantheon can be found in the liturgy at the annual convention of the Catholic Theological Society of America. Each year, the society shares a mass together on the Saturday evening of the conference, and most members attend, hundreds strong. And each year, this mass has never failed to evoke a deep emotional response from me. Assembled are Catholic theologians representing almost every point of view in theology in the United States. Some theologians are apparently quite "traditionally" pious, some are under investigation by Rome, some have been unofficially silenced. More than a few harbor personal beliefs unacceptable to the hierarchy. Many hold views simply uncomprehended by the official theology, often known only by a very close and psychologically aware reading of these theologians' texts, or known only by their intimate friends, or known only to themselves in the most private of personal depths, or not even known at all, but silently held. So many gods present at this Catholic theological mass. The inner landscape of each theologian becomes an inner pantheon, a personal and psychic history brought to the mass as much as we each bring ourselves physically. Karl Rahner famously argued that one theological reason for holding that love of neighbor is love of God, is that when one genuinely accepts another in love, what is being co-accepted is the divine in and through that person, the image of God that makes that person the loveable being that they are.[27] Just as in saying yes to God in the Pantheon one consents to a world of gods one does not understand, one consents "proleptically" to the gods of other theologians in that mass, loves a strange world that makes us even more strange to each other, if we will but consider this more seriously. Despite all the gods present, all consent, in their way, to the ritual. A ritual shared and unshared.

> One of the most important things about the Pantheon is that it was created . . . at a turning point in history, when rites and rules drawn from a very long past were not yet abandoned, but when the surge of a new and utterly different age was already being felt. Because of this, the Pantheon is suffused with a quality of seeking. . . .[28]

EVANGELIZATION

Witnessing to dispossession is a genuine form of evangelization possible for Christians today. For many, it will be the only intellectually credible and emotionally compelling form.

Conversion has long been valorized over against its silent other—one of its many silent others—deconversion.[29] This time of a "new evangelization" in the Roman Catholic Church of postmodernity must also be a time of availability for deconversion, as the "missiological" counterpart to the Christian spirituality of dispossession. This is a missiology to and for the "already converted," sharing in the conviction of recent catechetical documents that due to the challenges to Christianity's vitality in Western culture, those Catholics raised in the faith themselves need a deeper evangelization, catechesis unending,[30] but now drawing a different inference: that a mature deepening of "faith" might in fact lead to a deconversion, faith's releasement.

Much of the ecclesial or theological literature concerning the situation of Christianity in a postmodern and religiously pluralistic context has contemplated the possibility and complexity of conversion from one religion to another religion, or a conversion to a second religious faith without giving up the first (for example, in many of the conversations about "multiple religious belonging"[31]). Theologies of inculturation share in this conversional rhetoric, typically framing the significance of attention to culture for the purpose of deeper conversion of the believer in a specific context.

We seem constantly, then, to be talking about the value of "ongoing conversion," whether within or, more cautiously in Catholic theology, between one religious tradition and another. But all this talk of movement in one direction, of a deepened faith that respects the given religious categories that will contain the new convert and allow a journey down into the depths of that tradition, signals a reluctance to explore the possibility of a backward breaking up, a dissolution, a fragmentation—a deconversion, a "holy departure" from religious belief, community, tradition.[32]

The processes of deconversion, the lives of those who "leave the faith," are almost never the focus of theological reflection, having disqualified themselves from the ability to bear a disclosure about the faith, and not just its aberrations or imperfections. "Ex-Catholics" or "Recovering Catholics" make even many Catholic theologians wince, and have yet to be generally seen as a potential source of real insight about the adult life of faith, indeed as one possible outcome of a Catholic theological life.[33] And yet, as John Barbour argues, the "insights of those who have conscientiously rejected Christian beliefs ought to play a role in Christian self-definition," especially if such definition is the work of a "self-critical Christian theology."[34] Dispossession shows us that the willingness to relinquish Christian faith to the service of a truth not comprehended by the faith that can be had today, can serve as a decompression chamber, of considerable length and complexity, into a new Catholic theology. This is a very particular way of saying that faith can be the midwife of doubt, that one can love the truth one learns in church so much that one experiences a commencement from the church. That one can fall so deeply for Christ that one falls through Christ (with Christ, and in Christ), into an unforeseen relationship to truth. Deconversion is of the spirit of a Foucauldian theological exposure, yet is a much broader contemporary phenomenon. As Barbour recognizes, deconversion "is a subtle yet pervasive impulse and theme . . . in a great deal of modern and postmodern thinking," recalling that it was "Nietzsche [who] first discerned that deconversion from all inherited beliefs could become a systematic program reflecting a scrupulous intellectual conscience."[35]

A PROVISIONAL VOCATION

Fear of the strong postmodernization of Catholic theology, which is still a palpable sentiment among both progressives and traditionalists in authority, and their admirers in ecclesial and theological societies, is often rooted in an appropriate, though finally mistaken, assumption: that the claim of Jesus' countercultural life and teachings will be muted or replaced entirely by something foreign to the gospel and more conducive to ideology. However, such a fear fails to fully appreciate what sort of spiritual discipline can be involved in an ongoing undoing or deconstruction of faith, in a restless and searching postmodern Catholic theology. As has been argued for two of the most well-known deconstructors of faith in recent decades, Jacques Derrida and Michel Foucault, the demands of thinking beyond the certitudes of the theological traditions, of suspending theology in favor of something other than its modern (or modernly romanticized premodern) versions can itself demand an *askesis* constitutive of exercises intellectual, ethical, and spiritual.[36] The *askeses* involved in the movements through the postmodern decompression chamber, and the new philosophies and theologies they let onto, cannot be prejudged as any less radical, courageous, or vital for Christians, or the larger culture, than a radical following of Jesus and his cross might like to suppose, or presuppose.

Thus can a witness to dispossession be a vocation for a postmodern theologian. Though it is not the only possible vocation for a postmodern or a theologian, it is one to which I have been led, however consciously, by my engagements with Foucault studies and immersions in practical and Catholic theologies. It makes little to sense to hold this vocation as a prescriptive norm or an obligatory intellectual allegiance. The engagement with the "postmodern" is still too new in American Catholic theology, the "postmodern" itself—not to mention the "Catholic" or the "theological"—too unstable to provide permanent residence for thought, and the cultural present for Catholic theology too rich in complexity for any single approach to a theology of culture. Postmodernity seems best rendered as something theology is undergoing and must undergo. Restoring theology to the mercy of the theologian's body[37] allows for multiple lived points of that undergoing: places where our positioning by cultural history and psychic life meets our cultural and psychic creativity in making a theology for the present. But—no confidence in a new theological totality. We theologize in memory of Bonhoeffer, with our own understanding of "no ground under our feet." As Michel de Certeau already saw several decades ago, and as American Catholic theology may yet discover, a witness to dispossession may live with Christian theology as a vertiginous, departing life.[38]

The style of Catholic theology after Foucault that is merely intimated in the essays in this book, and schematized in the present chapter, is thus a pre-Christian Catholic theology (in implicit distinction from a gathering alternative postmodern position, a postliberal Catholic theology[39]). It is so in several interrelated senses: first, in its Foucauldian genealogical orientation that experiences theological thought's ethical exertion not primarily in justifying, warranting, applying, or interpreting theological claims, but on an interdisciplinary-historical suspension of theological claims to attention, in the interest of understanding how these claims on Christian attention have emerged, a therapy for allowing theology a more critical, self-aware, and freeing role in our present lives; second, in its particular commitment to liquidating Christianity of its presumed essences, rooting them especially in what is thought of as "secular," "pagan," or, in that formulation as common as it is intellectually thorny, even and especially among liberal theologians, the "non-theological." Correlative to these points is a third: the priority of research on "indigenous" religions, philosophies, and cultures, from Greek and Roman antiquity to contemporary aboriginality—the focus remaining on the importance of situating Christianity's antecedent beliefs and practices.

This pre-Christian Catholic theology, then, focuses on the constitution of practice (including and especially Catholic theological practices) through a critical account of theological knowledge, attempting to test how Catholic theology can make critical, and particularly reflexive, sense of practice in faith and culture.

It might be asked what would qualify such a practical theology as "Catholic." In reply, it should be asked what is at stake in the very response to such a question. That is, who wants to know, and why? Who has the privilege of access to this truth, and with what effects? Such responses to the demand for a confession of Catholic identity are too seldom attempted by Catholic theologians, educators, or pastors. It is often oddly assumed that the question of criteria for Catholic theological statements itself is natural, neutral, necessary, or obligatory. Ascertaining both the available reasons that people are expected to declare the Catholicity of their theology, as well as the historical conditions positioning Catholic power and knowledge that make such a question askable, helps clarify whether and how one might reply. Many requests to justify the Catholicity of theology disqualify themselves as fearful attempts to control theology by an aggressive demand for Catholicity (typically clothed, of course, in the velvet glove of love for the church). It is therefore important to place the Catholicity of theology as a category marked by historicity, diversity, and ambiguity. As Kathryn Tanner has so well explained in her recent theology, these "[p]ostmodern ideas about culture suggest what historical studies of Christianity confirm,"[40] namely, what "disciplines such as sociology and anthropology reveal: the often messy, ambiguous and porous character of the effort to live Christianly." "Theologians," she adds, "have yet to make the leap."[41] In so doing, one cannot avoid the conclusion that there is no deciding finally, now, what will count as Catholic for the future. One must respond from the paradoxical principle that no theology is Catholic as such. And it is not necessary to know in advance what Catholicism is in order to be available to the discoveries of dispossession and a possible future Catholicity. One's theology can only be accounted Catholic insofar as it gets distributed as Catholic in the cultural practices and networks of discourse in a specific cultural situation. Theology cannot attempt to defend itself as Catholic, in other words, without a simultaneous critique of the attempt to govern theology through the element of orthodoxy. It would thus seem that spreading out the power to denominate a theology as Catholic, rather than concentrating it in the hands of those with the authority, official or unofficial, to demand an answer, is a better way to honor the complexities intrinsic to the Catholicity of theology. Prayer and argument over time, including the very exposure to which this book is dedicated, may perhaps provide ways of avoiding the failures of courage and generosity ingredient in demands for Catholicity in theology.

Notes

Introduction

1. Rainer Maria Rilke, "[I find you, Lord, in all Things and in all]," *The Selected Poetry of Rainer Maria Rilke*, edited and translated by Stephen Mitchell (New York: Random House, 1982), p. 5.

2. Johannes Baptist Metz, "Facing the Jews: Theology After Auschwitz," in Johann Baptist Metz and Jürgen Moltmann, *Faith and the Future: Essays on Theology, Solidarity, and Modernity* (Maryknoll, Orbis: 1995), p. 41.

3. The psychologist Mary Gail Frawley-O'Dea, in her study of the psychological causes of the Catholic sex abuse scandal, argues that, based on the limits of church reporting about abuse, and various kinds of underreporting on the part of victims, that the approximately 11,000 victims reported by the John Jay College of Criminal Justice study represents only a portion of probable victims between 1950 and 2002, and that it is "reasonable to estimate that over fifty thousand young people were abused by priests over the fifty years encompassed by the [John Jay] study." Mary Gail Frawley-O'Dea, *Perversion of Power: Sexual Abuse in the Catholic Church* (Nashville, TN: Vanderbilt University Press, 2007), p. 6.

4. Stephen Pattison, "'Suffer Little Children': The Challenge of Child Abuse and Neglect to Theology," in Stephen Pattison, *The Challenge of Practical Theology: Selected Essays* (Philadelphia: Kingsley, 2007), pp. 164–184, at p. 166.

5. James Alison, *On Being Liked* (New York: Crossroad, 2003), pp. 98, 96.

6. I cannot think of one analysis of the crisis, of which I am aware, that has not implicitly or explicitly regarded attention to the issue of power in Catholicism as the central, or one of the central, problems to be comprehended. See, for example, Frawley-O'Dea, *Perversion of Power*; Mary Gail Frawley-O'Dea and Virginia Goldner (eds.), *Predatory Priests, Silenced Victims: The Sexual Abuse Crisis and the Catholic Church* (Mahwah, NJ: Analytic Press, 2007); Myra L. Hidalgo, *Sexual Abuse and the Culture of Catholicism: How Priests and Nuns Become Perpetrators* (New York: Haworth, 2007); Frank Bruni and Elinor Burkett, *A Gospel of Shame: Children, Sexual Abuse, and the Catholic Church* (New York: Perennial, 2002); David France, *Our Fathers: The Secret Life of the Catholic Church in an Age of Scandal* (New York: Broadway Books, 2004); A.W. Richard Sipe, *Sex, Priests, and Power: Anatomy of a Crisis* (New York: Brunner/Mazel, 1995); Jason Berry, *Lead*

Us Not Into Temptation: Catholic Priests and the Sexual Abuse of Children (Urbana, IL: University of Illinois Press, 2000).

7. The recent president of the Catholic Theological Society of America, Daniel Finn, has called for Catholic theologians to include a much more serious concern for power in their theologies and academic-ecclesial practices. See Daniel Finn, "The Catholic Theological Society of America and the Bishops," *Origins* 37:6, June 21, 2007, pp. 88–95.

8. Karl Rahner, "The Theology of Power," in Karl Rahner, *Theological Investigations IV: More Recent Writings*, trans. Kevin Smyth (Baltimore: Helicon Press, 1966), pp. 391–409, at pp. 403, 402.

Chapter 1—Foucault Teaching Theology

1. Michel Foucault, "The History of Sexuality," interview by Lucette Finas, in Michel Foucault, *Power/Knowledge*, ed. Colin Gordon and trans. L. Marshall (New York: Pantheon, 1980 [1977]), pp. 183–193, at p. 189.

2. Michel Foucault, *The History of Sexuality: Volume 1: An Introduction*, trans. Robert Hurley. New York: Vintage (1990 [1976]), p. 93.

3. Michel Foucault, "Clarifications on the Question of Power," interview by Pasquale Pasquino, in *Foucault Live*, ed. Sylvère Lotringer and trans. James Cascaito (New York: Semiotext[e], 1996 [1978]), pp. 255–263, at p. 258.

4. Foucault, *The History of Sexuality: Volume 1*, p. 96.

5. Michel Foucault, "Intellectuals and Power: Discussion with Gilles Deleuze," in Michel Foucault, *Language, Counter-Memory, Practice*, ed. Donald F. Bouchard and trans. Donald F. Bouchard and Sherry Simon (Ithaca, NY: Cornell University Press, 1977 [1972]), pp. 205–217, at p. 213.

6. Foucault, *History of Sexuality: Volume 1*, p. 94.

7. Ibid.

8. Foucault's struggle to get beyond Marxism is also evident in his attempt to free himself from "the old concept of ideology," a concept that encouraged "playing reality against false interpretations of reality," in a way that ignored the power-knowledge forces at work in the supposedly nonideological description of "reality" (Foucault, "Clarifications on the Question of Power," p. 260).

9. Foucault, *History of Sexuality: Volume 1*, pp. 94, 136.

10. "The traditional conception of power [is] an essentially judicial mechanism . . . which lays down the law, which prohibits, which refuses, and which has a whole range of negative effects: exclusion, rejection, denial, obstruction. . . ." (Foucault, "The History of Sexuality," p. 183).

11. Michel Foucault, "On the Genealogy of Ethics," in Hubert Dreyfus and Paul Rabinow, *Michel Foucault: Beyond Structuralism and Hermeneutics* (Chicago: University of Chicago Press, 1983), pp. 231–232.

12. Foucault, "The History of Sexuality," p. 189.

13. "One needs to be nominalistic, no doubt: power is not an institution, and not a structure; neither is it a certain strength we are endowed with; it is the name that one attributes to a complex strategical situation in a particular society" (Foucault, *The History of Sexuality: Volume 1*, p. 93).

14. Ibid., p. 94.

15. Ibid.

16. Ibid., p. 95.

17. Ibid.

18. On this theme, see J. Joyce Schuld, *Foucault and Augustine: Reconsidering Power and Love* (Notre Dame, IN: University of Notre Dame Press, 2003).

19. Foucault, *History of Sexuality: Volume 1*, p. 96. "Are there no great radical ruptures, massive binary divisions, then? Occasionally, yes. But more often one is dealing with mobile and transitory points of resistance." Revolution, however unlikely, is possible through a "strategic codification of . . . points of resistance" (p. 96).

20. Ibid., p. 101.

21. Jeremy Carrette, *Foucault and Religion: Spiritual Corporality and Political Spirituality* (New York: Routledge, 2000).

22. Foucault, *History of Sexuality: Volume 1*, p. 98.

23. Ibid., p. 99.

24. James Bernauer, *Michel Foucault's Force of Flight: Toward an Ethics for Thought* (Atlantic Highlands, NJ: Humanities Press International, 1990), p. 107.

25. Foucault, "Talk Show," interview by Jacques Chancel, in *Foucault Live*, ed. Sylvère Lotringer and trans. Phillis Aronov and Dan McGrawth (New York: Semiotext(e), 1996 [1975], pp. 133–145, at p. 138.

26. Foucault, *Discipline and Punish: The Birth of the Prison*, trans. Alan Sheridan (New York: Vintage, 1978 [1975]), p. 222.

27. Foucault, *Madness and Civilization,* trans. Richard Howard (New York: Vintage, 1988 [1961]), p. 247.

28. Ibid., p. 261.

29. Ibid., p. 265.

30. Ibid., p. 135.

31. Ibid., p. 130.

32. Ibid., p. 276.

33. Foucault, *Discipline and Punish*, pp. 3–31.

34. Ibid., pp. 29–30.

35. Ibid.

36. Ibid., pp. 170–194.

37. Ibid., p. 177.

38. Ibid., pp. 195–230.

39. Foucault, *History of Sexuality: Volume 1*, p. 20.

40. *Episteme* is Foucault's term for the entire set of relationships in a given period that governs what gets counted as knowledge across diverse cultural-political-scientific terrain, "the lateral relations that may exist between epistemological figures or sciences in so far as they belong to neighbouring, but distinct, discursive practices" (Michel Foucault, *The Archaeology of Knowledge*, trans. A.M. Sheridan Smith [New York: Pantheon, 1972], p. 191).

41. Foucault, "Nietzsche, Genealogy, History," in *The Foucault Reader*, ed. Paul Rabinow and trans. Donald F. Bouchard and Sherry Simon (New York: Pantheon, 1984 [1971]), p. 88.

42. The phrase is from The Bible and Culture Collective, *The Postmodern Bible* (New Haven, CT: Yale University Press, 1995), p. 50, in reference to their critique of the reader-response criticism of Wolfgang Iser.

43. David Tracy, *Plurality and Ambiguity: Hermeneutics, Religion, Hope* (Chicago: University of Chicago Press, 1987).

44. I borrow and redirect the term from the Bible and Culture Collective, *The Postmodern Bible* (p. 63), who employ it in their discussion of the work of Jonathan Culler.

45. One example: while Judith Berling rightly observes that "The power issue cannot be evaded; it is a reality of the way courses work," she then suggests that there is required an "active intentionality on the part of the teacher to *relinquish some of that power* and to devise effective ways to *empower the students* in a collaborative learning environment." While a Foucauldian approach would suggest that it is impossible for us to conceptualize the teacher "relinquish[ing]" power in a way that would not itself be a reinscription of power, albeit perhaps in a more subtle way, the claim of "empower[ing]" students also needs nuance in a post-Foucauldian theological pedagogy. "Empowerment" as the leading metaphor for the redistribution of power in the classroom still suggests the bestowal of power "onto" students, and seems to bear traces of nostalgia for a top-down model of power (and of teaching, and hence of learning), which conceives of power as something disseminated downward from an authority figure. (See Berling, "Getting Out of the Way: A Strategy for Engaging Students in Collaborative Learning," *Teaching Theology and Religion* 1:1 (1998), pp. 31–35, at p. 32).

46. Foucault, "Talk Show," p. 144.

47. Foucault, "Intellectuals and Power," p. 208.

48. Foucault, *History of Sexuality: Volume 1*, p. 97.

49. Foucault, *Discipline and Punish*, p. 27.

50. From a Foucauldian perspective, John Ransom in *Foucault's Discipline* (Durham, NC: Duke University Press, 1997) notes that it is better to see that real change typically happens incrementally and unstably, across a variety of practices and fields that may contradict and contend with each other.

51. In the piquant words of John Ransom (ibid., pp. 120–121), as he refuses to savor the alluring "retreats to normativity" found in some "politics of difference."

52. Foucault, "Intellectuals and Power," p. 209.

53. It is worth noting that liberal dialogue-based pedagogies fall under the Foucauldian critique as inadequately attentive to power relations: "In traditional academic spiritualist philosophy, relations among individuals are viewed essentially as dialogues, relations of understanding, verbal, discursive: either you understand each other or you don't" (Foucault, "Talk Show," p. 143).

Chapter 2—Multiple Theological Intelligences?

1. From "Cosmos," in Micheal O'Siadhail, *Hail! Madam Jazz: New and Selected Poems* (Newcastle: Dufour, 1992), p. 149, cited in Begbie, "Theology and the Arts: Music," in David F. Ford (ed.), *The Modern Theologians* (Cambridge, MA: Blackwell, 1997) p. 696.

2. René Char, "Partage Formel," #XXII, translated and cited in James Miller, *The Passion of Michel Foucault* (New York: Simon and Schuster, 1993), p. 108.

3. On a "history of the present," see Foucault, *Discipline and Punish,* trans. Alan Sheridan (New York: Vintage, 1978), p. 31.

4. James Bernauer, *Michel Foucault's Force of Flight: Toward an Ethics for Thought* (Atlantic Highlands, NJ: Humanities Press, 1993), pp. 180–181.

5. "Postscript: An Interview with Michel Foucault," in *Death and the Labyrinth,* trans. Charles Ruas (New York: Doubleday and Co., 1986), p. 184.

6. Jean-Paul Aron, *Les Modernes* (Paris: Gallimard, 1984), pp. 64–65, cited in Didier Eribon, *Michel Foucault*, trans. Betsy Wing (Cambridge, MA: Harvard University Press, 1991), p. 65.

7. Relevant passages in the major biographies include Eribon, *Michel Foucault*, pp. 64–68, 83; David Macey, *The Lives of Michel Foucault* (New York: Vintage, 1995), pp. 50–54, 399; and Miller, *Passion*, pp. 79–81, 89–92, 408 n.68.

8. Eribon describes Foucault in Uppsala as determinedly writing "always to music. Not an evening went by that he did not listen to the *Goldberg Variations*. Music for him meant Bach or Mozart" (p. 83; also p. 66). According to Macey, Foucault "idolised Beethoven" and enjoyed Mahler and Wagner (see *Lives*, pp. 51, 399).

9. See Foucault and Pierre Boulez, "Contemporary Music and the Public," in Lawrence D. Kritzman (ed.), *Michel Foucault: Politics, Philosophy, Culture* (New York: Routledge, 1988). Macey reports that Daniel Defert, Foucault's partner of two decades, once took Foucault to a David Bowie concert. Anyone who knows something of Bowie's theatrical gender-bending can only wonder what this experience must have been like.

10. Eribon, *Michel Foucault*, p. 65.

11. Cited in ibid., p. 66.

12. Ibid., p. 67.

13. Macey, *Lives*, p. 53. Miller (*Passion*, p. 79) quotes the interview: "[T]he French serialists and deodecaphonic musicians [provided] the first 'tear' in the dialectical universe in which I had lived."

14. Maurice Blanchot, "Michel Foucault as I Imagine Him," trans. Jeffrey Mehlman, in *Foucault/Blanchot* (New York: Zone, 1987), p. 74. For an interpretation of the relation of Foucault's thought to negative theology, see Bernauer, *Michel Foucault's Force of Flight*.

15. Blanchot, "Michel Foucault," p. 75.

16. For evidence of this influence, see the list of Gardner's works, works by others, and workshop presenters that defend and elaborate his theories, in Gardner, *Multiple Intelligences: The Theory in Practice* (New York: Basic Books, 1993), pp. 281–297. As examples of his appropriation in Christian religious education settings, see Carl J. Pfeifer and Janann Manternach, "The Processes of Catechesis," in Thomas Groome and Michael J. Corso (eds.), *Empowering Catechetical Leaders* (Washington, DC: National Catholic Education Association, 1999); Ronald Nuzzi, *Gifts of the Spirit: Multiple Intelligences in Religious Education*, 2nd edition (Washington, DC: National Catholic Educational Association, 2005). Leading religious education theorist Thomas Groome endorses Gardner's seven intelligences in *Educating for Life: A Spiritual Vision for Every Teacher and Parent* (Allen, TX: Thomas More Press, 1998), p. 101. For a helpful application of Gardner's multiple intelligence theory to university teaching of religion, see Paul F. Aspan and Faith Kirkham Hawkins, "After the Facts: Alternative Student Evaluation for Active Learning Pedagogies in the Undergraduate Biblical Studies Classroom," *Teaching Theology and Religion* 3, no. 3 (October 2000): 133–151.

17. Jean-Luc Marion, *God Without Being: Hors-Texte*, trans. Thomas Carlson (Chicago: University of Chicago Press, 1991), p. 1.

18. Ibid.

19. Howard Gardner, *Frames of Mind: The Theory of Multiple Intelligences* (New York: Basic Books, 1993 [1983]).

20. Ibid., p. 365.

21. Ibid., p. 4.

22. Ibid., p. x. This definition is from his introduction to the 1993 edition.

23. Ibid., pp. 25–27.

24. I have abstracted these from ibid., pp. 60–62. Gardner does not enumerate them.

25. Ibid., p. 61.

26. Ibid.

27. The following examples are taken from ibid., pp. 63–67.

28. Ibid., p. 65.

29. Ibid., p. 70.

30. Hence Gardner's claim in ibid., p. 27: "In monitoring the prodigy as he advances, one glimpses a 'fast-forward' picture of what is involved in all educational processes." See William James, *The Varieties of Religious Experience* (New York: Vintage, 1990 [1902]), p. 436, wherein observation of the most intense form of a religious phenomenon becomes the ideal mode for its study.

31. Gardner, *Frames of Mind*, p. 27.

32. Ibid., p. 28.

33. There are many examples of this overindividualization of intelligence in *Frames of Mind*. See, for example, p. 148, where Gardner ignores any social or cultural influences that may have functioned to allow or disallow the "faith in the power of one's own intuitions concerning the ultimate nature of physical reality" in certain prodigious scientists; or p. 289, where Gardner claims that with respect to truly original thinking, "it is up to the skilled practitioner himself [sic] whether he in fact produces original work or is simply satisfied with realizing a prior tradition."

34. See, for instance, Gardner's alarming statement in ibid., p. 311: "It is given to only a few individuals in most cultures to reach the apogee of symbolic competence and then to move off in unanticipated directions, experimenting with symbol systems, fashioning unusual and innovative symbolic products, perhaps even attempting to devise a new symbol system." While this observation may be statistically "true" ("a few individuals"), it fails to critically investigate why so "few" exhibit this creativity with respect to experimentations with knowledge—other than presupposing the tautology that prodigious individuals are rare.

35. Among other places, see ibid., p. xii, ". . . efforts to *define* intelligence . . . ," and p. xvi: "intelligences are always *expressed* in the context of . . ." Further, see Gardner (with Joseph Walters), "A Rounded Version," in *Multiple Intelligences*, p. 16: ". . . the biological proclivity to participate in a particular form of problem solving must also be coupled with the cultural *nurturing* of that domain." (Italics mine.)

36. For example, see Gardner's interpretations of culture in *Frames,* pp. 57, 98, 164, 242. Typical is the claim in *Frames*, p. 242, that "symbolization [is] of the essence in the [intra- and inter]personal intelligences. Without a symbolic code supplied by the culture, the individual is confronted with only his [sic] most elementary and unorganized discrimination of feelings: but armed with such a scheme of interpretation, he has the potential to make sense of the full range of experiences which he and others in his community can undergo." Gardner's assertion that several of the intelligences are essentially acultural is thus equally problematic. He argues that musical and linguistic intelligence, for example, are "not closely tied to the world of physical objects," having "an essence that is equally remote from the world of other persons" (ibid., p. 98). He argues that only logical-mathematical, spatial, and bodily intelligences are formed through interaction with objects in the world (ibid., p. 235).

37. Gardner and Walters, "Questions and Answers," in Gardner, *Multiple Intelligences*, p. 37. See also in *Multiple Intelligences*: Gardner, "The Relation of Intelligence," pp. 50–51, and Gardner, "Assessment in Context," pp. 172–173.

38. Gardner's definition of symbol is too thin to do the work he wants it to do (defining it as "any entity material or abstract) that can denote or refer to any other entity") and frequently vague, even appearing naïve at times ("a symbol can convey some mood, feeling, or tone . . . just so long as the relevant community chooses to interpret a particular symbol in a particular way"). See Gardner, *Frames*, p. 301.

39. Gardner, *Frames*, p. 300.

40. Ibid., p. 242.

41. Gardner argues (ibid., p. 284) that "[w]hat is crucial is not the label but, rather, the conception: that individuals have a number of domains of potential intellectual competence which they are in the position to develop, if they are [']normal['] and if the appropriate stimulating factors are available." From this definition, the "domains of competence" seem to exist prior to and may "develop" largely independent of external power-knowledge relations.

42. Gardner in many places gives a largely uncritical and politically agnostic reading of the history of intelligence tests in the past, oblivious to their socializing and normalizing functions. See, for example, ibid., pp. 14–17, and Gardner, "Intelligences in Seven Phases," in *Multiple Intelligences*, pp. 215–230. A more critical view appears in Gardner, Kornhaber, and Krechevsky, "Engaging Intelligence," in Gardner, *Multiple Intelligences*, pp. 238–243.

43. Gardner, *Frames*, pp. 28–29, italics mine.

44. Ibid.

45. Educators must not only enter the conversation by merely receiving the authorized foundation statements of science, "build[ing] upon a [scientific] knowledge of . . . intellectual proclivities and their points of maximum flexibility and adaptability" (ibid., p. 33), but must undertake a constant criticism of them as well.

46. *Contra* Gardner in ibid., p. 68: "Intelligences are best thought of apart from particular programs of action."

47. In this respect, the politics of Gardner's own text often protects reigning knowledge brokers of society: "Those individuals most directly charged with the maintenance of cultural knowledge and tradition . . . are well-equipped to know, and to evaluate, the dances, dramas, and designs fashioned by members [of a culture]" (ibid., p. 300).

48. This distinction relates "cognitive potential" to Gardner's more recent definition of intelligence as "a *biopsychological potential*," in Gardner and Walters, "Questions and Answers," p. 36.

49. My initial thinking in this area was influenced by many helpful verbal musical conversations and nonverbal musical collaborations with theologian and percussionist Loye Ashton.

50. Gardner discusses the evidence for musical intelligence in *Frames*, pp. 99–127.

51. Jeremy Begbie, "Theology and the Arts: Music," in David F. Ford (ed.), *The Modern Theologians: An Introduction to Christian Theology in the Twentieth Century* (Cambridge, MA: Blackwell, 1997), p. 695.

52. David Sudnow, *Ways of the Hand: The Organization of Improvised Conduct* (Cambridge, MA: Harvard University Press, 1978), p. 150, italics mine. "Joint knowing" is of course a pun: much musical knowing depends on unselfconscious attention to physical sensations at the joints—of fingers, arms, shoulders.

53. Ibid., p. 13.

54. Ibid., p. 152. Sudnow's book also shows how new domains of knowing have political implications for the institutional identity of academic theologians. One

mentor "enabled me to realize the consequences of allowing the keyboard, and not an academic discipline, to tell me where to go" (ibid., p. viii).

55. Martin Heidegger quoted in ibid., p. ix.

56. Karl Barth in Richard Viladesau, *Theological Aesthetics: God in Imagination, Beauty, and Art* (New York: Oxford University Press), 1999, pp. 4–5.

57. Barth, *Final Testimonies*, ed. Eberhard Busch and trans. Geoffrey W. Bromiley (Grand Rapids, MI: Eerdmans, 1977), pp. 20–21.

58. Viladesau, *Theological Aesthetics*, p. x. For Viladesau, music does not necessarily constitute a distinct "domain" of knowledge. Rather, he frequently turns (via Thomism) to "feeling" and "affect" as other "modes" of intelligence, cutting across the boundaries of more familiar formulations, such as Gardner's, of bodily, musical, personal intelligences, etc. (See Viladesau, ibid., p. 85.)

59. Ibid., p. 180.

60. Gardner and Walters, "A Rounded Version," p. 20.

61. Viladesau, *Theological Aesthetics*, p. 149.

62. Theodore Jennings, "On Ritual Knowledge," *Journal of Religion* 62 (1982), p. 115, in Richard Gaillardetz, *Transforming Our Days: Spirituality, Community and Liturgy in a Technological Culture* (New York: Crossroad, 2000), p. 117.

63. See David Tracy, *The Analogical Imagination: Christian Theology and the Culture of Pluralism* (New York: Crossroad, 1991), and Kathryn Tanner, *Theories of Culture: A New Agenda for Theology* (Minneapolis, MN: Fortress Press, 1997).

64. Tracy, *The Analogical Imagination*, pp. 112–113.

65. See Margaret Miles, *Image as Insight: Visual Understanding in Western Christianity and Secular Culture* (Boston: Beacon, 1985), pp. xi, 9.

66. Musicality may fail to appear to most theologians as a mode for theology not because of music's inherent deficiencies as a cognitive practice, but because of the reigning knowledge paradigms in which modern theology and theological education are invested. Of pivotal importance here is the often-biased pedagogical training of academic theologians. The question of the possibility that musicality and bodily knowledge, for example, may manifest or develop their own unique critical practices, analogous to linguistic-logical "critical thinking," cannot be adjudicated, indeed can hardly get a fair hearing, under current norms for theological work, under the distortions present by the powers of musical-bodily restriction and linguistic-logical production and domination in modern subjects of theology.

67. For example, the musical concept "overtone," derived from musical experience, can function as an alternative to the hermeneutical concept "correlation," as in Begbie, ". . . striking theological overtones emerge in any study of improvisation" ("Theology and the Arts," p. 693). Viladesau wisely observes that "Unless they take refuge in a totally negative theology . . . neither philosophy nor theology can do without metaphor—and metaphor cannot be controlled or communicated without art of some kind" (*Theological Aesthetics*, p. 209).

68. Viladesau summarizes the work of neurologist Antonio Damasio, whose survey of brain research, recalling that of Howard Gardner, indicates that "knowledge, 'which exists in memory under dispositional representation form, can be made accessible to consciousness . . . virtually simultaneously' in both verbal and nonverbal versions. Hence the coexistence in individual minds of different kinds of symbolic mediations of thought—heuristic and conceptual, pictorial and verbal, felt and formulated—allows for comparison and dialectic between our various symbolic 'languages,' so that no one of them can be absolutely determinative of our interpreta-

tion of experience" (Viladesau, *Theological Aesthetics*, p. 81, citing Antonio Damasio, *Descartes' Error: Emotion, Reason, and the Human Brain* [New York: Avon Books, 1994], p. 166). Note that Viladesau's claim here touches only upon cognitive operations in general—not upon theological knowledge in particular. However, it seems to me appropriate to find in the construction of theological knowledges an analogical relationship to what can be known neurobiologically about human cognitive operations. This appropriateness issues from at least two sides: from the side of responsibility to the body's own unique learning processes manifest in the mind/brain; and from the side of the legitimate (natural and cultural) diversity of human ways of knowing, ways that take on a heightened significance when viewed as rooted in some sense in the dignity of being created in the image of God—an argument for another time and place.

69. Foucault, "The Discourse on Language," in *The Archaeology of Knowledge*, trans. A.M. Sheridan Smith (New York: Pantheon, 1972), pp. 226–227.

70. Foucault in Miller, *Passion*, p. 93.

71. James Bernauer and Michael Mahon, "The Ethics of Michel Foucault," in *The Cambridge Companion to Michel Foucault*, ed. Gary Gutting (New York: Cambridge University Press, 1994), p. 147.

72. There arises here the important question of whether verbal-linguistic-conceptual knowledge does and should have a priority in the work of academic theology. A full treatment of this important question is beyond the scope of this chapter. Let me briefly note that the reasons for *granting* such a priority, and therefore for relegating all other domains of knowledge to a secondary status, include the following:

(1) the traditional priority of linguistic, verbal or conceptual knowing for theology's dominant modes of practice;

(2) the purported immediacy of nonlinguistic, nonverbal domains of knowing to "originating" religious experience, rendering them inadequate in serving the necessity of a critically systematizing, "second-order" dimension for theology, or, at the limit, a "metaphysical" task, which is most adequately carried out in linguistic-conceptual modes. As Viladesau writes, "Thematically reflexive, discursive thought is the exceptional mode of rationality—one to which we refer when doubt is introduced, when critical control is needed, or when system is desired" (*Theological Aesthetics,* pp. 85, 86–89). Viladesau endorses Paul Ricoeur's case for the priority of linguistic expression and perception in the adequate rendering of meaning. Viladesau recalls Ricoeur's argument that "the word can generally represent absent realities, abstract ideas, analogies, and judgments in a more clear and direct way than spatial images." Further, the "capacity of word to express judgments of being and of doing make it the normal (although not exclusive) medium of ontological and ethical thought." And finally, "word's unique ability to express negation directly makes it capable of expressing inverse insight and transcendence" (Viladesau, *Theological Aesthetics*, p. 89, summarizing Ricoeur, *Fallible Man*, trans. Charles Kelbley [New York: Regnery, 1965], p. 27).

(3) the broadly public (and hence accessible to general argument) character of linguistic or verbal knowledge, a character that does not obtain with respect to other domains, such as the musical;

(4) the training of contemporary theologians, which precludes facility with nonverbal knowledge domains.

For myself, these positions are very nearly persuasive for the priority of verbal, linguistic or conceptual knowledge for theological work, and so for theological pedagogy. However, reasons for *questioning* such a priority can be formulated as problematizations of the aforementioned claims:

(1) While a theology in service of a tradition must take particular methodological care to foster exposure to that tradition's orienting claims, it is the question of what in fact constitutes the orienting claims of a given theological tradition—*and the knowledge domains mediating those claims*—that is raised by the positing of nonverbal ways of knowing as legitimate theological knowledges.

(2) It seems an open question whether musical knowing, as discursively situated, is any closer to "originating" religious experience than (discursively situated) linguistic-verbal knowing. Moreover, there may be forms of dialectic and criticism unique to nonverbal domains, such as the tendency toward the dialogical "undistorted communication" that may be immanent in improvisatory instrumental work (Begbie, "Theology and the Arts," p. 694). It bears asking whether the modern tradition of critical thought has been too narrowly restricted to the realm of the verbal, and whether Viladesau and Ricoeur overclaim for the precision of the word. There is a need for research on quasi-metaphysical operations in the domains of music and the body.

(3) I take the need for critical and publicly accessible language for theology to be the greatest challenge to the epistemologically leveling prospects of my proposal. At the same time, proficiency in nonverbal knowing, such as the capacity for perfect pitch, may be more widespread than is recognized in the general population. Such proficiency may be a cognitive potential in our students to a greater extent than we typically assume. We lack critical pedagogical means to inquire whether the dominant domains of theological knowledge merely mirror (while developing and intensifying) the dominant knowledge domains in the larger culture in which theology takes place.

(4) Work on the three questions above has implications for the training of theologians. Certainly, academic fragmentation and intratheological balkanization have not provided conditions favorable for the present proposal. The lack of intimate work between contemporary liturgical and systematic theologians is just one example of a hindrance in this regard. A much greater fluidity among the contemporary divisions of theology would be necessitated by my approach.

In sum, the dialectic expressed in this note suggests that the present proposal needs further exploration as a new question. What seems to be needed is much more time to allow nondominant domains of knowledge an extended opportunity to make real contributions to theology. Some sort of "affirmative action" for these heretofore nondominant domains may be programmatically required in order to give them a fair chance at proving their truth-bearing possibilities. Only then can the many quandaries raised in this note be adequately answered.

73. Gardner, *Frames*, p. 353.
74. Gardner and Walters, "A Rounded Version," p. 14.
75. Viladesau, *Theological Aesthetics*, p. 20.

76. David Shutkin, "The Deployment of Information Technology," in *Foucault's Challenge: Discourse, Knowledge and Power in Education*, ed. Thomas S. Popkewitz and Marie Brennan (New York: Teachers College Press, 1998), p. 207.

77. Aspan and Hawkins, "After the Facts," p. 134, referencing Cleo Cherryholmes, *Power and Criticism: Poststructural Investigations in Education* (New York: Teachers College Press, 1988), p. 171.

78. Gardner, *Frames*, p. 365.

79. Foucault, "Two Lectures," in *Power/Knowledge: Selected Interviews and Other Writings 1972–1977*, ed. Colin Gordon, trans. Alessandro Fontana and Pasquale Pasquino (New York: Pantheon, 1980 [1977]), p. 81.

80. Gardner, *Frames*, pp. 208–209, quoting Frederic Bartlett, *Thinking* (New York: Basic Books, 1958), p. 14.

81. It is worth noting the way in which critical pedagogies and critical forms of religious education, that rightly prize critical reception of knowledge, may unwittingly reinscribe the authority of logical-mathematical and/or verbal domains of theological knowledge, insofar as those may be the domains most appropriate for such critical pedagogies. Other domains may not conform neatly to such a critical epistemological model. For example, Gardner argues that bodily-kinesthetic intelligence is developed through practices of mimicking and imitation, which may imply that "imitative teaching and learning may be the most appropriate way to impart skill in this domain." The problem for some critical pedagogies is that "the ability to mimic, to imitate faithfully, is often considered a kind of arrogance or a failure to understand, rather than the exercise of another form of cognition which can be highly adaptive" (see *Frames*, pp. 228–229, taking cues from John Martin's *Introduction to the Dance* [New York: Dance Horizons, 1965]). Overall, Gardner and Walters provide a helpful warning:

> The kind of thinking required to analyze a fugue is simply different from that involved in observing and categorizing different animal species, or scrutinizing a poem, or debugging a program, or choreographing and analyzing a new dance. There is little reason to think that training of critical thinking in one of these domains provides significant "savings" when one enters another domain . . . [Each form] of critical thinking must be practiced explicitly in every domain where it might be appropriate. ("Questions and Answers," p. 44).

This signal insight needs much more development if the project I am describing here is to have merit.

82. Foucault in Miller, *Passion*, p. 79.

Chapter 3—Is Your Spirituality Violent?

1. Tom Beaudoin, *Consuming Faith: Integrating Who We Are with What We Buy* (Lanham, MD: Rowman and Littlefield, 2004).

2. See Darren C. Marks (ed.), *Shaping a Theological Mind: Theological Context and Methodology* (Burlington, VT: Ashgate, 2002); Gesa E. Thiessen and Declan Marmion (eds.), *Theology in the Making: Biography, Contexts, Methods* (Dublin, Ireland: Veritas, 2005); and the several theologians writing in *Jesuit Postmodern: Scholarship, Vocation, and Identity in the 21st Century* (Lanham, MD: Lexington Books, 2006).

3. The report from the National Labor Committee is available at http://www.nlcnet.org/article.php?id=239 (accessed July 29, 2007).

4. See the essays in Seán Hand (ed.), *The Levinas Reader* (Cambridge, MA: Blackwell, 1989).

5. Michel Foucault, *Discipline and Punish: The Birth of the Prison,* trans. by Alan Sheridan (New York: Vintage, 1978), p. 272; cf. the French original: Foucault, *Surveiller et punir: Naissance de la prison* (Gallimard, 1975), p. 317. The term is not in quotation marks in the French.

6. Foucault, *Discipline and Punish*, p. 199.

7. Ibid., p. 279; *Surveiller et punir*, p. 325. It is Sheridan's translation of *marquages* and *marquée* (from *marquer*, "to mark") as "branding" that first gave me the idea of associating these passages in Foucault with contemporary branding practices.

8. Ibid., pp. 279–280.

9. Ibid., p. 281. Dorothy Day, when describing her arrest as an alleged prostitute, says that she was "branded" in that experience, imprinting the status of outcaste on her in a permanent way. See Dorothy Day, *The Long Loneliness* (New York: HarperCollins, 1997), p. 100.

10. Tom Beaudoin, "The Iraq War and Imperial Psychology," *America* 192:2 (January 17, 2005), pp. 14–16.

11. Many contemporary thinkers have treated violence as a theological and religious problem. This is not the place to adequately appreciate the diverse but deeply substantial contributions of such philosophers of religion and violence that have influenced my thinking such as Marjorie Hewitt Suchocki, *The Fall to Violence: Original Sin in Relational Theology* (New York: Continuum, 1994); René Girard, *Violence and the Sacred*, trans. Patrick Gregory (Baltimore: Johns Hopkins University Press, 1977); Grace Jantzen, *Death and the Displacement of Beauty* (New York: Routledge, 2004); Richard Horsley, *Jesus and the Spiral of Violence* (San Francisco: Harper and Row, 1987); Wendy Farley, *Tragic Vision and Divine Compassion: A Contemporary Theodicy* (Louisville, KY: Westminster John Knox, 1990). Even more consciously determinative for me have been Bonhoeffer and Metz. There is Dietrich Bonhoeffer's theological life in the face of the violence of Nazi Germany, and the many ways he enacted a theological disobedience in face of both church and state in response to the impossible call of God. Basic references include Bonhoeffer, *Ethics*, trans. Reinhard Krauss, Douglas Stott, Charles C. West, ed. Clifford Green (Minneapolis, MN: Augsburg Fortress, 2004); Bonhoeffer, *Letters and Papers from Prison*, ed. Eberhard Bethge (New York: Macmillan, 1972); Eberhard Bethge, *Dietrich Bonhoeffer: A Biography*, ed. Victoria J. Barnett (Minneapolis, MN: Augsburg Fortress, 2000). There is also Johannes Baptist Metz's theology as theodicy in face of Jewish suffering, his intellectual-spiritual atonement for his own guilt in serving the German army and for Christianity's preparation of the ground for modern anti-Semitism. Basic references include Metz, *Faith in History and Society: Toward a Practical Fundamental Theology*, trans. David Smith (New York: Seabury, 1979); Metz, *Faith and the Future: Essays on Theology, Solidarity, and Modernity* (Maryknoll, NY: Orbis, 1995); Metz, *A Passion for God: The Mystical-Political Dimension of Christianity*, ed. and trans. J. Matthew Ashley (New York: Paulist, 1998); James Matthew Ashley, *Interruptions: Mysticism, Politics, and Theology in the Work of Johann Baptist Metz* (Notre Dame, IN: University of Notre Dame Press, 1998).

12. J. Joyce Schuld, *Foucault and Augustine: Reconsidering Power and Love* (Notre Dame, IN: University of Notre Dame Press, 2003).

13. See Jantzen, *Death and the Displacement of Beauty.*

14. An internet search for the phrase "violent spirituality" turned up only six different examples of the phrase itself. And while it is easy to think of thousands of everyday questions that return literally millions of "hits" on searches, I found that the specific question "is your spirituality violent?" returned zero. (Searches using www.google.com on February 15, 2006.)

15. Jeremy Carrette and Richard King, *Selling Spirituality: The Silent Takeover of Religion* (New York: Routledge, 2005).

16. For a provocative recent journalistic essay on the tensions involved in America's self-proclaimed Christianity, see Bill McKibben, "The Christian Paradox: How a Faithful Nation Gets Jesus Wrong," *Harper's Magazine*, August 2005, pp. 31–37.

17. Bob Herbert, "No Justice, No Peace," *New York Times*, 23 February 2006, p. A27.

18. From a statement made to the American Civil Liberties Union, excerpted in "Extraordinary Rendition," *Harper's Magazine*, February 2006, pp. 21–22, 24.

19. Ian Austen, "Deported Canadian Was No Threat, Report Shows," *New York Times*, August 10, 2007, p. A9.

20. Anthony Lagouranis, "Tortured Logic," *New York Times*, February 28, 2006, p. A23.

21. I borrow the phrase from bioethicist Steven Miles. See the interview with him, "The Torture-Endangered Society," by Richard Thieme, in *National Catholic Reporter*, January 13, 2006, pp. 12–14, at p. 14.

22. Kate Zernike, "Detainees Describe Abuses by Guard in Iraq Prison," *The New York Times*, January 12, 2005, at www.nytimes.com (accessed August 15, 2007).

23. George Steiner, *Lessons of the Masters* (Cambridge, MA: Harvard University Press, 2003), p. 14.

24. I am grateful to the Association of Jesuit Colleges and Universities for their provision of data.

25. See the 2006 to 2007 "Trends in College Pricing" report at http://www.collegeboard.com/prod_downloads/press/cost06/trends_college_pricing_06.pdf (accessed July 30, 2007).

26. See *Conversations on Jesuit Higher Education*, "Marketing and Mission," No. 25 (Spring 2004).

27. On an "economy of grace," see Kathryn Tanner, *Economy of Grace* (Minneapolis: Fortress, 2005).

28. Anya Kamenetz, *Generation Debt: Why Now Is a Terrible Time to Be Young* (New York: Riverhead, 2006).

29. See the discussion in Neil Howe and Bill Strauss, *Millennials Rising: The Next Great Generation* (New York: Vintage, 2000).

30. See Fr. Kolvenbach's 2000 address at Santa Clara University, "The Service of Faith and the Promotion of Justice in American Jesuit Higher Education," at http://www.scu.edu/ignatiancenter/bannan/eventsandconferences/justiceconference/nationalconference/kolvenbach.cfm (accessed July 30, 2007).

31. John W. O'Malley, *The First Jesuits* (Cambridge, MA: Harvard University Press, 1993), p. 219.

32. There can never be too much remembering of what we know of the basic facts: According to the official John Jay study, between 1950 and 2002 there were allegations of sexual abuse against 4,392 priests, made by some 10,667 people. According to their best estimates, approximately 4 percent of priests have been accused.

It is highly likely that not all victims have yet come forward (indeed, "more than 25 percent of the allegations were made more than 30 years after the alleged abuse began" [see the Executive Summary, p. 7]). See also the "Supplementary Data Analysis" of 2006. The original 2004 report may be found at http://www.usccb.org/nrb/johnjaystudy/ (accessed July 30, 2007). The supplementary report may be found at http://www.usccb.org/ocyp/JohnJayReport.pdf (accessed July 30, 2007).

33. This sentence was inspired by repeated listenings of the song "Faceless Man" by Creed, from the album *Human Clay* (Wind-up, 1999).

Chapter 4—Popular Culture Research and Theology

1. The quotation from Teresa of Avila can be found in *The Life of Saint Teresa of Ávila,* translated by J.M. Cohen (New York: Penguin, 1957), p. 123.

2. While the literature is already too voluminous to present economically, some recent noteworthy broad studies include Gordon Lynch, *Understanding Theology and Popular Culture* (Oxford, U.K.: Blackwell, 2005); Kelton Cobb, *The Blackwell Guide to Theology and Popular Culture* (Malden, MA: Blackwell, 2005); Bruce David Forbes and Jeffrey H. Mahan (eds.), *Religion and Popular Culture in America* (Berkeley, CA: University of California Press, 2000); Peter Horsfield, Mary E. Hess, and Adan M. Medrano (eds.), *Belief in Media: Cultural Perspectives on Media and Christianity* (Burlington, VT: Ashgate, 2004).

3. Representative of such studies are Eric Michael Mazur and Kate McCarthy (eds.), *God in the Details: American Religion in Popular Culture* (New York: Routledge, 2001); Jolyon Mitchell and Sophia Marriage, *Mediating Religion: Conversations in Media, Religion, and Culture* (London: T&T Clark, 2003); Michael Gilmour (ed.), *Call Me the Seeker: Listening to Religion in Popular Music* (New York: Continuum, 2005); Clive Marsh and Gaye Ortiz (eds.), *Explorations in Theology and Film: Movies and Meaning* (Malden, MA: Blackwell, 1997); John May (ed.), *New Image of Religious Film* (Kansas City, MO: Sheed and Ward, 1997); Richard Flory and Donald E. Miller (eds.), *GenX Religion* (New York: Routledge, 2000).

4. There is, of course, the widespread institutional-academic demand to overproduce edited works to fulfill publishing quotas so as to meet the necessary but ambiguous requirements of "tenure" and "promotion." Such pressures can forge the strangest of roommates in a single text, not to mention a single conference panel, and should not necessarily be confused with the publication of a coherent project belonging to a "field."

5. Simon Frith, "Popular Culture," in Michael Payne (ed.), *A Dictionary of Cultural and Critical Theory* (Cambridge, MA: Blackwell, 1996).

6. David Tracy, *Blessed Rage for Order: The New Pluralism in Theology* (New York: Seabury Press, 1975).

7. Lynch, *Understanding Theology and Popular Culture*; Cobb, *The Blackwell Guide to Theology and Popular Culture.*

8. Cobb, *The Blackwell Guide to Theology and Popular Culture*, p. 294.

9. Bruce David Forbes, "Introduction," in Forbes and Mahan (eds.), *Religion and Popular Culture in America*, pp. 1–20, at p. 17.

10. Margaret Miles, *Seeing and Believing: Religion and Values in the Movies* (Boston: Beacon Press, 1996), pp. xi–xii.

11. Randall Holm, "'Pulling Back the Darkness': Starbound with Jon Anderson," in Michael Gilmour (ed.), *Call Me the Seeker: Listening to Religion in Popular Music*, pp. 158–171, at p. 160.

12. Robin Sylvan, *Traces of the Spirit: The Religious Dimensions of Popular Music* (New York: New York University Press, 2002), pp. 214–215.

13. On fan culture as a complex domain of creative and conflicted meanings, and the construction of the popular culture "fan" over against the popular culture "academic," see Matthew Hills, *Fan Cultures* (New York: Routledge, 2002).

14. Forbes, "Introduction," p. 17.

15. For a recent example, see Dominic Strinati, *An Introduction to Theories of Popular Culture* (New York: Routledge, 2004).

16. Kathryn Tanner, *Theories of Culture: A New Agenda for Theology* (Minneapolis, MN: Fortress, 1997).

17. Michel Foucault, *Society Must Be Defended: Lectures at the College de France, 1975–1976*, Mauro Bertani and Alessandro Fontana (eds.), David Macey (trans.) (New York: Picador, 2003); Foucault, *Abnormal: Lectures at the College de France, 1974–1975*, Valerio Marchetti and Antonella Salomoni (eds.), Graham Burchell (trans.) (New York: Picador, 2003); Foucault, *Securite, territoire, population: Cours au College de France (1977–1978)*, Francois Ewald and Alessandro Fontana (eds.) (Paris: Gallimard, 2004). See also Graham Burchell, Colin Gordon, and Peter Miller (eds.), *The Foucault Effect: Studies in Governmentality* (Chicago: University of Chicago Press, 1991).

18. Michel Foucault, *Discipline and Punish: The Birth of the Prison*, Alan Sheridan (trans.) (New York: Vintage, 1978).

19. Foucault, *Abnormal*, p. 181.

20. Some recent examples of the academic concern with the popular as a form of social control include major studies on the faith of American teenagers and young adults, which have proven very influential among leaders of Christian denominations in the United States, and which incorporate problematic presuppositions about what constitutes "orthodox" belief and practice, reinforcing a conservative politics of religious identity in the American context. For critiques, see Tom Beaudoin, "In Praise of Young Adult Faith," in *Celebration: An Ecumenical Worship Resource* 33(6), 2004; Beaudoin, "Believing What They Need To," *America* 193(7), September 19, 2005: 24–25.

21. Foucault, *Discipline and Punish*, p. 191.

22. His later research was grounded not only in ancient philosophy but in early Christianity, from which he had learned substantially. See James Bernauer, "Michel Foucault's Ecstatic Thinking," in James Bernauer and David Rasmussen (eds.), *The Final Foucault* (Cambridge, MA: MIT Press, 1994), pp. 45–82.

23. The last several years of Foucault's Collège de France courses promise to yield rich material on the topic of Foucault's understanding of spiritual exercises. The 1982 course has recently been published in English as Michel Foucault, *The Hermeneutics of the Subject: Lectures at the College de France, 1981–1982*, Frederic Gros (ed.), Graham Burchell (trans.) (New York: Palgrave-Macmillan, 2005). See also on this theme Edward McGushin, *Foucault's Askesis: An Introduction to the Philosophical Life* (Evanston: Northwestern University Press, 2007); Jeremy Moss (ed.), *The Later Foucault: Politics and Philosophy* (Thousand Oaks, CA: Sage, 1998); Diana Taylor and Karen Vintges (eds.), *Feminism and the Final Foucault* (Urbana: University of Illinois Press, 2004); Bernauer and Rasmussen (eds.), *The Final Foucault.*

24. See James Bernauer, *Michel Foucault's Force of Flight: Toward an Ethics for Thought* (Atlantic Highlands, NJ: Humanities Press International, 1990).

25. Michel Foucault, *The Use of Pleasure*, trans. Robert Hurley (New York: Vintage, 1990), p. 8.

26. Foucault, *The Use of Pleasure*, p. 9.

27. James Miller, *The Passion of Michel Foucault* (New York: Simon and Schuster, 1993), p. 331.

28. Ibid., pp. 332, 342–344, 360.

29. Ibid., pp. 372–373.

30. Ibid., p. 459 n. 73.

31. For a critique of Miller, see Jeremy Carrette, "Prologue to a Confession of the Flesh," in Michel Foucault, *Religion and Culture by Michel Foucault*, Jeremy R. Carrette (ed.) (New York: Routledge, 1999), pp. 15–32.

32. David Halperin, *Saint Foucault: Towards a Gay Hagiography* (New York: Oxford University Press, 1995).

33. Ibid., p. 77.

34. Ibid., p. 105.

35. Ibid., p. 106.

36. Ibid.

37. Todd May, "Philosophy as a Spiritual Exercise in Foucault and Deleuze," *Angelaki* 5(2), August 2000, pp. 223–229, at p. 225.

38. Ibid., p. 225.

39. Michel Foucault, "Preface," in Gilles Deleuze and Felix Guattari, *Anti-Oedipus: Capitalism and Schizophrenia*, Robert Hurley, Mark Seem, and Helen R. Lane (trans.) (Minneapolis: University of Minnesota Press, 1983), pp. xi–xiv, at p. xiii.

40. Ibid., p. xiv; May, "Philosophy as a Spiritual Exercise in Foucault and Deleuze," pp. 226–227.

41. From February 1983 until Foucault's death just over a year later, Hadot was Foucault's colleague at the Collège de France. Foucault acknowledges that "I have benefited greatly from the works of Peter Brown and those of Pierre Hadot, and I have been helped more than once by the conversations we have had and the views they have expressed" (*The Use of Pleasure*, p. 8). As the understatement implies, it was much more than once. For example, in the 1982 course *The Hermeneutics of the Subject*, Foucault quotes Hadot over a dozen times.

42. Pierre Hadot, *Philosophy as a Way of Life: Spiritual Exercises from Socrates to Foucault*, ed. Arnold Davidson (Cambridge, MA: Blackwell, 1995); Hadot, *Exercises spirituels et philosophie antique* (Paris: Éditions Albin Michel, 2002 [1981]).

43. Pierre Hadot, *Qu'est-ce que la philosophie antique?* (Paris: Éditions Gallimard, 1995), pp. 355–378; Hadot, *What Is Ancient Philosophy?*, trans. Michael Chase (Cambridge, MA: Harvard University Press, 2002), pp. 237–252.

44. Aside from this advantage being presumed in most if not all theological interpretations of popular culture, the presumption is more striking in scholarship or pastoral texts that take spiritual exercises as part of their methodological approach, for example Teresa Blythe and Daniel Wolpert, *Meeting God in Virtual Reality* (Nashville, TN: Abingdon Press, 2004); John J. Pungente and Monty Williams, *Finding God in the Dark: The Spiritual Exercises of Saint Ignatius Go To the Movies* (Ottawa, Ontario, Canada: Novalis, 2004); Edward McNulty, *Praying the Movies: Daily Meditations from Classic Films* (Louisville, KY: Geneva Press, 2001); Michael Paul Gallagher, SJ. 1997, "Theology, Discernment, and Cinema," in John R. May (ed.), *New Image of Religious Film* (Kansas City, KS: Sheed and Ward, 1997), pp. 151–160.

45. Foucault, *The Use of Pleasure*.

46. Pierre Hadot, "Reflections on the Notion of the 'Cultivation of the Self'," in Timothy J. Armstrong (ed. and trans.), *Michel Foucault Philosopher* (New York: Routledge, 1992), pp. 225–232.

47. Bernard J.F. Lonergan, *Method in Theology* (Toronto, Ontario, Canada: University of Toronto Press, 1990).

48. Further in regard to ethics, there remains the serious problem of exercises as enactments of misogynistic power in antiquity. See the views in recent studies in Foucault and feminism, especially Taylor and Vintges and now Jantzen (*Death and the Displacement of Beauty* [New York: Routledge, 2004]), which I read as arguing that ancient spiritual exercises in philosophy are marked by a thoroughgoing misogyny. The complexity of the challenge constitutes part of the future task of thinking through our work as a spiritual exercise. I hope that my proposal gives an experiential vantage point for future explorations in this regard. To argue for a consciousness of spiritual exercises as intrinsic to the writing and reading in our field is not to argue for a repetition of what was misogynistic in their ancient practice.

49. See, for example, Russell McCutcheon, *Manufacturing Religion: The Discourse on Sui Generis Religion and the Politics of Nostalgia* (New York: Oxford University Press, 1997); McCutcheon, *The Discipline of Religion: Structure, Meaning, Rhetoric* (New York: Routledge, 2003).

50. The concern to show that one is a real scholar and not a dilettante is a frequent motif in popular culture studies in theology and religion, giving a slight *frisson* to the work of scholars who wear the "dilettante" label proudly (for example, Holm, "'Pulling Back the Darkness': Starbound with Jon Anderson," p. 160).

51. Lynch, *Understanding Theology and Popular Culture*, p. 41.

52. Miles, *Seeing and Believing*, p. xi.

53. Karl Rahner, *Faith in a Wintry Season: Conversations and Interviews with Karl Rahner in the Last Years of His Life*, ed. Paul Imhof and Hubert Biallowons, trans. ed. Harvey D. Egan (New York: Crossroad, 1990), p. 19.

54. Georges Friedmann, *La Puissance et la sagesse* (Paris: Gallimard, 1970), as quoted in Hadot, *Philosophy as a Way of Life*, p. 70.

55. Johann Wolfgang von Goethe, *Conversations with Eckermann, 1823–1832*, trans. John Oxenford (San Francisco: North Point Press, 1984 [1850]), quoted in Hadot, *Philosophy as a Way of Life*, p. 109.

Chapter 5—Reflections on Doing Practical Theology Today

1. *Histoire de la folie à l'âge classique* (Éditions Gallimard, 1972), ET *Madness and Civilization*, trans. Richard Howard (New York: Vintage, 1988), p. 117.

2. For Foucault, the historical practices of power/knowledge that go into the constructing of oneself as a subject, in both the negative sense of "control by others" (limits that constrain) and the positive sense of "self-control" (limits that enable) fall under the notion of "subjectification," or *assujettisement*. Among many loci in his texts, see, for example, *L'Usage des Plaisirs* (Éditions Gallimard, 1984), ET *The Use of Pleasure*, trans. Robert Hurley (New York: Vintage, 1985), p. 27.

3. A "historical *a priori*" is "not a condition of validity for judgments, but a condition of reality for statements." By this concept, Foucault is trying to delimit what rules of practice made it possible in history for one thing or another to be stated as part of our relation to reality. How did these discursive practices and not others come to mold who we are today? "[D]iscourse has not only a meaning or a truth, but

a history, and a specific history that does not refer it back to the laws of an alien development" (*Archaeology of Knowledge*, p. 127).

4. See the discussion of Foucault, Augustine, and original sin in J. Joyce Schuld, *Foucault and Augustine: Reconsidering Power and Love* (Notre Dame, IN: University of Notre Dame Press, 2003), especially pp. 59–65.

5. Foucault's research led him to call for an "insurrection of subjugated knowledges" (see "Two Lectures," in Foucault, *Power/Knowledge*, ed. Colin Gordon and trans. L. Marshall [New York: Pantheon, 1980], p. 81). Avital Ronel reminds us that "If reading Foucault does not produce an effect of scandal, then his discourse has been sanitized, neutralized, expulsed from the filth and aberration which it at one point wanted to let speak" (*The Telephone Book: Technology, Schizophrenia, Electric Speech* [Lincoln: University of Nebraska Press, 1989], p. 429). Due to the place of the person, self or subject in contemporary Catholic theology, Foucault's attention to a philosophy of the practice of subjectivity could be of special interest to Catholic practical theologians. His critical deconstruction of subjectivity leads him to a strong critique of hermeneutics and transcendental philosophy, topics the significance of which few contemporary Catholic theologians ignore. Foucault's approach to practices can be understood as moving beyond a hermeneutical model. How we relate to ourselves is shaped by power that traverses our practice of self at a nonconceptual level. What we are able to make of ourselves is predenominated for us by past configurations of power that regulate and delimit what becomes possible to think, feel, perceive, and interpret about ourselves afterward, especially when past configurations migrate from the territory of moral regulation to natural, medical, or even metaphysical imperative. *The "meaning" of a practice*, so central to contemporary hermeneutical theologies, is from this perspective a problem, not an interpretive anchor. The meaning of a practice may be the surface effect of configurations of power; the meaning of a practice will most likely not be evident to those involved in it, whose identities are enmeshed in it, or even to those whose interpretive skills (e.g., practical theologians) depend on the naturalizing of practices as sites of deposits of meaning available to the theologian for their correlations. (Foucault argues that it is "a matter of analyzing, not behaviors or ideas, nor societies and their 'ideologies,' but the *problematizations* through which being offers itself to be, necessarily, thought—and the *practices* on the basis of which these problematizations are formed" [*Use of Pleasure*, p. 11]). Finally, he was very suspicious of a transcendental approach to subjectivity because it tended to occlude the strongly practical character of subjectivity, shielding us from our investment in power through knowledge practices through which we grid ourselves and our world. Foucault's approach to practices was meant to address what he considered the philosophical "crisis" in contemporary thought "that concerns that transcendental reflection with which philosophy since Kant has identified itself; which concerns that theme of the origin, that promise of the return, by which we avoid the difference of our present; which concerns an anthropological thought that orders all these questions around the question of man's being, and *allows us to avoid an analysis of practice . . . which, above all, concerns the status of the subject*" (*Archaeology of Knowledge*, p. 204, italics mine). This is why we must

> free the history of thought from its subjection to transcendence . . . to analyze this history, in the discontinuity that no teleology would reduce in advance; to map it in a dispersion that no preestablished horizon would embrace; to allow it to be deployed in an anonymity on which no transcendental constitution

would impose the form of the subject; to open it up to a temporality that would not promise the return of any dawn. My aim was to cleanse it of all transcendental narcissism; it had to be freed from that circle of the lost origin, and rediscovered where it was imprisoned. (*Archaeology of Knowledge*, p. 203)

6. James Bernauer, *Michel Foucault's Force of Flight: Toward an Ethics for Thought* (Atlantic Highlands, NJ: Humanities Press, 1993), p. 184.

7. See Paul Lakeland, *The Liberation of the Laity: In Search of an Accountable Church* (New York: Continuum, 2003). "Secular reality," he argues, "is the only reality we can experience" (p. 157).

8. In this respect, I would like to respond to Gordon Lynch, the respected scholar of religion and contemporary society, who has suggested in discussing my proposal for a consideration of such scholarship as a spiritual exercise, that we still must contest the "show and tell" quality of some work in this discipline, specifically in popular culture studies. (See Gordon Lynch, "Some Concluding Reflections," in Gordon Lynch (ed.), *Between Sacred and Profane: Researching Religion and Popular Culture* (London: IB Tauris, 2007), pp. 157–163, at pp. 157–158. My contention is that one way to hear it differently than as "show and tell" is to hear it therapeutically—in the critical sense intended by the present chapter. Moreover, this hearing of research in the register of spiritual exercises is precisely a "public" kind of discourse, as opposed to a merely private one. This is a way of attentive and public listening that Lynch himself seems to model in hearing carefully the new spiritual movements in his recent *The New Spirituality: An Introduction to Progressive Belief in the Twenty-First Century* (London: IB Tauris, 2007).

9. David Tracy, *The Analogical Imagination: Christian Theology and the Culture of Pluralism* (New York: Crossroad, 1991), chapter 1.

10. Tracy has more recently suggested that serious attention to the spirituality of the theologian has diminished considerably in modernity as theology gained a more academic, scientific status. He expresses a "hope for the reunion of theory and exercises in the theological education of the twenty-first century. . . . [T]he need to rethink the *relationship* of education and exercises corresponds to the ancient insistence on the role of intellectual exercises for personal intellectual self-appropriation." See David Tracy, "On Theological Education: A Reflection," in Rodney L. Petersen and Nancy M. Rourke (eds.), *Theological Literacy for the Twenty-First Century* (Grand Rapids, MI: Eerdmans, 2002), pp. 13–22, at p. 20 and p. 19.

11. Cf. Gerben Heitink, *Practical Theology: History, Theory, Action Domains*, trans. Reinder Bruinsma (Grand Rapids, MI: Eerdmans, 1999), p. 27.

12. Foucault, "What Is Enlightenment?" in Paul Rabinow (ed.), *The Foucault Reader* (New York: Pantheon, 1984), p. 47.

13. Echoing Foucault's famous formulation in *Surveiller et punir: naissance de la prison* (Gallimard, 1975), ET *Discipline and Punish: The Birth of the Prison*, trans. Alan Sheridan (New York: Vintage, 1978), p. 30.

14. Karl Rahner, "The Logic of Concrete Individual Knowledge in Ignatius Loyola," in *The Dynamic Element in the Church* (London: Burns and Gates, 1964), pp. 84–170.

15. Chris Pitt, "Peculiarly Participating in Practical Theology," 12 November 2004, "Practical Theology" course, Santa Clara University, Fall 2004.

16. Anonymous, "Practical Theology" course, Santa Clara University, Fall 2004.

17. Emory Lynch, "Practical Theology Journal," 12 November 2004, "Practical Theology" course, Santa Clara University, Fall 2004.

18. Soren Kierkegaard, *Purity of Heart Is to Will One Thing*, trans. Douglas Steere (New York: Harper and Row, 1956), p. 187.

Chapter 6—The Ethics of Characterizing Popular Faith

1. See Robin Sylvan, *Traces of the Spirit: The Religious Dimensions of Popular Music* (New York: New York University Press, 2002).

2. Tom Beaudoin, "Popular Culture Scholarship as a Spiritual Exercise: Thinking Ethically With(out) Christianity," in Gordon Lynch (ed.), *Between Sacred and Profane: Researching Religion and Popular Culture* (London: IB Tauris, 2007), pp. 94–110.

3. One way to allow ethical questions to register in the overlapping fields in studies of faith, popular culture, media, and religion is to begin to admit more carefully the "literary" character of our work, insofar as it finds the exertion of its experimentation, and its creditable expression as a scholarly "contribution," in writing. This implies thinking through what our being literary does to our work, and thus, to see our work as a literary exercise, a discipline of and on ourselves as writers and readers. We too often background the strangeness of the literary quality of our respective vocations, leading us to see the exertion and creditability of researching and contemplating in specific *products*—and not a *process* heavily traveled in literary *askeses*. This despite the focus of so much work in cultural studies in religion on the processes at work in popular culture, as distinct from its products. We study processes of identity performance, meaning making, "faithing," traditioning, poaching, living religion—so that to learn to study mediated popular faith and the sacred is to learn to value rich complexities of material processes, to register them intellectually through our models, even to represent these cultural processes to our own educational institutions (that is, those processes of which we may be "fans").

4. Christian Smith and Melinda Lundquist Denton, *Soul Searching: The Religious and Spiritual Lives of American Teenagers* (New York: Oxford University Press, 2005).

5. Ibid., pp. 118–171.

6. I am grateful to Terri Clark of the National Study of Youth and Religion for providing access to these compilations.

7. I wish to express gratitude to Dr. Kenda Creasy Dean of Princeton Theological Seminary for a helpful conversation about the conclusions of *Soul Searching* for church life today. Even in my own Roman Catholic Church, so often averse to creative and serious attention to the faith lives of young people, the NSYR data has received considerable attention. As of April 2007, there have been presentations to a group of Catholic bishops, to diocesan youth ministry leaders, and in thirty dioceses to pastoral ministry leaders. The National Federation for Catholic Youth Ministry (NFCYM) has been instrumental in arranging these presentations. See Charlotte McCorquodale, Victoria Shepp, and Leigh Sterten, *National Study of Youth and Religion: Analysis of the Population of Catholic Teenagers and Their Parents* (Washington, DC: National Federation for Catholic Youth Ministry, 2004); Robert McCarty, *The National Study of Youth and Religion: Analysis of the Population of Catholic Teenagers and Their Parents: A Brief Summary* (Washington, DC: National Federation for Catholic Youth Ministry, 2005). I am grateful to NFCYM Executive Director Robert McCarty for his overview of these activities.

8. United States Conference of Catholic Bishops, *United States Catholic Catechism for Adults* (Washington, DC: USCCB, 2006). Denton and Smith acknowledge the link between sociological research in religion and the formulation of social policies and practices that affect those studied. When encouraging parents of teenagers to cooperate in such studies, they counsel, "It may be helpful to stress that participation is important because the research will be used to help generate better policies or resources for teens and parents." Melinda Lundquist Denton and Christian Smith, "Methodological Issues and Challenges in the Study of American Youth and Religion" (University of North Carolina—Chapel Hill: National Study of Youth and Religion, 2001), p. 13 (www.youthandreligion.org/docs/methods.pdf, Accessed December 5, 2007).

9. From my perspective, the achievements of *Soul Searching* include a remarkably comprehensive presentation of teenage faith, surpassing the scope of all previous studies: the quotation of a great diversity of adolescent voices; exhaustive cross-analyses of data; productive categories for analysis (such as grouping teen beliefs according to "traditionally Christian," "non-Christian," and "paranormal" [p. 43]); productive internal comparisons, such as the description of similarities between young Catholics and Jews in religious practices and identities (e.g., p. 46); considerations of wider factors of influence on teenagers, such as the authors' argument that the moral rules that teenagers rehearse are strongly informed by lessons learned about drugs and sexuality (p. 155), or the evidence for how overrun explicitly religious practice is by popular electronic media (e.g., p. 179). These are just a few examples.

10. See Courtney Bender, *Heaven's Kitchen: Living Religion at God's Love We Deliver* (Chicago: University of Chicago Press, 2003). Bender argues that "an absence of straightforward discourse signaled neither the total absence of moral discourse nor empty or ineffectual religious talk" (p. 116).

11. The quoted terms are from Nancy T. Ammerman, "Studying Everyday Religion: Challenges for the Future," in Nancy T. Ammerman (ed.), *Everyday Religion: Observing Modern Religious Lives* (New York: Oxford University Press, 2007), p. 226. As Ammerman writes, a "person may recognize moral imperatives that have a transcendent grounding without ever having a 'religious experience' or being able to articulate a set of doctrines about God" (p. 226).

12. Lynn Davidman, "The New Voluntarism and the Case of Unsynagogued Jews," in Nancy T. Ammerman (ed.), *Everyday Religion: Observing Modern Religious Lives* (New York: Oxford University Press, 2007), pp. 51–67, at p. 65.

13. See, for example, the work of theologian Riet Bons-Storm, who found in her interviews of Dutch women that it took at least a full hour of conversation before she could even begin to have access to the "survivor theology" of those she interviewed—by which she meant the personal beliefs that do not necessarily square with the perception of the received tradition on the part of the interviewees. These "survivor theologies" are the hard-won fruit of having gone through difficult life experiences and reworking personal belief systems as a result. These were typically buried below more official sounding reports of their beliefs during the first hour. (Riet Bons-Storm, "Practical Theology in a Secularized World: Beyond the Obsession with Guilt and Atonement," paper presented at the International Academy of Practical Theology, Berlin, Germany, 30 March 2007. See also Bons-Storm, *The Incredible Woman: Listening to Women's Silences in Pastoral Care and Counseling* [Nashville, TN: Abingdon Press, 1996]). From a different perspective, this claim

has also been developed for nearly three decades in the work of psychoanalyst Ana-Maria Rizzuto, who has argued that personal images of God and individual religious beliefs cannot be read off people's conscious speech. "Believing has complex unconscious components and the resulting belief content may remain completely unconscious for the believer. . . . Most beliefs require psychic work to become consciously verbalized descriptions. . ." (Ana-Maria Rizzuto, "Believing and Personal and Religious Beliefs: Psychoanalytic Considerations," *Psychoanalysis and Contemporary Thought*, v. 25, no. 4, Fall 2002, pp. 433–463, at p. 443 and p. 436.) For a fascinating and bewildering compilation of attempts by social scientists to measure faith, from a psychology of religion perspective broadly construed, see Peter C. Hill and Ralph W. Hood, Jr. (eds.), *Measures of Religiosity* (Birmingham, AL: Religious Education Press, 1999).

14. Smith and Denton, *Soul Searching*, p. 27.

15. Ibid., p. 42. Note the double qualification, which is a clue to the moral burden of the book. Such judgments are anchored in these sorts of rhetorical formulations.

16. Ibid., p. 88.

17. Ibid., p. 44.

18. Ibid., p. 136.

19. Ibid., p. 74.

20. Ibid., pp. 156–158.

21. Ibid., p. 150. Note again the qualifier "something of" that both allows the subtle moral claim and renders difficult or impossible any assessment of it.

22. Ibid., p. 76.

23. See D.F. Pilario, *Back to the Rough Grounds of Praxis: Exploring Theological Method with Pierre Bourdieu* (Leuven, Belgium: Leuven University Press, 2005).

24. Smith and Denton, *Soul Searching*, p. 136.

25. For a recent attempt to read Christian history through the "popular culture" of material Christian practices, see Colleen McDannell, *Material Christianity: Religion and Popular Culture in America* (New Haven: Yale University Press, 1995). On recent historicisms, see Sheila Greeve Davaney, *Historicism: The Once and Future Challenge for Theology* (Minneapolis: Fortress Press, 2006).

26. See Catherine Cornille (ed.), *Many Mansions? Multiple Religious Belonging and Christian Identity* (Maryknoll, NY: Orbis, 2002).

27. Smith and Denton, *Soul Searching*, p. 32.

28. Ibid.

29. Ibid., p. 79.

30. For example, ibid., p. 42.

31. Ibid., p. 41.

32. Ibid.

33. Ibid., p. 44.

34. Ibid., p. 154.

35. Ibid.

36. Ibid.

37. Ibid., p. 171, italics mine.

38. Ibid., p. 322, n. 21.

39. Ibid., p. 42.

40. Ibid., p. 83.

41. Ibid., p. 95. Cf. pp. 131, 132.

42. Of course, a mature moral philosophy that turns out to lack "solid grounding" is quite different from what many seventeen-year-olds might articulate. The point is that a discussion of theological literacy would be better served by a different kind of attention to what teenagers say and how they live, including attention to the analogies between complexities in their own praxis and that of their elders.

43. Smith and Denton, *Soul Searching*, p. 156.

44. The importance of listening for "nonreligious" language used by people in secular culture as ways of talking about faith, religiousness, or spirituality is recognized in Christian pastoral care and counseling, and spiritual direction. See, for example, Janet Ruffing, *Uncovering Stories of Faith* (Mahwah, NJ: Paulist, 1989), pp. 132–133, on everyday "secular" phrases that may hold and signal a religious significance in individuals' faith lives.

45. For example, Janet Ruffing suggests that the delicate task of "eliciting the unsaid" is essential in attempting to round out the depth of individual faith stories in spiritual direction (*Uncovering Stories of Faith*, pp. 102–104), and reminds readers that "experiences of God are among the most difficult to tell for many people. . . . [S]tories of falling into the realm of a strangely loving mystery which subtly allures one and insists on response are not easily told even in the direction situation. There are no cultural forms for these highly personal and unique encounters with the holy" (p. 127).

46. Donna Freitas, *Sex and the Soul: Juggling Sexuality, Spirituality, Romance, and Religion on America's College Campuses* (New York: Oxford University Press, forthcoming), p. 53. I am grateful to Dr. Freitas for providing access to the manuscript in advance of publication.

47. Smith and Denton, *Soul Searching*, p. 140, italics in original. See all of Chapter Four, "God, Religion, Whatever," pp. 118–171, for dozens of examples of teen faith testimonies that could benefit from a more generous, patient, and theologically informed ear.

48. Ibid., p. 67.

49. I cannot help but think of Nick Couldry's suggestion for the academic analysis of the cultural practices of "others": "every attempt to describe others must allow them the complexity of voice that one requires to be acknowledged in oneself." See Nick Couldry, *Inside Culture: Re-Imagining the Method of Cultural Studies* (Thousand Oaks, CA: Sage, 2000), p. 127.

50. Quotations from Smith and Denton, *Soul Searching*, p. 163.

51. Ibid.

52. Namely individualism, consumerism, technology; see ibid., pp. 172 ff.

53. Ibid., pp. 156–158.

54. Ibid., p. 157.

55. Ibid.

56. R. Laurence Moore, *Selling God: American Religion in the Marketplace of Culture* (New York: Oxford University Press, 1994).

57. Note the information about the reception of *Soul Searching* in ecclesial circles on pages 79–80 above. Tina Besley, in *Counseling Youth: Foucault, Power, and the Ethics of Subjectivity* (Westport, CT: Praeger, 2002), provides a recent discussion on the long history of American concern about the "moral constitution of youth." This history of moral concern is frequently part of larger attempts to manage the intimate lives of youth. Citing the work of Kenneth Thompson, one frequent theme in such attempts is the invocation of "moral panic," in which the emphasis on the disintegration of the old order be-

comes paramount. (See Thompson, *Moral Panics* [New York: Routledge, 1998].) When this happens, writes Besley, the "ideal is often portrayed as some past, halcyon time of moral certainty, so there is often an appeal to a simplistic 'back to basics'. . ." (*Counseling Youth*, p. 152).

58. Don Browning, *A Fundamental Practical Theology: Descriptive and Strategic Proposals* (Minneapolis, MN: Fortress Press, 1991).

59. See Kathryn Tanner, *Theories of Culture: A New Agenda for Theology* (Minneapolis, MN: Fortress Press, 1997).

60. Michel Foucault, *Discipline and Punish: The Birth of the Prison*, trans. Alan Sheridan (New York: Vintage, 1978), p. 30. In taking this stance, I am doing no more than affirming what Denton and Smith wrote most advisedly elsewhere, that "religion is often an understated influence in people's lives, and people—perhaps especially youth—are not always fully conscious about the ways in which it affects them" (Melinda Lundquist Denton and Christian Smith, "Methodological Issues and Challenges in the Study of American Youth and Religion" (NSYR, 2001), p. 11, www.youthandreligion.org/docs/methods.pdf (accessed December 5, 2007).

61. Sharon Welch, "Lush Life: Foucault's Analytics of Power and a Jazz Aesthetic," in Graham Ward (ed.), *The Blackwell Companion to Postmodern Theology* (Oxford, UK: Blackwell, 2001); Jeremy Begbie, *Sounding the Depths: Theology Through the Arts* (London: SCM, 2002); Robert Beckford, *Jesus Dub: Theology, Music, and Social Change* (New York: Routledge, 2006).

62. Especially with regard to the psychological question, I find helpful the conclusion of Stephen Pattison in his book *Shame: Theory, Therapy, Theology* (New York: Cambridge University Press, 2000), in which he charts and charters a new relationship to himself through the scholarship on shame that he undertakes, which yields for Pattison the individual yet public insight that, in so many words, sometimes a Christian must, on Christian grounds, divest oneself of Christ. This psychological discussion affords a productive re-reading of Pattison's scholarship as the venture of that divestment, registering the work that is part of the author's life. The only thing I would like to know is *how* Pattison modulates from this work to his life. What is the technique of that modulation? What are the ways of making explicit for life what is implicit in the writing? What disciplines are involved in making subjectivity the seismograph of thought, which itself is the "real" work?

63. James Keenan, "Church Leadership, Ethics, and the Future," *The Santa Clara Lecture*, Santa Clara University, Vol. 12 (March 7, 2006).

64. Matt Hills, *Fan Cultures* (New York: Routledge, 2002).

65. Ibid., p. 183.

66. See Nick Couldry's excellent discussion of some approaches to reflexivity in Chapter Six, "Accounting for the Self," in Nick Couldry, *Inside Culture*, pp. 114–133.

67. Hills, *Fan Cultures*, p. 183. It is difficult to imagine such a thing as "reflexivity" as such, despite how it is commonly and perhaps increasingly used in research discourses. Reflexivity seems a rather mobile concept that can be marshaled for all sorts of different cultural work, identity straitening, or enforcements of knowledge. One can imagine, or reference, many kinds of reflexivity, though often enough having a similar function: failing to interrupt the scholarly understanding and practice of work. This can be the case particularly if reflexivity means the invocation of popu-

lar culture pleasures without analysis, or merely a report about that increasingly unhelpful category called one's "social location."

I advocate here a specific meaning of reflexivity, that of making fan studies into studies of academics as fans, in their academic and non-academic fandoms, because of the ethical questions posed to our common work, questions that come to us first in a general acknowledgement of an unacknowledged placement of our subjectivity in our scholarship, leaving our understanding of our work incomplete if we cannot begin to think through its *askesis* on us; and second, because of what we can see happening concretely with the way knowledge of popular religious practice can be constructed, through a work like *Soul Searching*, which may leave us desirous of a way to pay attention to the power we indulge in such thinking. Such intellectual work needs *this* reflexivity, this self-examination as fans of our academic and non-academic disciplines, because cultural studies, sociology, and theology, in their own ways, claim for themselves the right and responsibility to tell other people the truth about themselves.

Nick Couldry's underscoring of the importance of the work of Kamala Visweswaran for theorizing reflexivity is germane to my present argument. Couldry notes that Visweswaran wants anthropologists to involve themselves in (in her phrase) "anthropology in reverse," by (in Couldry's telling) "questioning the process by which she came to be in a position to write about culture" (Couldry, *Inside Culture*, p. 124). See Kamala Visweswaran, *Fictions of Feminist Ethnography* (Minneapolis, MN: University of Minnesota Press, 1994), especially pp. 101–106.

68. On the fetishization of the monograph and contemporary academic overinvestments in university presses, see Lindsay Waters (of Harvard University Press), *Enemies of Promise: Publishing, Perishing, and the Eclipse of Scholarship* (Chicago: Prickly Paradigm Press/University of Chicago Press, 2004).

69. John B. Thompson, *The Media and Modernity: A Social Theory of the Media* (Stanford, CA: Stanford University Press, 1995), pp. 222–223.

70. Tony Becher and Paul R. Trowler, *Academic Tribes and Territories: Intellectual Enquiry and the Culture of Disciplines*, 2nd ed. (Philadelphia: Open University Press, 2001).

71. Elizabeth Ann Ellsworth, *Teaching Positions: Difference, Pedagogy, and the Power of Address* (New York: Teachers College Press, 1997); and on the dangers of the temptation to recover personal losses through teaching, see also Madeleine Grumet, *Bitter Milk: Women and Teaching* (Amherst: University of Massachusetts Press, 1988).

72. Hills, *Fan Cultures*, p. 131.

73. See Smith and Denton, *Soul Searching*, pp. vii–viii, and Denton and Smith, "Methodological Issues and Challenges," pp. 29–30, for the lists of individuals consulted on the project. I note that on my (fallible) reading, the list of consultors includes many Protestants, including many Protestant theologians, far fewer academically or ministerially identified Catholics, and no self-identified Catholic theologians that I could recognize.

74. Nancy T. Ammerman, "Studying Everyday Religion: Challenges for the Future," in Nancy T. Ammerman (ed.), *Everyday Religion: Observing Modern Religious Lives* (New York: Oxford University Press, 2007), p. 224. In line with the critique developed in the present chapter, Ammerman argues that the prevailing methods "privilege religious adherence and institutional affiliation as measures of religion's

strength." Likewise, "[d]efining strong religion in terms of 'strict' [read 'orthodox'] beliefs and practices leaves much of everyday religion unanalyzed" (p. 224).

75. Simon Frith, *Performing Rites: On the Value of Popular Music* (Cambridge, MA: Harvard University Press, 1996).

76. Hills, *Fan Cultures*, p. 66.

77. Ibid., p. 67. Compare the many quotations in *Soul Searching* wherein teens express bewilderment, and then appear to fall back on certain formulas as a way of explaining their faith.

78. Ibid., p. 112, italics mine.

79. Michel Foucault, *Madness and Civilization*, trans. Richard Howard (New York: Vintage, 1988 [1961]), p. 276.

80. I have in mind here works like Becher and Trowler, *Academic Tribes and Territories*; Sheila Slaughter and Larry L. Leslie, *Academic Capitalism: Politics, Policies, and the Entrepreneurial University* (Baltimore: Johns Hopkins University Press, 1997); Sheila Slaughter and Gary Rhoades, *Academic Capitalism and the New Economy: Markets, State, and Higher Education* (Baltimore: Johns Hopkins University Press, 2004); Jennifer Washburn, *University, Inc.* (New York: Basic Books, 2005); Benjamin Johnson, Patrick Kavanagh, and Kevin Mattson (eds.), *Steal This University: The Rise of the Corporate University and the Academic Labor Movement* (New York: Routledge, 2003). Such studies have hardly begun to deeply influence the everyday consciousness of those who toil in academic fields. If we imagine our identities as "including" all that has been kept from our attention, this helps explain why learning the histories of the study of religion and of academic practices can feel unnerving, or an act of hostility, and occasionally therapeutic or liberating.

81. Though it lies beyond the scope of the present writing to settle, could what Hills discusses as the religiousness of fandom, in this case for method in sociology of religion, be sustained in part by the religious quality, by which I mean religious genealogy, of sociology of religion, in its investment in Christian assumptions about religious practice? Among others, sociologist Lynn Davidman has suggested that "Most sociological studies of religion, and the methods used to study religion, have been based on assumptions derived from Protestant theology and praxis. As the dominant religion in the United States, Protestantism has shaped sociological study, often presuming to stand for religion in general." (Lynn Davidman, "The New Voluntarism and the Case of Unsynagogued Jews," in Nancy T. Ammerman [ed.], *Everyday Religion: Observing Modern Religious Lives* [New York: Oxford University Press, 2007], pp. 51–67, at pp. 64–65.) Substantiating Davidman's claim is social theorist Philip Mellor, who argues that various "constructive conceptions" of the relationship between faith or religion and culture that are used by otherwise nonconfessional social theorists have a "recognizably Protestant character, even if this is generally concealed by a representational system that is, ostensibly, religiously neutral." (Philip Mellor, *Religion, Realism, and Social Theory: Making Sense of Society* [Thousand Oaks, CA: Sage, 2004], p. 149.)

82. Might we even have to speak of a "secondary secondary," which would allow consideration of an indirect approach to one's secondary objects? Such a neologism might be required insofar as one cannot know, short of psychological intimacy with the scholar, such as a good therapist, autobiographer, partner, friend or spouse might have, what the true secondary object is for which the academic object and its discipline stands in. But Hills' work seems to invite such a slippage/development of the concept.

83. Taking such an approach makes our fields into sites of transport to fundamental questions in the study of religion, and that also connect us to family resemblances of problems in other fields. The disciplines addressed here are not the only ones that are poised to begin to bring the ethics of academic practice itself into its "subjects" and "objects" of study. Motivated by the turn in philosophy to spiritual exercises, a small group of philosophical theologians and philosophers of religion in the United States have begun meeting to study philosophy together as a way of acceding to wisdom in their own lives and, one hopes, of letting through that accession into a critical refiguring of their profession. This group, called Synousia, has been meeting together for several years. (I am grateful to Dr. Jason Smick of Santa Clara University for information about the group.) And in literary theory, there is a robust conversation about literature and ethics, with rich development of theories about the ways that reading and writing effect changes in writers and readers, from the Aristotelian approaches of novelistic literature as space for instruction in practical wisdom of Martha Nussbaum, to this same literature as space for radical suspension of all moral certitudes, literature becoming a holding place for an ethical reordering for the subjects who are willing to let the text lead them into its difference from our maps for valuing. (See Liesbeth Korthals Altes, "Some Dilemmas of an Ethics of Literature," in Gaye Williams Ortiz and Clara A.B. Joseph [eds.], *Theology and Literature: Rethinking Reader Responsibility* [New York: Palgrave, 2006], pp. 15–31). Theology and the study of religion now have the opportunity for deep listening and engagement in these discussions, an opportunity occasioned by the turn to the popular in sociology and religion, a turn which can become the beginning of a reflexivity that allows us to rethink our own work and our larger fields as such.

84. Matt Hills, *Fan Cultures*, pp. 183–184.

85. Here paraphrasing Georges Friedmann, *La Puissance et la sagesse* (Paris: Gallimard, 1970), as quoted in Hadot, *Philosophy as a Way of Life: Spiritual Exercises from Socrates to Foucault*, ed. Arnold Davidson, trans. Michael Chase (New York: Blackwell, 1995), p. 70.

Chapter 7—I Was Imprisoned by Subjectivity and You Visited Me

1. See Michel de Certeau, *The Practice of Everyday Life,* trans. Steven Rendall (Berkeley: University of California Press, 1988), pp. 165–176.

2. *Dietrich Bonhoeffer Werke* 10:285, cited in Eberhard Bethge, *Dietrich Bonhoeffer: A Biography,* trans. Eric Mosbacher, ed. Victoria J. Barnett (Minneapolis, MN: Augsburg Fortress, 2000), p. 115.

3. Foucault, "What Is Enlightenment?" in Paul Rabinow (ed.), *The Foucault Reader* (New York: Pantheon, 1984), p. 46.

4. Dietrich Bonhoffer and Maria von Wedemeyer, *Love Letters from Cell 92,* eds. Ruth-Alice von Bismarck and Ulrich Kabitz, trans. John Brownjohn (Nashville, TN: Abigdon Press, 1995), p. 43.

5. Bethge, *Dietrich Bonhoeffer*, p. 528.

6. Theodor Adorno, *Minima Moralia: Reflections from Damaged Life*, trans. E.F.N. Jephcott (New York: Verso, 1974), p. 50.

7. Foucault, *Discipline and Punish: The Birth of the Prison,* trans. Alan Sheridan (New York: Vintage, 1978), p. 222, italics mine.

8. See Foucault, *The Use of Pleasure,* trans. Robert Hurley (New York: Vintage, 1990), pp. 26–32.

9. Ibid., p. 28.

10. James Bernauer, "Michel Foucault's Ecstatic Thinking," in James Bernauer and David Rasmussen (eds.), *The Final Foucault* (Cambridge, MA: MIT Press, 1994), pp. 46–47.

11. Foucault, "Technologies of the Self," in Luther H. Martin, Huck Gutman, and Patrick H. Hutton (eds.), *Technologies of the Self: A Seminar with Michel Foucault* (Amherst: University of Massachusetts Press, 1988), p. 18.

12. As this volume evidences, Foucault undertook many studies in this regard. He levied a critique of the trinity sex-self-truth that had come to so dominate psychoanalytic and religious discourses in modernity. Early in his career he sought to show how a certain bourgeois morality had helped to create the modern idea of the soul in French penal and prison codes, such that the soul became "the prison of the body." He sought to show how sex was an historically constituted discourse, and that the confession of the truth of one's self as a sexual discourse was the heritage of Christian medieval confessional practices that reappeared in psychotherapy. He called attempts to manipulate the inner life of adherents, by first maintaining power/knowledge practices that *created* such an inner life and positioned us to see it as the seat of our truth, exercises of "pastoral power" (see "Omnes et Singulatim," pp. 300–303, 308–311, and "The Subject and Power," pp. 333ff., in Michel Foucault, *Power,* ed. James D. Faubion, trans. Robert Hurley et al. (New York: The New Press, 2000).

13. The notion of a technology of self implies a contested character of the self. This contested character comes from the self being deeply embedded in history, from being so immersed in power/knowledge formation; in historically specific "games of truth," that one is oriented to oneself in and through historical practices that are dangerous because so tangled in power/knowledge matrices. In a sense, the "negative" aspect of the notion of a technology of the self is the control of subjectivity revealed by the genealogies of our self-identities. The "positive" aspect is the necessity of, and freedom for, taking up a relation to ourselves in order to displace the truths into which we have been subjectified, and into a more nondominative relationship to ourselves and others.

14. On his family's muted habits of self-disclosure, his reserved relation to his parents and to Maria von Wedemeyer, see Bethge, *Dietrich Bonhoeffer*, pp. 837–840.

15. de Certeau, *The Practice of Everyday Life*, p. xv.

16. Dietrich Bonhoeffer, *Letters and Papers from Prison,* ed. Eberhard Bethge (New York: Macmillan, 1971), pp. 34–35.

17. Ibid., p. 34.

18. Ibid., p. 16.

19. Ibid., p. 35.

20. Ibid., p. 109.

21. Ibid., p. 236.

22. Bonhoeffer and von Wedemeyer, *Love Letters from Cell 92*, p. 95.

23. Ibid., pp. 36, 38.

24. Ibid., p. 73.

25. Bonhoeffer, *Letters and Papers from Prison,* p. 129.

26. Ibid., p. 160.

27. Bonhoeffer and von Wedemeyer, *Love Letters from Cell 92*, pp. 246–247.

28. Bonhoeffer, *Letters and Papers from Prison*, p. 319, italics mine.

29. "The past . . . retain[s] its immediacy if we are profoundly, unselfishly grateful for God's gifts and regretful for the perverse way in which we so often vitiate

them" (Bonhoeffer in Bonhoeffer and von Wedemeyer, *Love Letters from Cell 92*, pp. 229–230).

30. Ibid., pp. 248–252.

31. Bonhoeffer, *Letters and Papers from Prison*, pp. 17, 361. See also Bethge, *Dietrich Bonhoeffer*, pp. 847–853.

32. Bonhoeffer, *Letters and Papers from Prison*, pp. 151–152.

33. Ibid., p. 134.

34. Ibid., p. 136.

35. Ibid., p. 124.

36. Ibid., p. 348.

37. Ibid., p. 162.

38. Ibid., pp. 231–232.

39. Ibid., p. 370.

40. Ibid., p. 162.

41. Ibid., p. 348.

42. Francis Fiorenza, "The Crisis of Hermeneutics and Christian Theology," in S.G. Davaney (ed.), *Theology at the End of Modernity* (Philadelphia: Trinity, 1991), p. 135.

43. I take the phrase from Judith Wallerstein, *The Unexpected Legacy of Divorce* (New York: Hyperion, 2000).

44. Bonhoeffer, *Letters and Papers from Prison*, p. 105.

45. Ibid., p. 150.

46. One reason that I argue for only "fragments" is that Bonhoeffer also manifests a very noncontested, relatively unhistorical interpretation of (him)self. Consider his letter to Bethge of 22 April 1944, where he opines that he has not changed much in his life. "Everything seems to have taken its natural course, and to be determined necessarily and straightforwardly by a higher providence" (*Letters and Papers from Prison,* p. 276; see also pp. 233–234, 295). Indeed, the Christian technology of the self that I am sketching here existed alongside less adventurous construals, one might say traditional kataphaticisms of the self, such as are manifest in his emphatic rendering of gendered marital tasks in his May 1943 wedding sermon (ibid., pp. 41–47). Yet even there, in the former example, we see another indication surface, in the statement that "continuity with one's own past is a great gift" (ibid., p. 276). It is perhaps this tension between an apophatics of the shifting self and the eschatologically promised stable self that is a keynote of Bonhoeffer's relationship with himself in *Letters and Papers from Prison.*

47. Ibid., p. 162.

48. Ibid., p. 157.

49. Ibid., p. 169.

50. Ibid.

51. Ibid., p. 344.

52. Ibid., p. 346.

53. Ibid., p. 341.

54. A question remains here: What role does original sin or the "fall" play in this technology of self? Is the self unknowable essentially due to the state of human corruption (see *Letters and Papers from Prison*, pp. 158–159)? In this strand of Bonhoeffer's thinking/writing, understanding the truth—presumably also about oneself—is a practice of realizing the limits of inquiry inherent in human fallenness, "showing respect for secrecy, intimacy, and concealment" (ibid., p. 159). Truth bears its own

cross. The truth of the self has an eschatological character. Foucault would say that a full and final exposure of the self's truth is usually in the interest of a historically contingent power/knowledge regime. Bonhoeffer writes that "exposure is cynical" (ibid., p. 158); one can only be most truly exposed to God. Yet it is not only the cross of concealment that negates the exposure of self-knowledge but solidarity with the suffering that produces the critical mass to begin with. "Our center is outside ourselves," in those whose sufferings we must share, fundamental teachers about the truth of our lives.

55. Ibid., p. 219.

56. Ibid.

57. Ibid.

58. Ibid., pp. 347–348.

59. Ibid., p. 348.

60. Ibid., p. 279.

61. Ibid., p. 279ff.

62. Ibid., p. 280.

63. Bonhoeffer in Bonhoeffer and von Wedemeyer, *Love Letters from Cell 92*, p. 32.

64. Bonhoeffer, *Letters and Papers from Prison*, p. 362.

65. Ibid., p. 369.

66. Ibid., p. 361.

67. Ibid.

68. Bonhoeffer did remark, apropos the Berneucheners, a Protestant liturgical reform movement, that "faith and style are mutually exclusive. My chief quarrel with the Berneucheners is that they saddle the Christian faith with a style, and thus prevent people from attaining full freedom under the word of God . . . I oppose all forms of stylization" (*Love Letters from Cell 92*, p. 229). Bonhoeffer here is of course referring to worship and not subjectivity. But insofar as these comments disclose his more general convictions in 1944 about the relationship between style and freedom, what I am arguing here is that, by contrast, a Foucauldian ethics of self sees stylization as intrinsic to freedom. I am further arguing that this approach is not necessarily in contradiction with Bonhoeffer's convictions about style and self-making, insofar as Foucault gets "behind" the subject in ways that Bonhoeffer presumed but never opened up in his thought. Foucault's ethics of self critically deepens Bonhoeffer's notion of "this-worldliness": "living unreservedly in life's duties, problems, successes and failures, experiences and perplexities" (*Letters and Papers from Prison*, p. 370). It offers to the thought of the self a realization of Bonhoeffer's "acceptance of the uncertain, the incomplete, and the provisional" (Bethge, *Dietrich Bonhoeffer*, p. 678). A Foucauldian technology of the self is an ethics that makes possible a "this-worldliness" "characterized by discipline and the constant knowledge of death and resurrection" (*Letters and Papers from Prison*, p. 369). That is to say, not only is a technology of self an ascetical practice, but an apophatic technology of self is one that continually deals with the death of self-identity while preparing a "transform[ation] . . . to . . . immortality" (Foucault, "Technologies of the Self," p. 18).

69. Foucault, "Technologies of the Self," p. 40.

70. Foucault, "Omnes et Singulatim," p. 312.

71. Foucault, "Technologies of the Self," p. 41.

72. Ibid., p. 42.

73. Ibid.

74. Foucault, "Omnes et Singulatim," p. 311.

75. Foucault, "Sexuality and Solitude," in Foucault, *Religion and Culture,* ed. Jeremy Carrette (New York: Routledge, 1999), p. 186.

76. Foucault, "Technologies of the Self," p. 43. See also Foucault, "Sexuality and Solitude," p. 183.

77. Bernauer, "Michel Foucault's Ecstatic Thinking," p. 53.

78. Mark Vernon, "I Am Not What I Am," in Foucault, *Religion and Culture,* p. 203.

79. Foucault, *The Use of Pleasure*, p. 9.

80. Foucault, "The Concern for Truth," in *Foucault Live,* ed. Sylvère Lotringer, trans. John Johnston (New York: Semiotext(e), 1996), p. 461.

81. Foucault, "The Subject and Power," in Hubert L. Dreyfus and Paul Rabinow, *Michel Foucault: Beyond Structuralism and Hermeneutics* (Chicago: University of Chicago Press, 1983), p. 216.

82. Cited in William R. Hackmann, "The Foucault Conference," *Telos 51*, Spring 1982, p. 196, quoted in David Macey, *The Lives of Michel Foucault* (New York: Vintage, 1995), p. 439.

83. Foucault interview with Rux Martin, "Truth, Power, Self: An Interview with Michel Foucault October 25, 1982," in *Technologies of the Self*, p. 9, italics mine.

84. Foucault, "Preface," in Gilles Deleuze and Felix Guattari, *Anti-Oedipus: Capitalism and Schizophrenia,* trans. Robert Hurley, Mark Seem, and Helen Lane (New York: Viking, 1977), p. xiii.

85. Foucault, "The Political Technology of Individuals," in *Technologies of the Self*, pp. 146, 153.

86. Ibid., p. 146.

87. Ibid., p. 153.

88. Bonhoeffer, *Letters and Papers from Prison*, p. 6.

89. And yet their lives also bore some striking similarities (the following examples and citations are suggestive, not exhaustive): Both had familiarity with and suspicions of psychoanalysis. Both were critical of humanism. Both were committed to interpreting history from the "underside," "from the perspective of those who suffer" (quoting Bonhoeffer, *Letters and Papers from Prison*, p. 17). Both were concerned or even preoccupied with death from an early age. Both were European intellectuals significantly marked by their experiences in the United States, and both made trips to Africa. Both thought their way out of the prevailing orthodoxies of their age, having made personal acquaintance with the representatives of those orthodoxies (for Foucault it was Sartrean thought; for Bonhoeffer it was liberal theology and Barthianism). Both were political activists against repression exercised by the state. Both saw their task as a personally and academically full struggle for life in their own present. Both were shaped at an early age by the experience and humiliation of war. Both of them made of their own life a project of transformation. (While this is often recognized for Foucault, it is worth remembering that for Bonhoeffer, "The driving force in his life was the need for unchallenged self-realization" [Bethge, *Dietrich Bonhoeffer*, p. 37]). For both, their academic work was wrapped up in this life transformation. Foucault called this being a "specific intellectual" (Foucault, "Truth and Power," in Foucault, *Power/Knowledge: Selected Interviews and Other Writings, 1972–1977*, ed. Colin Gordon, trans. Alessandro Fontana and Pasquale Pasquino [New York: Pantheon, 1980] pp. 109–133, at pp. 126–128). As for

Bonhoeffer, "As a Christian theologian of the resistance, he did not simply observe and analyze from an aloof and critical perspective, but shaped viable formulas in the midst of action" (Bethge, *Dietrich Bonhoeffer*, p. 796). Both distanced themselves from works already published and looked forward to the next new project (Foucault, "Truth, Power, Self" in *Technologies of the Self*, p. 11; Bethge, *Dietrich Bonhoeffer*, p. 131). Both engaged the question of truth-telling at the end of their lives. Both died much too young.

90. David Tracy, "Foreword" to Marion, *God Without Being: Hors-Texte,* trans. T. Carlson (Chicago: University of Chicago Press, 1991), p. xiii.

91. James Bernauer, *Michel Foucault's Force of Flight: Toward an Ethics for Thought* (Atlantic Highlands, NJ: Humanities Press, 1993), pp. 180–181.

92. Bonhoeffer, *No Rusty Swords: Letters, Lectures and Notes, 1928–1936,* ed. Edwin H. Robertson, trans. Edwin H. Robertson and John Bowden (New York: Harper and Row, 1965), pp. 191–192, quoted in Bethge, *Dietrich Bonhoeffer*, p. 21.

93. Foucault, "Truth, Power, Self," in *Technologies of the Self*, pp. 10–11.

Chapter 8—The Struggle to Speak Truthfully

1. Michel Foucault, "Politics and Reason," in Michel Foucault, *Politics, Philosophy, Culture: Interviews and Other Writings, 1977–1984*, ed. Lawrence D. Kritzman (New York: Routledge, 1988), pp. 58–85, at p. 83.

2. See Christian Smith and Melinda Lundquist Denton, *Soul Searching: The Religious and Spiritual Lives of American Teenagers* (New York: Oxford University Press, 2005).

3. As differently articulated in Don Browning, *A Fundamental Practical Theology: Descriptive and Strategic Proposals* (Minneapolis, MN: Fortress Press, 1991), and Gerben Heitink, *Practical Theology: History, Theory, Action Domains*, trans. Reinder Bruinsma (Grand Rapids, MI: Eerdmans, 1999).

4. Lectures at the University of California, Berkeley in 1983, published as *Fearless Speech*, edited by Joseph Pearson (Los Angeles: Semiotext[e], 2001). The following summary of the qualities of *parrhesia* are drawn from pp. 11–24.

5. Ibid., p. 16.

6. Ibid., p. 17.

7. Ibid., p. 18.

8. Ibid., p. 17.

9. Stanley Marrow,"*Parrhesia* and the New Testament," *Catholic Biblical Quarterly*, 44 (1982), pp. 431–446.

10. Ibid., p. 444.

11. Ibid., p. 441.

12. Ibid., pp. 440–441.

13. Ibid., p. 441.

14. Ibid., p. 442.

15. Ibid., p. 439.

16. Ibid., p. 440.

17. Ibid., p. 442–443.

18. Ibid., p. 439.

19. Foucault's remarks on the confessional are brief but provocative and were intended to introduce the confessional recommendations of St. Charles Borromeo, who instructs that confessors should lead penitents in an examination of conscience.

20. Michel Foucault, *Abnormal: Lectures at the Collège de France 1974–1975*, ed. Valerio Marchetti and Antonella Salomoni, trans. Graham Burchell (New York: Picador, 2003), p. 181.

21. Foucault, *Abnormal*, p. 181.

22. Ibid., pp. 181ff.

23. Ibid., p. 202, italics mine.

24. In Jason Berry and Gerald Renner, *Vows of Silence: The Abuse of Power in the Papacy of John Paul II* (New York: Free Press, 2004), p. 52. For the record, a spokeswoman for Law says he has a "vague recollection of such an encounter but no memory of the words exchanged." But, she adds, Law would never have counseled anyone to remain silent about abuse (see Bella English, "I Wanted to Run," *Boston Globe*, May 15, 2002; accessed March 1, 2007).

25. "Sex Crimes and the Vatican," BBC 1 television special, October 1, 2006; available at http://news.bbc.co.uk/1/hi/programmes/panorama/5402928.stm (accessed July 19, 2007).

26. Teresa of Ávila, *The Life of Saint Teresa of Ávila*, trans. J.M. Cohen (New York: Penguin, 1957), p. 88.

Chapter 9—Faith and Apocalypse

1. I am indebted to the excellent study of Metz by J. Matthew Ashley, *Interruptions: Mysticism, Politics, and Theology in the Work of Johann Baptist Metz* (Notre Dame, IN: University of Notre Dame Press, 1998). Also very helpful to me was Alan Revering's paper, "'God Bless America': Patriotism and Political Theology," presented at the 2002 Annual Meeting of the American Academy of Religion, Toronto, Ontario, Canada. For recent collections of Metz's work in English, see Johann Baptist Metz, *A Passion for God: The Mystical-Political Dimension of Christianity*, ed. and trans. J. Matthew Ashley (New York: Paulist, 1998); Johann-Baptist Metz and Jürgen Moltmann, *Faith and the Future: Essays on Theology, Solidarity, and Modernity* (Maryknoll, NY: Orbis, 1995).

2. James W. Fowler, *Stages of Faith: The Psychology of Human Development and the Quest for Meaning* (San Francisco: Harper and Row, 1981).

3. Ibid., p. 208.

4. Ibid., p. 204, with acknowledgement of H. Richard Niebuhr's notion of "radical monotheism."

5. Ibid., p. 199.

6. Ibid., p. 207.

7. See Catherine Cornille (ed.), *Many Mansions?: Multiple Religious Belonging and Christian Identity* (Maryknoll, NY: Orbis, 2002).

8. See Jeannine Hill Fletcher, *Monopoly on Salvation? A Feminist Approach to Religious Pluralism* (New York: Continuum, 2005).

9. John Henry Newman, *An Essay on the Development of Christian Doctrine* (Notre Dame, IN: University of Notre Dame Press, 1989 [1845]).

10. See, for example, John T. Noonan, Jr., *A Church That Can and Cannot Change: The Development of Catholic Moral Teaching* (Notre Dame, IN: University of Notre Dame Press, 2005).

11. Mark D. Jordan, *The Silence of Sodom: Homosexuality in Modern Catholicism* (Chicago: University of Chicago Press, 2000), p. 227.

12. While not all former Catholics define themselves as "recovering Catholics," there are more former Catholics than ever in the United States. As of 2008, according

to one major study, those who have left Catholicism make up about about one-tenth of the entire American population. (See Neela Banerjee, "A Fluid Religious Life Is Seen in U.S., With Switches Common," *New York Times*, February 26, 2008, pp. A1, A12.)

13. Michel de Certeau, *The Mystic Fable*, trans. Michael B. Smith (Chicago: University of Chicago Press, 1992), p. 299.

14. Michel de Certeau, "Mystic Speech," in Michel de Certeau, *Heterologies: Discourse on the Other*, trans. Brian Massumi (Minneapolis: University of Minnesota Press, 1986), p. 83.

15. Certeau, *The Mystic Fable*, p. 299.

16. Tool, "Schism," in *Lateralus* (Volcano, 2001).

Conclusion

1. Michel Foucault interview with Christian Delacampagne, "The Masked Philosopher," Sylvère Lotringer (ed.), *Foucault Live*, pp. 302–307, at pp. 306–307. Trans. by John Johnston.

2. Teresa of Avila, *The Life of Saint Teresa of Ávila*, trans. by J.M. Cohen (New York: Penguin, 1957), pp. 112, 127, 145.

3. Inspired by Martin Heidegger: "Every motion of the hand in every one of its works carries itself through the element of thinking; every bearing of the hand bears itself in that element." (See Martin Heidegger, *What Is Called Thinking?*, trans. Fred Wieck and Glenn Gray (New York: Harper and Row, 1968), p. 16.

4. Dietrich Bonhoeffer, *Letters and Papers from Prison,* ed. Eberhard Bethge (New York: Macmillan, 1971), pp. 281, 337.

5. Ibid., p. 3.

6. Ibid., p. 297.

7. Ibid., p. 286.

8. Quoting Jonathan Malesic, "Bonhoeffer's 'Secret Discipline': The Duty to Conceal Christian Identity" (unpublished paper), p. 11, which denotes well Bonhoeffer's intention. See also Malesic, *Secret Faith: The Responsibility to Conceal Christian Identity in Public Life* (Grand Rapids, MI: Brazos, forthcoming).

9. See Thomas A. Carlson, *Indiscretion: Finitude and the Naming of God* (Chicago: University of Chicago Press, 1999); Marcella Althaus-Reid, *Indecent Theology: Theological Perversions in Sex, Gender, Politics* (New York: Routledge, 2000).

10. Sigmund Freud, in Peter Gay, *Freud: A Life for Our Time* (New York: Norton, 1998), p. 132.

11. A visit to the Pantheon with my wife Martina Verba in December 2004 sparked these reflections. I am indebted to the following architectural and historical research in my thinking about the Pantheon: William L. MacDonald, *The Pantheon: Design, Meaning, and Progeny* (Cambridge, MA: Harvard University Press, 1976); Kjeld de Fine Licht, *The Rotunda in Rome: A Study of Hadrian's Pantheon* (Copenhagen: Gyldendal, 1968); Richard Wrigley and Matthew Craske (eds.), *Pantheons: Transformations of a Monumental Idea* (Burlington, VT: Ashgate, 2004). Just how innovative the temple porch and rotunda combination is, remains a topic of some dispute. MacDonald, *The Pantheon*, highlights its uniqueness in the history of ancient architecture. Edmund Thomas, "From the Pantheon of the Gods to the Pantheon of Rome," in Wrigley and Craskey, pp. 11–34, at p. 27, relying on research from the later 1980s and 1990s, identifies a possible precursor for the unusual design of a structure in the agora at Stymphalos.

12. For the physical specifications, see MacDonald, *The Pantheon*, pp. 33, 35, and the helpful plan on p. 21.

13. I take my claim here as a summary of the present volume's registration of difference from Daniel Finn's recent framing of the need for a Catholic theological engagement with power. Finn persuasively argues that power has not been central enough to Catholic theological analyses of society, and of Catholic structures of governance themselves. He then characterizes the work to be done in this way: "If theology is to fulfill its mission, it must make power visible and examine it in the light of Christian doctrine." Whether theology can render power available for thought without also submitting 'Christian doctrine,' and especially the way it is employed as a 'light' for 'examin[ation,]' to the same power analysis—seems to me impossible. (See Daniel Finn, "The Catholic Theological Society of America and the Bishops," *Origins* 37:6, June 21, 2007, pp. 88–95, at p. 95.)

14. MacDonald, *The Pantheon*, p. 34.

15. Ibid., p. 67. Here as elsewhere I put MacDonald's architectural language to theological work.

16. See the *locus classicus* for the idea in Vitruvius, *Ten Books on Architecture*, trans. Ingrid D. Rowland (New York: Cambridge University Press, 1999), Book 3, Chapter 4, §1–4, p. 47. See also Charles Nicholl, *Leonardo da Vinci: Flights of the Mind* (New York: Viking, 2004), pp. 245–247. My discussion here was occasioned by, and is an expansion of, MacDonald's discussion in *The Pantheon*, pp. 70–71.

17. Thomas, "From the Pantheon of the Gods to the Pantheon of Rome," p. 28.

18. MacDonald, *The Pantheon*, p. 91.

19. See Roger Miller Jones, "Posidonius and Solar Eschatology," *Classical Philology* 27:2 (1932), pp. 113–135.

20. MacDonald, *The Pantheon*, p. 89.

21. Too late did I discover two recent works that promise a serious enrichment on the matter of a necessary pluralism of identity within Christian life: Lisa M. Cataldo, "Multiple Selves, Multiple Gods? Functional Polytheism and the Postmodern Religious Patient," (paper delivered at the 2007 Annual Meeting of the American Academy of Religion), and Laurel C. Schneider, *Beyond Monotheism: A Theology of Multiplicity* (New York: Routledge, 2008).

22. See de Fine Licht, *The Rotunda in Rome*, pp. 44–47; the quotation is from MacDonald, *The Pantheon*, p. 63.

23. MacDonald, *The Pantheon*, p. 88.

24. Ibid., p. 77: "What we perhaps most need to know about the meaning of the Pantheon, the gods' names and positions, is lost, in all likelihood forever." However, MacDonald argues, "It is perhaps reasonable to suppose that the planetary deities were represented, however hopeless the task may be of trying to assign them places in the rotunda. They were Mercury, Mars, Venus, Jupiter, the Moon, the Sun, and Saturn. . . ." On this reading, Zeus would not have a statue himself, but would be "the void seen through the oculus" (MacDonald, p. 89).

25. See the discussion in MacDonald, *The Pantheon*, pp. 76–78. See Thomas, "From the Pantheon of the Gods to the Pantheon of Rome," pp. 15–16, 18–19, for examples of ancient temples that predate the Roman Pantheon in which were placed statues of kings, generals, and other political or military figures. I have bracketed a complex story about the Pantheon's provenance here, which it seems best to do so as not to distract from my main focus. Suffice it to say that it seems that Hadrian built the Pantheon on the site of at least one earlier pantheon presumably constructed by Agrippa,

and commissioned by Augustus, in the mid-to-early first century BCE. (See de Fine Licht, *The Rotunda in Rome*, pp. 180–190; MacDonald, *The Pantheon*, pp. 11–14; see Thomas, "From the Pantheon of the Gods to the Pantheon of Rome," for a fascinating proposal regarding the possible influence of the "Tychaion" in Antioch on Agrippa's and then Hadrian's Roman Pantheon.) I would like in future work to incorporate another architectural background for the Pantheon, Roman markets, into this theological interpretation. See the discussion of the debt of the Pantheon to the early second-century Markets of Trajan in MacDonald, pp. 56–58.

26. In the end, the ideas were abandoned. See MacDonald, *The Pantheon*, pp. 111–112. That, of course, did not put an end to a remarkable European history of building chapels and churches on the model of the Pantheon.

27. Karl Rahner, "The Unity of Love of God and Neighbor," in Karl Lehmann and Albert Raffelt (eds.), and Harvey D. Egan (trans.), *The Content of Faith: The Best of Karl Rahner's Theological Writings* (New York: Crossroad, 1994), pp. 579–587.

28. MacDonald, *The Pantheon*, p. 89.

29. See John D. Barbour, *Versions of Deconversion: Autobiography and the Loss of Faith* (Charlottesville: University Press of Virginia, 1994).

30. This is an important theme of the authoritative catechetical document by the Congregation for the Clergy, *General Directory for Catechesis* (Washington, DC: United States Catholic Conference, 1998).

31. Catherine Cornille (ed.), *Many Mansions? Multiple Religious Belonging and Christian Identity* (Maryknoll, NY: Orbis, 2002).

32. The music of another call can incite this leave-taking, this "holy departure". Indeed, Rainer Maria Rilke found music itself the agent of this dispossession: "You stranger: music You heart-space / grown out of us. The deepest space *in* us, / which, rising above us, forces its way out,— / holy departure: / when the innermost point in us stands / outside, as the most practiced distance, as the other / side of the air: / pure, / boundless, / no longer habitable." See Rilke, "To Music," *The Selected Poetry of Rainer Maria Rilke*, edited and translated by Stephen Mitchell (New York: Random House, 1982), p. 147.

33. See Earnie Larsen and Janee Parnegg, *Recovering Catholics: What to Do When Religion Comes Between You and God* (San Francisco: HarperSanFrancisco, 1992); Joanne H. Meehl, *The Recovering Catholic: Personal Journeys of Women Who Left the Church* (Amherst, NY: Prometheus Books, 1995).

34. Barbour, *Versions of Deconversion*, p. 6.

35. Ibid., p. 210.

36. For example, in the work of James Bernauer and John Caputo.

37. See Louis-Marie Chauvet, *The Sacraments: The Word of God at the Mercy of the Body* (Collegeville, MN: Liturgical Press, 2001).

38. See Michel de Certeau, *The Mystic Fable*, trans. Michael B. Smith (Chicago: University of Chicago Press, 1992).

39. See Robert Barron, *The Priority of Christ: Toward a Postliberal Catholicism* (Grand Rapids, MI: Brazos Press, 2007).

40. Kathryn Tanner, *Theories of Culture: A New Agenda for Theology* (Minneapolis, MN: Fortress Press, 1997), p. 110.

41. Kathryn Tanner, "How I Changed My Mind," in Darren C. Marks (ed.), *Shaping a Theological Mind: Theological Context and Methodology* (Burlington, VT: Ashgate, 2002), pp. 115–121, at pp. 120–121.

Acknowledgements

Chapter 1 is published, with permission, as a revised version of a chapter first published as "Foucault-Teaching-Theology," in *Religious Education* 98:1 (2003), pp. 25–42. The Web site of the journal is www.informaworld.com.

Chapter 2 is published, with permission from Ashgate (www.ashgate.com), as a revised version of a chapter first published as "From Singular to Plural Domains of Theological Knowledge: Toward a Foucaultian New Question," in James Bernauer and Jeremy Carrette, eds., *Michel Foucault and Theology: The Politics of Religious Experience* (Burlington, VT: Ashgate, 2004), pp. 171–190.

Chapter 4 is published, with permission, as a revised version of "Popular Culture Scholarship as a Spiritual Exercise: Thinking Ethically With(out) Christianity," in *Between Sacred and Profane: Researching Religion and Popular Culture*, edited by Gordon Lynch (New York: I.B. Tauris, 2007), pp. 94–110.

Chapter 7, is published, with permission from *Currents in Theology and Mission*, as a revised version of an article titled "I Was Imprisoned by Subjectivity and Jesus Visited Me: Bonhoeffer and Foucault on the Way to a Postmodern Christian Self," *Currents in Theology and Mission*, October 2002, pp. 341–361.

Index